Emergent Conflict and Peaceful Change

Also by Hugh Miall

CONTEMPORARY CONFLICT RESOLUTION (*co-author with Oliver Ramsbotham and Tom Woodhouse*)

REDEFINING EUROPE: New Patterns of Conflict and Cooperation (*editor*)

MINORITY RIGHTS IN EUROPE: The Scope for a Transnational Regime (*editor*)

SHAPING THE NEW EUROPE

THE PEACEMAKERS: Peaceful Settlement of Conflicts since 1945

BEYOND DETERRENCE: Britain, Germany and the New European Security Debate (*co-author with Oliver Ramsbotham*)

NUCLEAR WEAPONS: Who's in Charge?

ENERGY EFFICIENT FUTURES: Opening the Solar Option (*co-author with David Olivier, François Nectoux and Mark Operman*)

Emergent Conflict and Peaceful Change

Hugh Miall

Professor of International Relations
University of Kent, UK

First published 2007 by
PALGRAVE MACMILLAN
Houndmills, Basingstoke, Hampshire RG21 6XS and
175 Fifth Avenue, New York, N.Y. 10010
Companies and representatives throughout the world

PALGRAVE MACMILLAN is the global academic imprint of the Palgrave Macmillan division of St. Martin's Press, LLC and of Palgrave Macmillan Ltd. Macmillan® is a registered trademark in the United States, United Kingdom and other countries. Palgrave is a registered trademark in the European Union and other countries.

ISBN-13: 978-0-333-98766-7   hardback
ISBN-10: 0-333-98766-7   hardback
ISBN-13: 978-0-333-98767-4   paperback
ISBN-10: 0-333-98767-5   paperback

This book is printed on paper suitable for recycling and made from fully managed and sustained forest sources.

A catalogue record for this book is available from the British Library.

A catalog record for this book is available from the Library of Congress.

10   9   8   7   6   5   4   3   2   1
16 15 14 13 12 11 10 09 08 07

Printed and bound in Great Britain by
Antony Rowe Ltd, Chippenham and Eastbourne

To Claire and Naomi

Contents

List of Tables

List of Figures

Preface

My interest in studying peaceful change and emergent conflict dates back to my PhD days, and I would like to acknowledge the inspiration of my then friend and supervisor, Paul Smoker, and of Michael Nicholson, who was also an important influence. I also acknowledge the life-work and inspiration of Adam Curle. Peace and conflict research in Britain is the poorer for the loss of these founding figures.

I have incurred many debts in the preparation of this book. I would like to acknowledge the friendship and support of colleagues at the Richardson Institute at Lancaster University, and at the University of Kent where the book was completed. I am very grateful to Duco Hellema and his colleagues Jolle Demers and Chris van der Bergh at the Centre for Conflict Studies at the University of Utrecht, who provided a wonderful setting for a period of sabbatical leave spent working on the book. I am very grateful to John Moolakattu of the School of Gandhian Thought & Development Studies in the Mahatma Gandhi University at Kottayam for his insights into the social transformation of Kerala and the contribution he made through a background paper on this topic. I am grateful to Oliver Ramsbotham for his comments on draft chapters. I would also like to acknowledge discussions with Ian Bellany, Peter Bennett, Michael Dillon, Mark Duffield, Diana Francis, Michael Grubb, Nigel Howard, Preston King, Judith Large, Claire Leggatt, Michael Lipton, Chris Mitchell, Gerd Nonneman, Heikki Patomäki, Roy Prosterman, Tom Woodhouse, Joseph Valadez, Ximena Vengoechea, Andrew Williams and Maurice Yolles. I am also indebted to the scholars on whose work I have drawn, the enthusiasm of students at Lancaster and Kent, my colleagues at the Oxford Research Group and the Royal Institute of International Affairs, the Conflict Research Society, and the donors who have supported peace and conflict research in Britain.

Most of all I would like to thank my wife Claire and daughter Naomi, to whom the book is dedicated.

This book was a long time in the gestation but abrupt in its ending. I hope that further publications will appear in due course to expand on the themes developed here.

HUGH MIALL
Canterbury
October 2006

1
Introduction

A harsh wind was blowing over the uplands, down from the snow-clad mountains. Change was on the way. The old dictator had fallen. The people had torn down the bridges, the irrigation works, the factories and collective farms. They destroyed everything that remained as a symbol of the hated past. Now it was time to rebuild. But the land would not sustain everyone who lived on it. There were too many people living on too small plots. Subsidies from the government were no longer coming. Something would have to change.

In Riogam, in northern Albania, the villagers faced this situation calmly and collectively. It was a poor village, but the inhabitants were resourceful and proud. The village headman was the teacher. Everyone respected him. He called a meeting to discuss the situation. The government had ordered that every household was to receive an equal minimum share of the land. The men discussed the situation, inside and outside the community hall. There was disagreement. Half the men supported the government's proposal for equal distribution. Half supported a return to the old boundaries. It was clear to the villagers that they would have to reach their own decision. Eventually a consensus was reached on dividing the livestock equally. Then it was realized that there was not enough land to graze them. Those who had owned the land before the communist government took over their former plots. The landless eventually left the village. Rough justice was done, but everyone accepted the outcome.[1]

In Golaj, also in northern Albania, there was a different outcome. A dispute developed between two clans over the redistribution.

After the collapse of communism, when collective ownership of the land was abolished, the Rrushis say the Bardhoshis 'occupied' a plot of

1

land that belonged to them. The Rrushis countered by seizing another plot of land belonging to the Bardhoshis, triggering the family feud. 'They started slapping and hitting. Then we got our weapons,' said Isuf Rrushi, 70, another family elder.

The Rrushis attacked in June 1992. They say three Bardhoshis died in the gun battle; the Bardhoshis insist that they lost four family members. According to the kanun, 'blood is paid for with blood.' An eye for an eye or, in the kanun, 'a head for a head.' Killing violates family honor, and 'an offense to honor is never forgiven.'

The Rrushi killers had to retreat into the confines of their home or face execution, because the Bardhoshis were entitled to avenge the deaths. According to the old kanun, only the killer could be targeted for revenge, but later versions extend the blood feud to all males in the family, which is interpreted to mean all males over 18.

Now the Rrushi men are pale from so much time spent inside. Their shoes are splitting and their clothes threadbare, a sign of their sore finances since only women and children in the family go outside to work.[2]

The two stories illustrate divergent responses to social change. They also illustrate the importance of conflict processes and contexts, and of social capacities to manage conflicts. Why are some social changes managed constructively while others lead to violent conflict?

Most societies are divided by conflicts of interest all the time. But from time to time, social changes create new emergent conflicts of interest. These conflicts may divide societies in new ways or intensify existing divisions. Sometimes they polarize societies into rival camps. It then becomes easy for one side to see a mortal threat in the opposition of others. Then they may feel compelled to resort to taking up weapons. They may find a path through the conflicts, negotiate, and manage to accommodate the interests of different groups. But often they fail to find such a path. Then, painfully and reluctantly, time and time again, they have chosen war.

In the first decade of the twenty-first century, it is possible to discern many existing and emergent conflicts of interest which divide our global society. As population rises and the weight of economic power gradually moves away from older centres, a shift in the balance of political power would be expected to follow. But control over the major levers of economic, political and military power has become very concentrated. The rich nations are growing richer and are placing barriers around themselves. The developing countries are struggling to tackle their internal problems and to gain access to the natural resources, capital and global markets they need for development. There are well-established economic, political and cultural divisions. One particular long-term problem, however, looms over many others. This is the issue of global climate change. Whether in the short or the long term, it will be necessary to achieve constraints on carbon emissions, adjusting the economic activities of all societies to respect sustainable limits. This creates clear conflicts of interest between countries and groups, regarding how and whether these emissions will be applied. If these conflicts are eventually accommodated through negotiations and agreement, the prospects for some form of sustainable and agreed system of global governance will be much improved. If, however, the conflicts of interest intensify and combine with other sources of cleavage in a divided world, they could become a new source of violent conflicts.

The question of how to manage long-term changes, at the national, international or global levels, is therefore a crucial issue for international society. Change and the conflicts that accompany it are unavoidable. Conflict may be desirable in many cases, especially when it is a condition for a necessary change. A central issue in international relations and conflict studies is therefore how change can proceed with conflict but without war. In order to answer this, it is necessary to explore the emergence of conflicts from the earliest stage and analyse the processes and contextual conditions that shape whether emergent conflicts become violent or are peacefully transformed. The issue of peaceful change is thus linked to the prevention of specific violent conflicts. It is also linked to the creation of political orders, or political communities, that can accommodate and foster social transformation. More generally, it is related to the wider question of whether, as Hannah Arendt puts it (1970: 5), a substitute for warfare as 'a final arbiter in international affairs' could become established on the political scene.

As the schema in Figure 1.1 suggest, emergent conflicts may follow two paths. One path is from an incipient conflict of interest towards an overt conflict, which may become polarized and lead to violence. Another path is towards negotiation and accommodation of the issues in conflict, leading to peaceful change. The dynamics of the conflict process and the context determine which path is taken. Some contexts reinforce the likelihood of violence, if the international, national or community setting is prone to war. Others channel conflicts into constructive directions and reinforce the tendency to peaceful change.

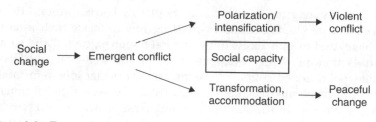

Figure 1.1   Two paths for conflict

The debate over peaceful change

The rapid pace of transformation in global society gives the question of peaceful change a particular significance today. But it is an old question. Thucydides posed it first, in his discussion of the origins of the Peloponnesian War. The change which struck fear in the hearts of the Spartans was the rise of a dynamic and expansionist Athenian democracy. Believing that the growing power of the Athenians could threaten their control of the Peloponnese and ultimately risk a rebellion of the Helots, the Spartans chose to go to war to protect their interests. In the view of Thomas Hobbes, who translated Thucydides into English, a 'warre of all against all' was an inevitable result of the conflict of interests between people unrestrained by sovereign authority. In contrast to Hobbes's interpretation, however, the Peloponnesian War is better understood not as the direct result of a situation of anarchy, but rather of a process of change which divided the Greeks into alliances with very specific conflicts of interest.

In the nineteenth century, another 'irrepressible' conflict developed in the United States, when social change and diversification brought about the growing conflict of interest and polarization between the slave-owning South on one hand and the industrial North and the small-holding Westerners on the other. Somewhat similar conflicts of interest between agricultural and industrial interests developed in nineteenth-century Britain and Germany, but with different results. In Britain, an accommodation was reached between these interests, assisted by the abolition of the Corn Laws, the shared interest in financing colonial and trading ventures overseas and a slow process of political reform. The association of liberalism with trading interests and capital led to a movement for the abolition of slavery, which was agreed by Parliament. In Germany, the Junkers made common cause with the industrialists in modernizing the state, though not in the way that the urban liberals or the industrial workers wished. The processes are not exact analogues, but the contrasts are instructive (Moore 1967).

Similar comparisons can be drawn in other cases and a number of significant studies have been made. Why was Estonia peaceful, and Chechnya violent? Why do some processes of change in the relative status of ethnic groups lead to accommodation and others lead to violence (Gurr 2000)? Why have certain Indian cities managed to accommodate their communal divisions with little violence while others have been torn with riots (Varshney 2002)? Why are some processes of rapid urbanization violent and others not (Homer-Dixon 2001)? Why are some riparian conflicts violent and others not (Libiszewski 1999)? What accounts for the different impact of industrialization, or decolonization, or globalization, in different settings? All have led to both violent and peaceful change. There is a large agenda here for comparative research.

The main question that has preoccupied the literature on peaceful change in international relations concerns change in the power of leading states. In particular, why are some power transitions peaceful, while others are not (Kupchan et al. 2001)? The rise to world power, or the fall from a dominating position, have frequently been occasions for war in world history. Why have some power transitions, such as the passing of primacy from the British Empire to the United States and the end of the Cold War, been peaceful, while others have been violent? What accounts for the peaceful changes?

The issue of peaceful change emerged in the international relations literature in the 1930s when the Western powers were facing the second challenge from a resurgent Germany (Crutwell, 1938; Carr, 1946). After a period of relative neglect from the Second World War to the end of the Cold War, the topic has re-emerged in recent years (Adler 1998; Adler and Barnett 1998; Patomäki 1995; Kacowicz 1994; Kratochwil 1998). Perhaps the preoccupation with emergent conflicts in the unsettled international order explains this new interest. Peaceful change was a central point of contention in the debate between idealists and realists, and now attracts interest from a variety of theoretical perspectives.

E.H. Carr and the debate between idealists and realists

In E.H. Carr's formulation (1939: 209), 'the problem of "peaceful change" is, in national politics, how to effect necessary and desirable change without revolution and, in international politics, how to effect such changes without war.' Carr steered a middle position between the idealists, who argued for international organizations, international law and the development of norms of peaceful change, and the realists, who argued that peaceful change was impossible to achieve in a world of clashing interests, since powerful groups would always use violent means in the last resort to defend their positions. Carr argues (1939: 209) that power has a necessary part to play in political change, but that group conflicts that are not settled through legislation offer the most interesting lessons for international relations. He cites the struggle between capital and labour, employers and employees, as a key case (1939: 212–3). Strikes and negotiations were a means to bring about contests and settlements without the use of military force. They certainly rested on implicit threats and power. Force was sometimes used to suppress strikes, but it usually proved to be unenforceable in the long term. Carr suggested that if international conflicts are to be settled by peaceful means, a similar process of bargaining, involving contests and power struggles of a non-military kind, was required.

Every community, argues Carr, must recognize that the good of the part may have to be sacrificed for the good of the whole (1939: 167). There is no naturally occurring harmony of interests. Harmony is achieved through voluntary self-sacrifice, or 'the realistic consideration that it is in the interest of the individual to sacrifice voluntarily what would otherwise be taken from him by force. Harmony in the national sphere is achieved by this blend of morality and power' (1939: 168). In order to preserve it, there must be some give-and-take between power holders and challengers. Thus, Carr argues, peaceful change in the national order depends on accommodation, as does peaceful change in international orders. 'Those who profit most by that order can in the long term only hope to maintain it by making sufficient concessions to make it tolerable to those who profit by it least; and the responsibility for seeing that these changes take place in an orderly way rests as much on the defenders as on the challengers' (1939: 169).

Carr rejects judicial settlement as a basis for peaceful change in international politics, since it fails to recognize the element of power which goes along with demands for change (1939: 218). He also rejects legislation because it presumes a legislative authority capable of binding decisions, which does not exist in international society. Bargaining then is the essential basis for peaceful change in international environments, but it 'can only be enforced by the power of the complainant'.

However, it is not possible to discuss peaceful change in terms of power alone. Carr argues that legitimacy is also important. 'If an orderly procedure of peaceful change is ever to be established in international relations, some way must be found of basing its operation not on power alone, but on that uneasy compromise between power and morality which is the foundation for all political life.' The establishment of peaceful procedures in international relations rested not only on the power balance in industry, but also a shared perception of fair outcomes, and of the value of give-and-take, so that some basis existed for discussing what was just. Carr points out that 'it is the embryonic character of this common feeling between nations, not the lack of a world legislature, and not the insistence of states on being judges in their own causes, which is the real obstacle in the way of an international procedure of peaceful change.'

Periodical or constant revision of existing rights is a prime necessity of an organized society. 'To bring about revision in the international society by means other than war is the most vital problem of contemporary international politics' (1939: 207). For this, some minimum level of political community is necessary. That is then a basis for creating a forum in which a sense of legitimacy, give-and-take and acceptance of procedures is possible.

Peaceful change then, as Carr suggests, requires means by which actors can pursue conflicts over their interests, by means of bargaining or by political means. It also requires an arena that provides a minimum sense of community so that some common rules and standards of mutually acceptable behaviour can be established. If the realm of peaceful change is to be extended, then the issue-areas in which such bargaining and resort to political means is an effective way of bringing about change must be enlarged.

As I illustrate in this book, peaceful change has been repeatedly achieved in history. Different communities and societies have developed their own means of preventing and handling conflicts. These include systems of governance, institutions and channels of communication, laws, rules and norms, dispute resolution procedures, and many distinctive means of dealing with change.

Karl Deutsch and security communities

Karl Deutsch made the second major contribution to the debate on peaceful change with his conception of 'security communities'. He conceived this as part of the study of integration (itself an important form of peaceful change). One form of integration that changes the context for conflict and creates a potential community of interest and an 'arena' with common rules and norms is the building of new political communities (whether these be empires, city-states, nations or states). But looser forms of integration are also important. Deutsch was interested in exploring the minimum form of association that could still be identified with the renunciation of violence as a means of change. This he called a 'pluralistic security community'. In Deutsch's words, a security community is

A social group of people which has become 'integrated'. By *integration* is meant the attainment, within a territory, of a 'sense of community' and of institutions and practices strong enough and widespread enough to assure, for a long time, dependable expectations of peaceful change among its population. By *sense of community* is meant that there is a belief on the part of actors that they have come to agreement on at least this one point: that common social problems must and can be resolved by processes of 'peaceful change'. By *peaceful change* is meant the resolution of social problems, normally by institutionalised procedures, without resort to large-scale physical force.

(Deutsch 1954: 4)

This definition could apply equally well to groups within societies as to societies in an international grouping of states. Indeed, Deutsch's reference to a sense of community within a territory suggests that he may have had domestic peaceful change in mind. But he applies the concept to the development of one grouping of states in particular, those that have lost the fear of fighting one another, the Euro-Atlantic states.

The idea of a 'security community', when Deutsch and his colleagues proposed it, was intended to look ahead at a possible future as much as to analyse existing trends. But with the development of 'zones of peace' in a number of areas, where international war appears to be falling into disuse (not only North America and Western Europe but also Latin America and the ASEAN countries), Deutsch's work is regarded as significant. It has helped to inspire efforts to build regional security-building communities, such as the OSCE. A recent wave of scholarship has begun to develop the concept, theoretically and empirically (Adler and Barnett 1998, Adler 1998).

With its emphasis on the scope for trust, co-operation and dependable expectation between states, the security community concept challenges traditional realism about behaviour between states. It is now embedded in part of a wider conceptualization of international relations, constructivism. This theory argues that, because states, relations between states and international systems are socially constructed, and are constituted out of beliefs, expectations and behaviour patterns, mankind is not necessarily doomed to endless war between states defending their relative power positions. States can construe their interests and identities in changing ways, and can construct new identities as members of associations of states. Because power and interests are not given by nature, but are 'constituted' out of ideas, culture and social patterns, the behaviour of states (and indeed the nature of states), both at the level of single states and as a collectivity, is ultimately malleable. Specifically, states can alter patterns of repeated mistrust and the security dilemmas these create through co-operation, reciprocity and the trust that flows from them (Wendt 1999).

Co-operation not only leads to the reciprocation of co-operation but 'enables states to overcome the fundamental problem of collective identity formation: overcoming the fear of being engulfed by the Other' (1999: 344). A security community is an example of a socially constructed system within a larger international society, which has the capacity to change the structure, culture and sense of identity of that larger society (Adler and Barnett 1998: 9–14).

Closely related to the idea of a security community, but with a rather broader application, is the notion of 'stable peace' (Boulding 1978, Kacowicz 2000). In Boulding's words (1978: 12–13), this is 'a situation in which the probability of war is so small that it does not really enter the calculations of any of the people involved.' The idea is very similar to Deutsch's 'dependable expectations of peaceful change'. But in the case of stable peace there is no presumption of integration, nor of the formation of a shared identity. Hence, security communities are included in 'stable peace', but 'stable peace' also applies to dyadic relationships between pairs of states and periods of prolonged absence of war between great powers, such as the Concert of Europe. Stable peace implies the acceptance of a norm of abstaining from war, and a degree of stability in this normative system (Kacowicz, 2000: 33). The researchers exploring this concept seek to understand how stable peace relations emerge, and what conditions consolidate them over time.

Heikki Patomäki and the republican approach

A third approach to the debate over peaceful change comes from the critical realist approach enunciated by Heikki Patomäki (1995). He explores peaceful change not in the sense of navigating a dangerous form of change, but rather 'as a general metamorphosis of a polity' (11–12). ' "Peaceful change" is seen as more than a way to avoid war, it also presupposes and implies an improvement in the political arena.' He cites Hannah Arendt, whose distinction between 'power' and 'violence' lays the basis for 'republican' politics. Arendt (1970) conceives of power as an exercise of collective capacity that does not require the use of force. If power is 'the human ability to act in concert' (44), then the use of violence undermines and destroys power (56). So war is not the continuation of politics by other means, but actually an obstacle to politics. 'Only if we succeed in ruling out war from politics altogether, can we hope to achieve that minimum stability and permanence of the body politic without which no political life and no political change are possible.' (Arendt, quoted by Patomäki 1995: 12). For Patomäki, peaceful change is about the possibility of opening up a new political arena in which politics, in

Arendt's sense, can take place. This conception goes beyond the idea of the security community as a transformed group of states, towards the Kantian idea of a community of citizens, acting across borders to create a new type of political domain. This is close to the ideas of the transformation of international politics by the construction of a transnational community, espoused for example by Linklater (1998).

The significance of the republican approach is that it changes the definition of the problem from the way in which realism has framed it. The realist assumption is that the interests of states (and other sovereign groups) are very durable. When there is conflict between them, these interests cannot readily be compromised. The constructivist argument is that interests and identities are changeable, so that states and other groups can in principle construct an arena in which peaceful change is possible. The republican view goes further and argues that it is possible to open a kind of political space in which only peaceful change is possible.

The meaning of 'peaceful change'

These debates about the feasibility and conditions of peaceful change all presume a shared understanding of the meaning of the term. Unfortunately 'peace', 'change' and 'peaceful change' are all imprecise and contested terms.

Carr's use of the term 'peaceful change' was at least clear-cut. The issue was whether the international system could undergo major changes (for example, in the relative power and economic weight of major powers) without conventional armed conflicts. At the national level, it was whether similar major changes (for example, in the relative economic and social status of major social classes or regions) could take place without a violent revolution. This 'negative' definition of peace as the absence of war or of violence is still the most widely used today.

However, it raises difficult questions. If coercion or the threat of force is used, can change be considered peaceful? In his study of peaceful change, Crutwell (1937) did not rule out cases where coercion was implicit in the situation, as it often is in international relations.

Deutsch, as quoted above, uses both a positive and negative definition. Peaceful change means 'the resolution of social problems, normally by institutionalised procedures, without resort to large-scale physical force'. Deutsch's successors have particularly emphasized the importance of norms in creating the habits and practice of peaceful resolution. To the extent that political communities share norms and goals and can 'read' one another's behaviour through shared forms of governance, they are more likely to have dependable expectations of one another (Adler 1998: 34–5).

Johan Galtung criticized the negative conception of peace by arguing that it refers only to the absence of direct violence, perpetrated by actors who intend the consequences. Instead he proposed an expanded conception of violence, on which he built an expanded conception of peace. 'Structural violence' refers to indirect harm, not necessarily perpetrated by actors and not necessarily intended. For example, the economic and political structures underlying the gulf between rich industrialized countries and poor developing countries are regarded as responsible for the suffering of people in the latter whose life potential is drastically restricted by their position in the global economy. Galtung then defines peace as the absence of both direct and structural violence. Later he extended the definition to include the absence of cultural violence (cultural traits that justify violence or disrespect the value and dignity of others), gender violence, and ecological violence against other species.

Patomäki (1995: 8–10) accepts Galtung's view that indirect harm should be considered violence, but is unwilling to adopt his broad definition of 'structural violence' on the grounds that (1) extending the concept 'violence' to cases where there are no identifiable agents extends its meaning too far, and so includes, for example, victims of pollution or malnutrition; (2) identifying peace with the absence of all 'bads' makes it a utopia (and one that depends on the author's view of goods and bads); (3) in particular, identifying peace with social justice does not solve the problems of definition, since justice is itself a contested concept.

Patomäki argues that the concept of 'structural violence' is problematical, because violence should not be defined in terms of its conditions, and because of the ultimately arbitrary notion of 'potential realization'. However, Galtung is surely right that peace cannot simply be the absence of direct violence. It seems inappropriate to describe changes that are brought about either through the intentional use of coercion or as a result of structures of domination as 'peaceful change'.

Moreover, the idea of peace should have some positive content. To define it merely as the *absence* of violence, however broadly the concept of violence is stretched, remains a negative definition. It also makes peace appear very elusive, since few societies have been without some structures that have had negative effects on the potential realization of some human beings. On the other hand, many structures and processes of change in history have had positive effects on the potential realization of human beings. Their presence, and not merely the absence of conditions of violence, have contributed to peace.

Building on Galtung's own conceptualizations, 'positive peace' involves mutual development, mutual trust, mutual respect and regard, and mutual co-operation.[3] It is possible that these conditions can be *present* at the same time as conditions of violence.

The notion of positive peace in this sense is close to Sen's (1999) idea of well-being and capabilities, or the idea of 'human flourishing' suggested by Pogge (2002: 27–31). Galtung's own idea of 'realization' is close to these notions.

The expression of individual realization collectively promotes the flourishing of the whole, and the flourishing of the whole enables the flourishing of individuals.[4] Positive peace thus has the sense of 'wholeness', or 'flourishing-within-wholeness'. The latter formulation links to the idea of peace as a process. 'Peace, in the strong sense of the term, is best thought of as a process in which people freely and responsibly cultivate shared commitments to common expressions, projects and practices' (Cox 1986: 129). The pursuit of common goals, in mutual co-operation and in awareness of the wholeness of society, is constitutive of peace. The adaptation to change in a way that fosters mutual co-operation in achieving common goals and develops friendly and co-operative relations is constitutive of peaceful change.

The UN Charter is notable for containing a positive statement on peaceful change. In the preamble, expressing the determination to rid mankind of the scourge of war, the Charter reaffirms faith in fundamental human rights, the dignity and worth of the human person and the equal rights of men and women. It aims 'to promote social progress and better standards of life in larger freedom'. And in Article 1 the UN sets out its principles as not only to achieve international peace and security, but also to develop friendly nations, achieve international co-operation and 'to be a centre for harmonizing the actions of nations in the attainment of these positive ends.'

So we need to have in mind peaceful change in both the weak and the strong senses. Peaceful change in the weak sense means that a major change is achieved without the use of direct violence. Peaceful change in the strong sense means that change not only avoids violence but fosters mutual development and friendly relations. The idea of peaceful change in the strong sense suggests a co-operative transformation of conflict. The idea of peaceful change in the weak sense means only avoidance of violent conflict.

These considerations suggest a refinement of the scope of the inquiry indicated in Figure 1.1. First, there is a process of social change, such as uneven development, a change in the relative status and standing of ethnic groups, a power transition, a change in the environment, the

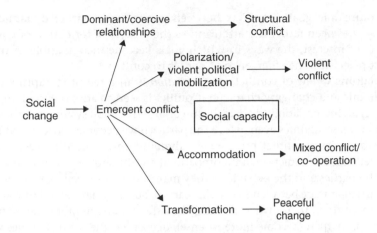

Figure 1.2   Four paths for conflict

development of a new mode of production, the formation of a new belief system, and so on. Secondly, this change may lead to the formation of a conflict if it creates a perceived conflict of interests, a feeling of hostility, or unfriendly actions. Alternatively, at this stage, society may adjust to the change by adapting existing practices, developing new institutions, by accommodation. This depends on social and political action. For a conflict of interest to become a violent conflict, protagonists have to act to mobilize violence (Tilly 2003). Alternatively they may be able to get their way through coercion; the mobilization of coercive instruments then leads to a situation of hegemony or structural conflict. A third alternative is that they may mobilize resources of negotiations, political procedures, and so on, to reach a negotiated accommodation. In this case a violent conflict is avoided. A fourth alternative is that the parties manage to deepen their co-operation and transform the emergent conflict in a way that is mutually beneficial. The outcome is then 'positive peace'. These different paths are illustrated in Figure 1.2.

Emergent conflict and conflict transformation

I must now consider what I mean by 'emergent conflict'. This concept is not as much contested as that of 'peaceful change', since the fact that conflicts somehow 'emerge' out of background conditions is a matter of common observation. Nevertheless, the process of emergence has attracted less theoretical attention than the process of conflict itself. Within conflict theory, there are well-developed ideas about conflicts of interest, incompatible goals, conflicts between actors, and conflict dynamics. There has been rather less attention to the process of formation of conflicts of interest, the ways in which goals become incompatible in the first place, and the emergence of parties to conflict.[5]

Galtung's view of conflict as a *formation* is an attempt to capture its dynamic and changing character. Conflict is seen to arise out of change when an incompatibility arises within an international system or a social structure, sometimes even before the parties have become conscious of it. He identifies a conflict process as a dynamic interaction between the underlying contradiction or incompatibility in the situation, the attitudes of the parties and the behaviour they manifest. Conflicts may start over a particular issue between particular parties, but they have an energy and momentum of their own and readily broaden (taking in more issues and actors), sharpen (become more intense), deepen (as the conflict comes to preoccupy those involved to a greater extent and dominate other cleavages) and spawn daughter conflicts.[6,7]

Conflicts emerge as a result of a combination of background factors, proximate causes and trigger events. Each is unique and has a particular relationship with its historical setting. Conflict is thus intricately linked with context: the historical setting forms the conflict, but the conflict also transforms the historical setting.

A conflict transformation is a change in the goals, structure, parties, or context of the conflict, which removes or changes the contradiction or incompatibility at its heart. Conflict transformation is therefore close to the meaning of peaceful change. If an emergent conflict can be transformed without violence, peaceful change is achieved. For this reason, this book is rooted in the theory of conflict and conflict transformation, and includes examples of conflict transformation in its case studies.

Social capacity and social context

The theory of conflict emphasizes the dynamic processes that develop between conflicting parties, such as escalation and de-escalation, the reciprocation of co-operation or conflict, and the interplay of moves between strategically interdependent actors. However, the social context of the conflict has an equally crucial significance. Some settings, like the clan structure in northern Albania, amplify the dynamics of conflict, so that trivial disputes lead to feuds lasting for generations. Other settings dampen emergent conflicts, as in 'peaceful societies' where social norms strongly reinforce peaceful behaviour and prevent the expression of violence. The capacity to manage conflicts is well-developed in modern societies, and includes flexible and legitimate institutions, forms of governance that allow representation and change, recognition and accommodation of diversity and difference. Within international systems, too, one can speak of capacity for managing conflicts, which is well developed in security communities and in other institutions that foster integration and co-operation between states, and poorly developed in 'raw anarchies' with strong rivalries and weak negotiating machinery.

Causes and Preventors of War

The complex causes that led to the First World War are a well-known example of a war-prone system. As A.J.P. Taylor tells the story, six schoolboys, members of a secret society called the Black Hand, lay in wait in different places as the Archduke Franz Ferdinand's motor car drove through Sarajevo on 28 June, 1914. One of them threw a bomb at the car, but it missed. It was pure luck that when the Archduke decided to drive straight out again, his car happened to stop next to a café where Princip, one of the conspirators, was sitting contemplating the failure of the assassination. Astonished to have a second chance, Princip stepped up to the car and shot the archduke.[8]

It is easy in retrospect to construct a version of events which would suggest that if the chauffeur had not stopped at the café, Princip would not have shot the Archduke; and there would have been no First World War.

If the causes of an event are arranged in a linear manner, then removing the trigger cause would appear to prevent the effect. But in reality there are multiple potential causal sequences, so that even if one sequence of events is prevented, another may take its place.

In 1914 the background and proximate causes were so well entrenched that it is likely that some kind of war would have taken place, but with a different trigger. If the proximate causes (Austria's forward policy in the Balkans, Germany's permissive attitude, Russia's support for Slav nationalism) had been different, a different kind of war might have occurred.[9] Only if the background conditions (such as the existence of highly armed and suspicious nation-states, the German ambition to take a more powerful position in the international system, the efforts of other states to thwart this, the strong identification of people with the defence of these nation-states that drove them to flock to the recruiting-halls, and so on) had been different is it likely that a war might not have taken place at all.

A cause of war is a factor that brings a war about. In a similar way, a 'preventor' is a factor that tends to preserve peace, at least in the negative sense. This is a more active idea than merely the absence of a cause.

A cause involves the idea of capacity – it has a causal power of bringing about an effect, in this case, war.[10] Similarly a preventor has the capacity to bring about the non-occurrence of war. Causes of war may only be effective when they operate together, and may depend on particular conditions (such as trigger conditions) to have their effects. Similarly preventors of war may need to act in combination, and may depend on contingent conditions. The idea of a preventor is therefore more active than merely the absence of a cause.

If we want to identify the factors that prevent wars, we cannot assume that they are necessarily the opposite of the causes of wars. Rather, they are likely to form part of a pattern of factors that work together to make a society peaceful.

Just as the causes of war are analysed at different levels (background, proximate and trigger causes), so we can look for preventors at similar levels. There are factors that tend to prevent a particular conflict-prone situation from falling into war, such as a successful piece of preventive diplomacy, or effective work by an agent or institution of conflict prevention. There are also more deeply entrenched structural characteristics of a society or an international system that tend to inhibit war. Good governance, development and democratization may be factors of this kind.

Spelt out in this way, it is immediately clear that the causes of war and the preventors of war are not exclusive categories. They co-exist. There may be many peaceful relations within a society which is nevertheless at war. Accepted institutions and agreed relationships may effectively manage some of the social conflicts. A great deal of potential violence is being prevented all the time. 'Peace', and 'peaceful change', are therefore not a utopia, but widely present conditions. However, they are intermixed with violence.

The ways in which the sphere of peaceful change and the sphere of violent change interact form an important part of the inquiry. Most societies experience both peaceful and violent change together, and the issue-areas that prompt violence themselves change with social conditions (Luard 1986).

In one view, all peaceful change rests ultimately on the threat of violence. In the view set out by Thomas Hobbes, order is a condition of peaceful change. Order in turn rests upon the concentration of coercive means in the hands of the sovereign. Without the sovereign the subjects would run amok. Peace therefore depends on the monopoly of violence in the hands of the sovereign.

In a radically different view order is seen to be located not in the sovereign but in the network of governmental relationships imprinted throughout society, which unwittingly uphold the social order. Foucault calls this 'disciplinary power', which has replaced the now obsolete 'sovereign power'. Even an apparently peaceful activity, such as making and selling shoes, is implicated in violence since all activities are related together by complex networks of governance. The sphere of peaceful change is therefore always implicated in violence and domination.

Between Hobbes on the one side and Foucault on the other, there is a large ground for middle views. Peaceful change and violent change exist together, but the sphere of either can be enlarged at the expense of the other. There is a capacity for self-organization, autonomy and free and friendly relations that are not tarnished by violence. Peaceful change, in short, is possible. The challenge is to expand its domain and exclude the prospect of violence from community and international affairs.

Conflict prevention and peace-building

The issue of peaceful change touches on two central features of contemporary conflict management. The first is conflict prevention, the second is peace-building. They are closely related, since conflict prevention aims at both avoiding wars and preventing the recurrence of wars once they have occurred. Operational conflict prevention aims to avoid a crisis becoming a war; similarly operational peace-building aims to prevent relapse into war. Structural conflict prevention and structural peace-building are both concerned with establishing what the EU calls 'structural stability'. This can be seen as the conditions for peaceful change – it is what enables societies to maintain trust, common values, shared institutions and public goods.

Conflict prevention, of course, explicitly aims at the prevention of violent conflict, particularly in situations that have not become violent. Peace-building equally aims at putting societies beyond the possibility of violence, and at creating dependable expectations that violence will not recur. As Elizabeth Cousens (2001: 12) notes, 'peace-building is not designed to eliminate conflict but to develop effective mechanisms by which a polity can resolve its rival claims, grievances and competition over common resources'. 'Although there will be many and various underlying causes of conflict, the proximate cause of internal violence is the fragility or collapse of political processes and institutions. The defining priority of peace-building thus becomes the *construction or strengthening of authoritative and, eventually, legitimate mechanisms to resolve internal conflict without violence*' (2001: 4). Both literatures therefore are concerned with the structural measures that can prevent violence and allow polities to manage their conflicts. Both are concerned with the creation of political space, procedures to place the conflicts in a political rather than a militarized arena, the establishment of acceptable institutions, the protection of human rights and provision of basic needs.

Conclusion

The main question this book seeks to explore, then, is: given that social and environmental change brings the interests of different social groups into conflicts, under what conditions can emergent conflicts be prevented from becoming violent? In particular, how do 'structural preventors' of war and the capacity for peaceful change contribute to keeping emergent conflicts on a peaceful track? In what ways can these apply to emergent global conflicts in the twenty-first century, as exemplified by the emergent conflicts arising from global climate change?

I shall argue that structural preventors already have a powerful effect on preventing wars. Moreover, peaceful change, and the development of the capacity to change peacefully, already takes place in many significant spheres. Responding to new forms of emergent conflict in the twenty-first century is a matter not only of addressing global and local conflict formations, but also of developing the capacity for peaceful change in a newly forming political space. This requires creating, at a global level, at least some of the norms, common understandings, public goods, co-operation and conflict handling capacity that exist at the level of domestic societies. This requires a sense of community of interest at the global level. In this sense, movement towards a 'positive peace' is closely associated with the prevention of war.

2
A Theory of Emergent Conflict

Introduction

This chapter and the next aim to develop a theoretical understanding of emergent conflict and co-operation. I will explore how parties to conflict form, how their interests come into conflict, how they formulate their goals, how polarization takes place, and how clashes of interest turn into contradictions. The purpose is to develop a conceptual framework that can capture the processes of conflict emergence and conflict transformation at an early stage.

Existing theories of conflict go a long way to examine how parties with incompatible goals develop latent conflicts of interest and how these conflicts of interest can escalate into fighting. But how do parties to conflict form in the first place? How does social change bring their interests into conflict? How do parties formulate their goals and what makes these goals incompatible? These are questions that an adequate theory of emergent conflict and conflict prevention needs to address.

The aim of this chapter is therefore to draw on and extend conflict theory to cover the emergent stages of conflict, focusing especially on conflict of interests. It starts from a review of existing theories of conflict, and how they bear on the question of conflict emergence. The following section outlines an original evolutionary theory of conflict. I propose a model of how actors and their interests continuously adjust to changing conditions, and of how conflicts of interest and sometimes new parties to conflict emerge. The third section links this evolutionary theory of conflict with a cognitive theory of goal formation. This treats conflict parties as not only reactive but also purposive, seeking to modify their environment as well as adapt to it. This allows for a consideration of conflict between aspirations and adaptive plans, as well as between existing interests. The fourth section explores how a conflict of interest can turn into overt conflict and, in some circumstances, a destructive struggle for survival. The fifth relates this to structural conflicts, in which relations of domination or coercion emerge and reproduce themselves, without necessarily involving physical violence. The sixth emphasizes the central significance of the political system and then discusses how the broader cultural and historical context shapes how interests are mobilized and conflicts form.

The next chapter turns to conflict transformation and peaceful change. Using the same theoretical framework, it shows how the ideas of conflict resolution apply even at the early stages of conflict emergence. It explores the co-evolution and co-ordination of interests in the context of social change, and discusses the significance of norms, common values, common goals and social action in underpinning co-operation and conflict resolution.

In outlining the general character of emergent conflict, I do not identify the immediate conditions that provoke or avoid direct violence. The purpose of this chapter is to explore the precursor conditions that make co-operation or conflict more likely. Social changes lead to co-operation, I argue, when complementary interests are more salient than conflicting interests, groups define their interests in a compatible way, there is a basis for identifying collective interests with other groups and there is social capacity for managing conflict. They lead to conflict when conflicting interests become salient, groups define their interests in incompatible ways, and society polarizes around parties which define their interests in terms of particular, conflicting interests. Such conflicts lead to violence when conflict handling capacity is overwhelmed and commitment to private goals overwhelms the sense of common good.

Lords of Milan

A well-known story in conflict resolution concerns the Lords of Milan. Two brothers strive to be lords of the city. Each seeks an outcome in which he becomes the lord and his brother does not. Their goals are incompatible. They see no possible resolution of their differences. They rule out mutually beneficial outcomes, such as both becoming lords of the city together. They are about to start to fight, even though a likely outcome of war is that both will be destroyed.

Galtung (1984: 71) represents the brothers' interests as in Figure 2.1. Brother A's interests are measured by the vertical utility axis, and Brother B's by the horizontal. The protagonists see the conflict in zero-sum terms (along the line from top-left to right-bottom where their interests

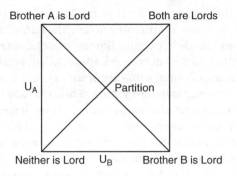

Figure 2.1   Lords of Milan

are diametrically opposed), but the nonzero-sum outcomes are equally important.[1] It is the task of conflict resolution to move from the likelihood of mutual loss in the bottom-left corner if the brothers fight to the possibility of mutual gain at the top-right.

I hope I will not spoil Johan Galtung's story by wondering how this conflict came about and what lay behind it. Could it have been prevented before getting to this point? Imagine the setting of the thirteenth and fourteenth centuries, when the development of the market was beginning to transform the traditional social structure in Milan and the countryside around it.[2] The lords needed to find money to pay for soldiers, luxuries and services, and were beginning to demand money to supplement feudal dues from their peasants. A new group of gentry and merchants were coming to dominate trade and financial services, and started to undermine the aristocracy's traditional sources of power.

A dispute develops, let us say, over the extortionate tolls that some aristocrats levy to gain a share of the profits of trade. The dispute is taken to the Council of the City, which finds a compromise. However, the underlying conflict of interest remains, and grows more intense. The gentry and merchants have an interest in the further development of the market. The aristocrats wish to maintain their traditional feudal basis of power, while also extending tribute to new forms of economic activity. The dispute becomes a struggle for power on the Council. There is a further uneasy compromise, representing a shift towards the gentry. Then, suddenly, the old Lord of Milan dies, triggering a succession struggle. Both parties line up between rival brothers, each favouring a different approach towards the key issues dividing them. The latent conflict comes to a head.

The theory of conflict and conflict resolution is well developed for zero-sum and nonzero-sum situations where the parties are well-defined and their goals are already in conflict. But theories of emergent conflict and conflict prevention are less developed. In the Milan story, as I have told it, the conflict emerges out of a process of social change, which generates a contradiction between different groups. This contradiction might have been resolved by co-operative action at an earlier stage. The landlords might have formed an alliance with the gentry and merchants, accepting the need to move towards more market relations in agriculture. The merchants might have used their money to buy estates and marry into the aristocracy. In this way, an accommodation between the two groups could have prevented the conflict. The question of the succession would then have lost its political significance, with no need for factions on either side to mobilize. With no particular political crisis following the accommodation, no great historical significance would be attached to it.

Peaceful accommodations do not take a striking place in the historical record. They receive less attention than wars, and than the conflict resolution that brings fighting to an end. Nevertheless, given the desirability of achieving conflict resolution at an early stage, the emergent stage of conflict merits more theoretical exploration than it has received in the conflict theory literature.

Theories of conflict

The classical theorists

The earliest theorists of conflict in the Western tradition were the Greeks, and the influence of the political tradition of classical Greece is plain to see in modern conflict theory as well as in modern politics. Plato and Aristotle both constructed their views of the ideal polity around the Greek *polis* (pl. *poleis*), a city-state which formed the political community for its citizens. They were both concerned with ethical principles and believed in a universal moral order that could be established by rational inquiry. They also saw association in *poleis* as a natural form of life which fulfilled the individual.[3] But there was a constant tension between the claims of justice and the needs of the state, which foreshadows contemporary concerns. Plato thought that disputes between city states that led to armed conflict were a sign of sickness affecting the social organization.[4] Thrasymachus defined justice as the interests of the state. Others, such as Democritus, held that self-interest would equate with common interest only in a law-governed state of educated citizens. If civil conflict arose, it was due to a lack of virtue in the citizens and their failure to abide by laws.[5] For Thucydides, however, there was a funda-mental conflict between the self-interest of city states and universal principles of justice, which was bound to lead to tragic consequences when, as in the Melian dialogue, the former overrode the latter.

Thucydides shows how this conflict plays out in his *History of the Peloponnesian War*. In Book One he explains how a combination of inter-mediate and trigger causes interacted with the existing propensity for war between the Athenian and Spartan alliances. Above all, conflict arose from the pursuit of self-interest by the *poleis*, and the clashes of interest that inevitably followed. The early part of his history gives 'an account of the causes of complaint' the Athenians and Peloponnesians had against each other 'and of the specific instances where their interests clashed'. But the real reason for the war, in Thucydides' view, was not these specific trigger events. 'What made war inevitable was the growth of Athenian power and the fear which this caused in Sparta.'[6]

Thucydides therefore saw emergent conflict as an outcome of a chan-ging balance of power, and the fear this provokes in the minds of decision-makers. He brilliantly evokes the mental worlds of the protagonists, by placing his own speeches in their mouths. His account of how the lead-ing decision-makers perceived their choices has not been surpassed. But, while he gives a compelling account of the origins of the second and larger Peloponnesian War, which tore the Greek city-states apart, he gives remarkably little attention to the first Peloponnesian War, which set the scene for the second. Nor does he say much about the precise fac-tors that brought their interests into conflict and made them vulnerable, nor of how the conflict of interest arose. I return to this below.

In recounting the decisions that led up to the war Thucydides intended a narrative not only about one particular conflict but about conflicts in general. Since 'the events which happened in the past ... (human nature being what it is) will, at some time or other and in much the same ways, be repeated in the future', his account 'was done to last forever'.[7]

Thucydides' view of international conflict has indeed lasted forever. Machiavelli echoed it in his writing on the Italian city-state princes, and he speaks like the Athenians to the Melians, in arguing that reasons of state must override moral considerations. Princes must pursue conflicts vigorously and ruthlessly in order to secure the common good of their citizens. Conflict thus arose naturally from fragmented sovereignty and competition for power. 'It is impossible for a state to remain for ever in the peaceful enjoyment of its liberties and its narrow confines; for, though it may not molest other states, it will be molested by them, and when thus molested, there will arise in it the desire, and the need, for conquest.'[8]

Hobbes took the same view. Nations 'live in the condition of perpetual war, and upon the confines of battel, with their frontiers armed, and cannons planted against their neighbours round about.'[9] Hobbes saw disorder and conflict as inevitable outcomes of anarchy, or lack of common government. Individuals and communities naturally tend to develop separate interests that come into conflict. They act on the basis of their own interests, seeking to protect them as best they can. Individuals and communities thus find themselves in a perpetual security dilemma. They expect others to act in their own self-interest and exploit any weakness they show. They therefore live in a state of mutual fear. Politics in the state of nature is a 'warre of all against all', alleviated only by strong government within states and by prudential considerations between them.

Thus the realist tradition in international relations sees emergent conflicts arising principally from competition for power. Since power determines security and the allocation of resources, changes in the balance of power, stemming from underlying social and economic changes, are the driving factor in emergent conflict. For neo-realists it is the structure and distribution of capabilities in the international system that is '*the* permissive cause' of war. International anarchy gives a 'final explanation' of the origins of war among states (Waltz 1959: 231).

Realists allow a place for human agency, but in the neo-realist scheme the influence of the international system outweighs the individual level. This echoes the determinism of nineteenth-century sociological theories, notably Marx's, which see violent social conflicts as a mechanistic outcome of social and economic change. 'In the social production of their existence, men inevitably enter into definite relations, which are independent of their will, namely relations of production appropriate to a given stage in the development of their material factors of production. The totality of these relations of production constitutes the economic foundation of society, the real foundation, on which arises a legal and political superstructure and to which correspond definite forms of social consciousness.'[10]

Marx's view of emergent conflict is closely integrated with his view of social structure. Observing the gulf that was developing between the factory owners and the working classes during the industrial revolution, Marx rejected the view of the liberal economists, who argued that the market's invisible hand would harmonize the interests of producers and consumers. Instead, Marx saw the social organization of production as the prime underlying factor in social and political conflict. Unequal control of the means of production made conflict endemic. In any era, the ruling classes would dominate the means of production in their own interests, exploiting the labour of the working classes to cream off the surplus for themselves. These conflicts of interest between classes, or 'contradictions' in Marx's terms, underlie political conflict, and give rise to revolutionary social change which transfers control of the means of production from one class to another.

Marx's model of conflict has had an enormous influence on sociological views of conflict. It has been widely criticized, but the critics often adopt important parts of Marx's point of view. For example Weber (1922) saw the pursuit of self-interest as a driving factor in society, but emphasized the variety of goals and interests that people have. He put more emphasis on ideas than Marx, and in particular stressed the norms associated with positions of authority. If rulers had legitimacy, they might well be accepted because societies accept the basis of their authority. Conflict emerges when new groups successfully deny the legitimacy of existing rulers and establish new norms. Weber rejected Marx's emphasis on the primacy of class conflict, believing instead in multiple sources of conflict, over values as well as other interests, between classes, parties and status groups. This was the beginning of a pluralist view of conflict.

Weber influenced many theorists of conflict. Dahrendorf (1959), for example, accepted his emphasis on authority and saw power itself (rather than control of the means of production) as the source of conflict. Power-holders would pursue their interests, the powerless would pursue theirs, and contests between them over authority and the control of power would be inevitable. His argument was that conflict groups would form if they held similar interests, if they could communicate easily, and if they stood in a similar relation to authorities.

Lewis Coser (1956, 1967) saw social conflict as an essential form of communication, and a means of bringing about constructive change in society. He stressed the functional as well as the dysfunctional aspects of conflict. Conflict emerges in part from its role in solidifying certain groups in society, and conflict can be a cohesive as well as a disruptive force. He quotes the anthropologist, Max Gluckman: 'men quarrel in terms of certain of their customary allegiances, but are restrained from violence through other conflicting allegiances which are also enjoined on them by custom ... Conflict in one set of relationships ... leads to re-establishment of social cohesion.' (Coser 1967: 2). Coser (1956) empha-sizes the importance of 'safety valve mechanisms' (or preventors, in this book's terms) – institutions that permit social and interpersonal conflict at minimal cost. He also drew on the work of George Simmell, who argued that co-operative relationships as well as conflict needed to be analysed: 'Social action always involves harmony and conflict, love and hatred' (Simmell 1964). Conflict emerged from cross-cutting cleavages, but people who are divided by some conflicts might be united by others. Coser thus sees conflict as a positive as well as a negative force, but sets great store on how it is conducted and the social institutions that regulate it. Later writers in the pluralist school (for example, Burton 1967, 1987; Mitchell 1981; Pruitt and Rubin 1986; Kriesberg 1998) emphasize the choices parties can undertake in the management of conflict, and reject the determinism that is implicit in structuralist and realist views.

These classical conflict theories can be grouped into three main schools – realism, pluralism, structuralism – each with their 'neo-' variants. Structural realism adds to neo-realism the concept of 'interaction capacity' and a more systemic view of the interaction between processes and structure (Buzan et al. 1993; Buzan and Little 2000). Neo-liberalism emphasizes the scope for co-operation and transnational interactions in international relations, which softens the rawness of anarchy (Keohane and Nye 1989; Keohane 2002). Constructivism follows pluralism in arguing that co-operative behaviour can construct and express identities collectively, thus 'overcoming the fear of being engulfed by the Other' (Wendt 1999: 344–6). Thus 'anarchy is what states make of it' (Wendt 1999). Post-structuralism follows structuralism by suggesting that sovereign power and its modern manifestation, disciplinary power, uses violence against internal and external challengers as a constitutive part of its being (Campbell and Dillon, 1993; Dillon and Reid, 2000).

Each of these schools, explicitly or implicitly, offers a view of conflict emergence in keeping with its world-view. What is striking about the early theories is how closely their view of conflict is integrated with a broader perspective on social or international change. In some theories, especially those of Marx and Dahrendorf, explanations of the genesis of conflict are intimately linked with explanations of the formation of political groups.

At the same time, many of these theorists paint with a very broad brush. Their theories of conflict stand or fall with their theories of society. In the 1950s a new set of conflict theories appeared which were not rooted in any monolithic view of social change or of the international system. They offered a new set of conceptual tools for thinking about conflict, and especially conflict processes, as general and particular phenomena.

Conflict theorists

The new theorists built on the classical approaches, but took a new approach to the understanding of conflict. Richardson (1960), Boulding (1962), Burton (1969), Galtung (1969, 1989), Axelrod (1970, 1984), Rapoport (1960, 1974, 1989) and others drew on interdisciplinary thinking and systems thinking to formulate a new approach to the analysis of conflict. In an attempt to capture the generic characteristics of conflict, they stripped conflict of its context and explored the dynamics of conflict processes in an experimental and theoretical way. They put the focus on the conflict parties and their interactions, exploring, for example, the strategic interdependence of goals using game theory, the escalation of conflict behaviour using differential equations, and the process of conflict resolution using social-psychological approaches. These theories generally start from parties to a conflict that already exists, and assume interests and goals that are already clearly formed and do not change. In emphasizing the generic characteristics of conflict and the process level dynamics, however, these theories tend to place less emphasis than the classical theorists on conflict emergence and on the social context of conflict.

I will pick out just three strands of this new thinking which are useful foundations for a theory of emergent conflict. These are bargaining theory, Boulding's theory of viability, and Galtung's theory of conflict formation.

Bargaining theory

Bargaining theory is a branch of game theory, which captures the conflict of interests between actors whose interdependent decisions determines outcomes that can be ranked in terms of the actors' preferences. In bargaining theory it is assumed that the actors have both common and conflicting interests. The analysis is intended to cast light on which bargains are likely to be preferred by both actors to the default option of no bargain, and what bargaining solutions are stable.

A particular 'game' is represented in a matrix, giving the payoffs from each outcome to each actor. Let us assume that in the Milan case the brothers are less bellicose than in Galtung's model, and both prefer rule by either or a condominium of both to the risk of war. However, although both wish to avoid war (and thus have an interest in common), they still each prefer to become the lord (and so have an interest in conflict). If we then plot the payoffs of Brother A against those of Brother B, we get a diagram as in Figure 2.2, where the possible outcomes are points W, A, C, B (representing war, Brother A is Lord, Condominium, Brother B is Lord). Brother A prefers all outcomes to the top; Brother B prefers all outcomes to the right. If we allow 'mixed strategies', whereby the brothers can choose between the outcomes with a certain probability, then any point within the 'bargaining set' formed by the lines between W, A, C, and B can be reached by some combination of mixed strategies.

Moves in the 'upwards and rightwards' direction are jointly beneficial. A 'Pareto optimal' position is reached where no joint improvement can

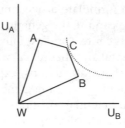

Figure 2.2   Payoffs for the war-averse Lords of Milan

be made. Nash (1951) showed that there is a unique point which provides a Pareto optimal solution to a bargaining game that has been 'normalized' to place the no-bargain solution at the origin. (In Figure 2.2, it occurs where the dotted line representing joint utility intersects the bargaining set: Nicholson 1989: 110–11.) Its significance is that a unique point can be identified with the normative property that it cannot be improved on by either actor. This does not, of course, mean that this outcome will necessarily be the one that is chosen.

Others, such as Zeuthen (1930), Nicholson (1989: 112–15) and Brams (1990), have modelled processes whereby 'rational' bargainers make successive 'moves' from a starting position in response to each other, reaching a unique solution.

These mathematically based 'solutions' are logical contenders for fair or stable outcomes, but the more significant achievement of bargaining theory is the light it shines on the bare structure of a conflict of interest. Figure 2.3 shows a general bargaining situation where the 'bargaining set' of possible outcomes lies along the curve UV and the 'no bargain' point lies at the origin. There is evidently a joint interest in moving from the origin towards the curve, but there is a conflict of interest along the curve. Changes in the shape of the curve which define the outcome possibilities will greatly change the amount of conflict. If the curve, or bargaining set, moves upwards and to the right, conflict tends to be reduced. At the limit, if the bargaining set becomes a square, enclosing A and B's best options, there is no conflict of interest at all. This is the 'win–win' outcome in the Lords of Milan case. On the other hand, if the bargaining set moves downwards and to the left, conflict of interest is increased. For example, if the payoffs of the brothers are adjusted so that they are in a prisoner's dilemma (Figure 2.4), there is more conflict of interest than in the bargaining situation of Figure 2.3. If the conflict reduces to completely polarized outcomes, for example, if the only possible

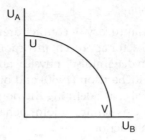

Figure 2.3 The general bargaining situation

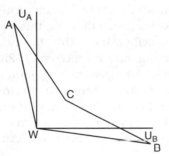

Figure 2.4 Lords of Milan as a prisoner's dilemma

outcomes are that brother A or brother B becomes Lord, there is no scope for compromise and conflict of interest is at a maximum. Axelrod (1970) has used these ideas to develop a measure of the amount of conflict of interest.

The assumption made in bargaining theory is that the goal of each side is to maximize its own utility and that the payoffs are fixed. The feasible bargains are determined by the payoffs and by the assumption of rational behaviour. The main role of the theory is to identify stable outcomes on the assumption that both parties act in accordance with their interests, and to account for bargaining behaviour given existing payoffs. The theory is also capable of giving a measure of the degree of conflict of interest in a conflict where the payoffs are known. But it clearly starts from the existence of parties with interests in conflict, and does not seek to show where these interests come from or what would happen if the interests were to change.

Boulding's theory of viability

Boulding's (1962) general theory of conflict drew on game theory in so far as he uses a rational actor approach, incorporating the idea of preferences and utility, and on deterministic physical and psychological models, as developed by Lewis Richardson (1960) and others. Boulding uses the concept of a behavioural space defining the possible movements of the parties, and analyses the dynamics of joint behaviour in this space arising from the parties' interactions.

The aspect of his work I will examine here is his theory of viability (Boulding 1962: 58–79), which builds on the economic theory of firms. Two firms are assumed to be competing in a market. Each firm's profits are determined by its own price and also by the price of the other firm. It stands to lose customers if the other firm undercuts its price. Competing firms may enter a price war, but if they take this too far they may become non-viable. Boulding demonstrates that the price war is a dynamic process, similar to the arms race as conceived by Richardson. Each party's reaction curves determine the trajectories of joint behaviour. Depending on these reaction curves, normal profit-maximizing behaviour can drive one firm or the other into extinction. If they get into a game of ruin they not only seek to maximize their profits, but also to drive the other out of business. Thus normal competitive behaviour can turn into destructive conflict.

Boulding's view of conflict behaviour as a dynamic set of trajectories, influenced by the underlying utility (profit) contours and determined by the moves the parties make, has been influential in process models of conflict. It has been taken further, for example, by Hirschleifer (2001). Boulding (1970) himself generalized his theory to an evolutionary theory of social dynamics. Although his conflict theory is rooted in classical economic equilibrium models, he does begin to explore what happens when parties change their preferences and when parties are driven into extinction. His theory of viability is a stepping stone towards an evolutionary conflict theory.

Galtung's theory of conflict formation

The third theory to be examined is Galtung's. In principle this is much closer to a theory of emergent conflict. Drawing on the structuralist and behaviouralist traditions, Galtung (1969, 1996: 72) saw conflict as a formation, a kind of energy that arises when living beings have their goals frustrated. It can be creative as well as destructive, he argues. The core of conflict is the contradiction, the incompatibility at its heart. Incompatibility goes beyond competition. In competition, a party cannot achieve as much of a particular goal as it wishes because the other party blocks it. When there is incompatibility, it cannot achieve its goal at all.

Conflict, however, is more than contradiction. It needs a conscious articulation and some kind of expression in action. Galtung uses his famous 'conflict triangle' (1969) to show that a latent conflict only becomes overt when an underlying contradiction, or conflict of interest, is reflected in conflict attitudes and conflict behaviour. This model has been influential in conflict theory and conflict resolution (Mitchell 1981; Miall 1992). But although Galtung gives a convincing account of how latent conflicts manifest themselves overtly, and also relates his theory to a larger theory of societal conflict, he does not offer a fully worked out idea of how the contradictions (or conflicts of interest) themselves emerge. Instead he sketches a theory of conflict and conflict transformation on a broad canvas.

Violent conflict, in Galtung's (1996) view, arises from conflict, polarization and legitimization of violence. Conflict can be removed as a source of violence by transforming the situation, so that the parties can handle their contradiction non-violently, empathetically and creatively. This will often entail looking for a way to transcend a contradiction. Polarization is removed as a source of violence by depolarization, linking positions, and flattening the gradient between Self and Other. Legitimization of violence is addressed by de-legitimizing it, at the cultural or the political levels. Conflict transformation may take place at any time. Before violence, creation of peaceful actors, peaceful structure and peaceful culture creates conditions for transformation. If conflict transformation is left until violence has broken out, there is a meta-conflict (over who wins), which often drives out the root conflict and inhibits conflict transformation. If conflict transformation is left until after violence is over, the secondary and tertiary conflicts created by the meta-conflict will also have to be addressed.

In summary, Galtung offers a theory of how latent conflicts become manifest, but his work gives little theoretical purchase on the question of how contradictions emerge. His work, together with that of other peace and conflict researchers, provides a powerful set of concepts for understanding conflict and its dynamics. But there is a gap in the existing theories in explaining how parties develop conflicts of interest in the first place. Precisely by attempting to take a general view of conflict as a generic process, conflict theory has downplayed the roots of conflict in specific social contexts. Conflict theory therefore needs to be extended to explain how conflicts of interest develop out of social change, in a way that brings the social context into the theory, and yet leaves open the question of whether social change leads to conflict, and whether conflict leads to constructive or destructive outcomes.

A theory of emergent conflict

Evolutionary interpretation of conflict

Building on these ideas, I want to construct a theory of how the interests and goals of parties change over time, how parties to conflict themselves form, and how changing interests lead to emergent conflict or co-operation.

I am concerned here, in the main, with conflicts of interest that develop over a long period, as a result of gradual changes in social or environmental conditions. Examples of such social changes are the rise of the market, the growth of urban population, the development of new production methods, industrialization and globalization. These processes alter social relations, redistribute economic and social power, and create potential conflicts between social groups.

In summarizing such social processes many separate details and events are rolled together. The rise of the market, for example, is a large story consisting of many discrete stories (Hicks 1969: 25–41). Examined closely it is discontinuous and episodic, with particular innovations playing their part in a larger story – the opening of new fairs, the establishment of trading guilds, specialization on new goods, the development of credit arrangements, and so on (Braudel 1979). In a longer perspective it is a clear trend. Here I want to stand back from the detail and see historical processes as trends.

I shall assume that social systems can be represented as a set of social organizations that alter their characteristics and rise and fall in importance in response to trends in historical circumstances. This is not to ignore the importance of discontinuous changes, as we shall see. But the perspective to be taken here is that of the *longue durée*. I will proceed by developing a simplified model to highlight the process by which conflicts of interest can emerge.

A change in historical circumstances may come from outside a society, for example, when an environmental change such as desertification upsets the balance between settled agrarian cultivators and pastoralists, or when an externally imposed economic change alters the social status of traditional sectors within a developing society. It may come about from structural change within a society, for example, through uneven development leading to a concentration of wealth and power in the hands of certain groups or regions at the expense of others. Or it may come about as a result of cultural or ideological change, as when a new religious movement spreads and a gulf appears with existing churches. In all of these cases an underlying change alters the relationships between people in such a way that groups may feel their interests to be damaged or threatened.

The social context both constitutes the set of groups that exist and influences their organization, their values and their sense of identity. Social and cultural change continuously alters the composition of society into groups and the structure and meaning of social relationships. Conflicts and contradictions appear as a result of turbulence and tensions, but at any time existing social relations are characterized by both conflicts of interest and common interests. When I speak of a newly emergent conflict, therefore, I mean some new conflict formation that brings about a significant change in existing relationships. Of course, new conflicts generally flow from previous conflict formations, and from 'knots' or contradictions in social development. I do not wish to suggest that conflict usually emerges as a result of change upsetting an existing harmony.

The emergence of conflict is an evolutionary process. This is not to suggest, of course, that social and biological processes are directly comparable:[11] random genetic mutation, sexual crossover and natural selection are very different processes from social learning, social innovation and the purposive adaptation of social groups. However, human organizations, like species, experience varying fitness, competitive pressures, the need to adapt, pressures to differentiate or to integrate, different types of emergent behaviour at different levels of aggregation, and continuous and discontinuous change. As systems theory and complex adaptive systems theory suggest, there are similar processes at work in different domains of evolutionary development (Bertalannfy 1968; Boulding 1970; Cedermann 1997; Holland 1995; Spruyt 1994).

Framework for the theory

In order to develop this theory, I start from the following propositions:

1. Social organizations in general are not to be regarded as fixed entities, but rather as states of a society in a continuous process of historical and social development.
2. A social organization can be defined by the position it takes on a set of variables or indicators of historical and social development.
3. Social organizations are affected by developments in their environments to which they must respond to by constant adaptation.
4. Social organizations tend to specialize in certain niches of the environment. They occupy a particular geographical, economic and social position in which they can make a living. Each organization is adapted to its own particular sub-environment, and is most responsive to circumstances affecting that sub-environment.

5. Social organizations are not only reactive, they are also purposive. They define their own interests and goals on the basis of their niche position, their needs, values and identity.
6. Social organizations are made up of sub-groups, which may respond differentially to change. Under pressure the sub-groups can take up distinct positions and may ultimately become new organizations, occupying new niches.
7. Social organizations are affected not only by exogenous change but also by the moves and positions of other organizations.
8. The set of organizations that are in existence at any one time, as well as the set of environmental variables on which they depend, are a function of previous historical developments and selective pressures. They are responsive to the environment but are shaped by their past history, which they carry with them.

Borrowing from theories of conflict and social dynamics (Boulding 1962, 1970) and from evolutionary theory (Levins 1968), we can characterize a social organization as a system that is adapted to certain values on a set of variables representing its environment and its social and historical context. It will do well under certain conditions and badly under others. At a given moment in time the organization will be able to survive and make its living in a certain range of conditions. Outside that range it will collapse. We can represent the range as the conditions under which the organization is viable. Its welfare, or success, or fitness varies over the range. Some points, at any given moment, will be best for it; at others it will be less viable. So we can represent the viability of the organization with respect to one particular variable as a curve, perhaps peaked as in Figure 2.5, or linear, or continuously rising, the shape of the curve depending on the particular case.

The height of the curve at any point represents the fitness, or viability, of the organization at that point. The area under the curve reflects the

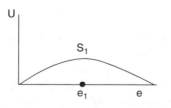

Figure 2.5   A viability curve

adaptiveness of the organization over a range of conditions. Social organizations cannot be viable to an unlimited extent over an unlimited range of environments.

At any time the character of an organization will determine the point on a particular variable that is best for that organization to occupy. For example, for a city-state of a given size, a certain size of fleet may be appropriate. Too small a fleet will be inadequate to carry out a trade, too large a fleet will be too costly to sustain. So with regard to its size a particular value for the fleet is ideal for the city-state. At points to either side, it will do less well. If the point e_1 in Figure 2.5 represents the value that the variable actually takes, and S_1 represents the city's optimum or goal on the variable 'fleet size' with respect to some other attribute 'city size', the viability of the city with respect to fleet size is some function of $(S_1 - e_1)$.

Social organizations will track change in their environment by moving towards positions that improve their fitness. Sometimes, however, the shape of the curve may alter. An organization may become specialized to a narrow range of the environment. Or it may increase its toleration to a wider range of environment, perhaps becoming unspecialized. If the environment is lumpy, it may pay different sub-groups within the organization to adapt to different values, so that the viability curve may become double-peaked. At this point, the pressure to adapt to different environments can lead to the formation of new organizations. This is social differentiation.

In general, social organizations will be tracking not one but may environments – and manipulating their environment at the same time. Moreover, other social organizations form a significant part of the environment. The viability of any social organization will be influenced by the actions of the others. Social organizations depend on each other and adapt to each other's capabilities.

When all is well, the social organization will be able to adjust smoothly to its changing environment, adapting continuously to complex changes, and altering its organization in the process. When times are hard, however, conflicting pressures in the environment may make adaptation difficult.

Consider a society or an organization facing rather different pressures from two environmental factors. Figure 2.6 shows the viability of the

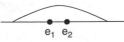

Figure 2.6   Adaptation to two environments

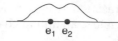

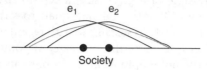

Figure 2.7   A double-peaked curve

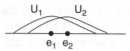

Figure 2.8   The social preference curve

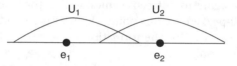

Figure 2.9   Sub-groups with similar interests

Figure 2.10   Sub-groups with different interests

organization that is adapting to two different pressures, e_1 and e_2. The curve has become flatter and broader. The organization has become less specialized. When the two environmental values move further apart, the viability curve becomes double-peaked, as in Figure 2.7.

Figure 2.8 shows an alternative representation of the same situation. Here the horizontal axis becomes some indicator of social variation, and the curves show which social attributes are most fit for each environment. Here the 'Society' dimension represents a range of possible social organizations. Figure 2.9 represents two potential sub-groups within the organization, that are adapted to the specialized environments. Figure 2.6 can be seen as a mean or 'social preference' of the two curves U_1 and U_2. While the two curves are relatively close together, a social compromise is possible. The social preference curve is single-peaked. When the two curves move further apart, as in Figure 2.10, the social preference line becomes double-peaked. At this point, differences within the

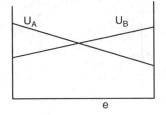

Figure 2.11   Conflict of interests

organization become harder to bridge and the sub-groups develop separate interests.[12]

No conflict need arise between sub-groups or separate organizations if they develop interests and occupy niches which are not in conflict. For example, agrarian and nomadic societies adopt different niches, but they do not usually threaten one another; indeed, they are often interdependent. However, at times, for example, when nomadic societies are forced to move from their grazing grounds, or when agrarian societies wish to irrigate common lands, conflicts of interest arise.

If the variable is one where only one possible value can be taken, then different interests lead to conflict. For example, if a society contains sectors which favour a low tariff and a high tariff, and only one tariff can be set, then organizations with different positions have a conflict of interests, and a widening of the gap between them, as in Figure 2.10, constitutes a widening of the conflict.

Figure 2.11 shows a conflict of interest on an issue e where U_A and U_B are utilities or interests of parties A and B on the issue. This is obtained by replacing the curves in the middle part of Figure 2.9 with lines, and limiting attention to a particular part of the range. This is the same diagram as the conflict of interest represented by two-person game theory (Luce and Raiffa 1957: 394–9). It can apply, for example, to territorial conflict, such as the conflict between Israel and Egypt over control of the territory of Sinai (Miall 1992: 57) or to competition for custom between firms (Boulding 1962: 72). If we now plot the utility of A in Figure 2.11 against the utility of B, we obtain the familiar bargaining line of a constant-sum conflict, as in Figure 2.12.

Similarly if we take the viability curves of Figures 2.9, and plot U_A against U_B, as in Figure 2.13, we obtain a bargaining curve similar to the bargaining set in Figure 2.3. Figure 2.13 is obtained from Figure 2.9 by transforming the ordinates of Figure 2.9 into the co-ordinates of Figure 2.13, and the ordinates into co-ordinates. Likewise Figure 2.14 is obtained from Figure 2.10 by the same procedure.

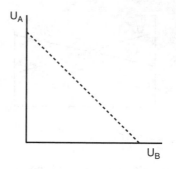

Figure 2.12   Conflict of interests in utility space

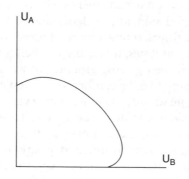

Figure 2.13   A convex conflict set

Axelrod (1970) has shown that it is possible to measure conflict of interest if the bargaining set is known. Using his measure and these transformations, it is possible to measure the changing conflict of interest as the parties' interests move apart.

As the interests of the two parties diverge, so that the utility curves move away from one another, the bargaining curve changes shape. In Figure 2.13 it remains convex, so that a single joint value can be found, which may be acceptable to both sides. In Figure 2.14, however, it becomes concave. A compromise or joint value is no longer acceptable: the parties have polarized around different outcomes. The shift from a jointly acceptable value to a growing gulf between the parties is underway. The point at which the curve moves from convex to concave may be taken as the point at which the possibility of a compromise collapses.

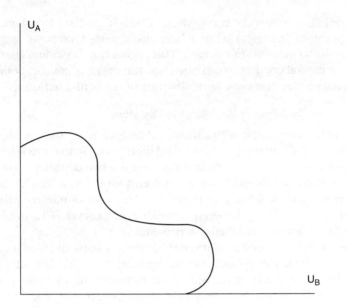

Figure 2.14   A concave conflict set

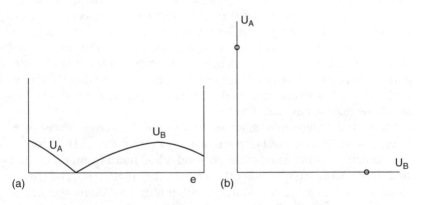

Figure 2.15   Complete incompatibility

As the curves continue to move apart, a point is reached where there is no longer any point of compatibility. At this point, a contradiction is reached, where there is no common ground between one party and the other (Figure 2.15a). The bargaining curve has shrunk from the unit square, representing common interests, to a bargaining curve where compromise is possible, to a concave curve where interests are hard to reconcile, to the point of incompatibility where each party's favoured outcome excludes the other (Figure 2.15b). This shows how a gradual change in environmental conditions can open up an increasing conflict of interest between parties; this can eventually turn into a contradiction.

Case study: the origins of the Peloponnesian War

To illustrate these ideas with a historical case, consider the development of the conflict of interest between Athens and Sparta preceding the Peloponnesian War. The long war between the two dominant powers in Greece broke out in −432 and did not end until −404. The immediate trigger was a civil war in Epidamnus (on the coast of modern Albania), which led to fighting between Corinth and Corcyra. This eventually brought in Sparta and Athens on rival sides.

The underlying conflict of interest between Athens and Sparta considerably preceded this episode. On the Spartan side a fundamental factor was the vulnerability of the Spartan community to a rebellion by the Helots (de Ste Croix 1989). As a militarized, collectivized community of warriors, the Spartans depended on the Helots to labour for them and grow their food. Helots outnumbered Spartans ten to one and, as many of them were former Greek citizens who had been captured and enslaved, they were ready to rebel when they had a chance. To protect against the risk of rebellions the Spartans kept a strong army and made military alliances with other cities in the Peloponnese. They therefore regarded maintenance of their military alliances and protection of the land-routes across the Peloponnese as vital interests. Conflicts involving their allies and other cities which appeared to them to threaten these interests would be regarded as vital threats.

Sparta and Athens were allies at the time of the Persian invasion of Greece, and Sparta and the Peloponnesian League took the lead in defeating the Persian invasion. At this time both sides had had a common interest in a strong Athenian fleet. After this victory, the Spartans returned home to deal with a Helot revolt, while the Athenians went on to liberate the Ionian cities from the Persians and brought them into her own Delian League. The allies of Athens were required to pay her tribute and contribute to the maintenance of her growing navy. In this way the Delian League became an Athenian empire. Meanwhile, the growing population of Athens had become dependent on imported corn. The most important source of grain was from around the Black Sea and the Athenian navy and the empire were regarded as vital necessities to protect this trade route. Just as Spartan dependence on the Helots made them committed to the Peloponnesian League, so Athenian dependence on the corn supply made it committed it to the Delian League.

A source of conflict between the two was soon to develop in the context of the −5th century struggle between democracies and aristocracies. Athenian democrats, including Pericles, overthrew the aristocratic Athenian leader, Cimon, who had championed the alliance with Sparta and pursued a pro-Spartan foreign policy. From this time, Athens withdrew from the alliance with Sparta and instead made alliances with Sparta's enemies. As early as −475 the Spartans considered a plan for a pre-emptive war with Athens. The seeds of conflict between an expansive, democratic, mercantile empire and a conservative, oligarchic, military alliance were already sown.

The First Peloponnesian War (−460 to −446/5), in which Athens fought mainly with Sparta's allies, reflected the sense of vulnerability of both sides. Athens feared it could easily be invaded by Sparta and so sought allies of her own (including Argos, Thessaly and Megara) in the Peloponnese; Sparta and especially Corinth resisted Athenian forward moves. When the Megarans returned to the Spartan fold, the Athenians were suddenly vulnerable to a Spartan attack, and the First Peloponnesian War came to an end when Pericles signed the Peace Treaty which led to the Thirty Years' peace.

The collapse of that peace, and the origins of the Second Peloponnesian War of −432, which formed the subject of Thucydides' narrative, involved a series of complex political moves and disputes between Athenian and Spartan allies. The manoeuvres involved were crucial in shaping the decisions for war. The context, however, was already set by the gathering strength of the Athenian Empire, and the threat that the Spartans perceived in it. Both *poleis* were vulnerable to each other: Sparta, because the power of the Delian League could attract away crucial allies; Athens because a threat to its naval power could undermine its empire and threaten its trade routes. Well before the Second Peloponnesian War started, the main elements of the conflict of interest between the two leading city states had already formed.

What made the conflict of interest reach the point of perceived incompatibility? For Athens, dependence on the empire and on the trade routes for the feeding of her population and the power and prosperity of the city made the maintenance of the empire and a pre-eminent fleet a vital interest. Pericles was therefore willing to intervene in the Corcyran dispute to avoid the Corcyran fleet falling into the hands of an ally of Sparta's. Although his intervention was deliberately limited, it inflamed the Corinthians who appealed to Sparta for support in their dispute with

Athens. The Spartan leadership decided that Athens had broken the terms of the Truce, and the war began.

Links between different interests

The emergent conflict preceding the Peloponnesian War highlights the importance of links between interests. Athens' growing trade and wealth increased her population, and this in turn made Athens dependent on the corn supply. Dependence on imported corn made the size of the fleet a vital interest. A rival fleet was then seen as a potential threat to the Athenians' vital interests. If population size, trade, and size of the navy are selected as variables to represent this situation, there are functional relationships between them, and the preferred size of the navy changes with the value of the other variables.

The overall viability of the Athenian city-state was a complex function of these variables. From the point of view of material interests, we could say that the goal of Athens with regard to the size of its navy is dictated by the volume of its trade. If we could correlate the size of the navy with the changing volume of trade, this would give a foundation for the argument that material interests determine political needs. But this would be to accept a deterministic view. I argue later that what matters politically was the Athenians' perceptions of their needs, and these are construed rather than objective.

Whether determined or construed, however, a chain of links between variables sets the interests and goals of the social organizations. A change of position by one actor, mediated by intermediate variables, can thus contribute to conflict of interest with another.

Conflict behaviour

So far, my theoretical discussion has assumed that, from the organization's viewpoint, the environmental changes are exogenous. But, of course, human organizations control their own environment. We need an open system theory of conflict that allows for both environmental change and the conflict behaviour of the parties. In short, as Galtung's triangle suggests, we need to go beyond identifying the conflict of interest, to consider how parties construe their interests and how they behave in response.

Exogenous changes are under the control of the environment. Endogenous changes are under the control of the organizations. Let us assume, then, that the values of certain variables are set by the organization's attributes and behaviour, and these variables will influence other organizations and can produce conflicts of interest and interdependence with others.

In a simple case a change in the behaviour of one organization upsets another, which has become adapted to the old behaviour. So this leads to conflict. It may be one-sided if the second organization cannot influence the first. It is two-sided if the second organization can react in a way that affects the first. Chapter 7 gives examples from the conflicts of interest over climate change.

In a complex system more representative of the real world, both environmental changes and behavioural changes occur together. Conflict may start when an environmental change precipitates a change of behaviour in one social organization, leading to a perception or construction of a conflict of interest by another, in turn leading to a change of behaviour by the other organization, and so setting up an action and reaction cycle. This is only a deterministic process if the organizations allow it to be. Arms races, like anarchy, are what states make of them. What is crucial is how the social organizations construe their reactions to one another.

Let us take a simplified case where two actors each control one environmental variable, and each is affected by the values of the environmental variable set by the other. A's preferences with respect to B's behaviour can be represented by a utility curve, that we can take to be linear for simplicity. B's preferences with respect to A's behaviour is another linear curve. If we then plot A's behaviour against B's behaviour from the utility curves, we arrive at the familiar Richardson diagram of an arms race.

Figure 2.16 shows the dynamic of conflict in Boulding's terms, where the isopreference curves are the payoffs or viability of two organizations with respect to two strategic variables each under the control of one of the organizations. If the organizations start at point a, they both have a common interest in moving to b, where their payoffs are higher.

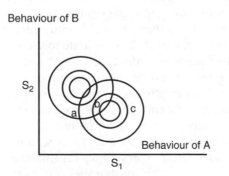

Figure 2.16   Viability curves on two variables

This is a compromise between their respective preferences, on the line between their preferred positions. However, from this point, party A can force a move to c, which may be no worse from its point of view but considerably worse from the other party's point of view. Similarly, party B can force the outcome into areas where party A is not viable. If each starts to behave in this kind of way, imposing costs on the other, an escalation of conflict can develop in which both end up worse off. The dynamic behaviour that follows is a Richardson process. (Boulding 1962, 37–8; Nicholson 1992; Binmore 1992: 290). Assuming that both parties seek to move in the direction of their highest payoffs, and that the payoff curves are static with respect to conflict behaviour, it is possible to plot the dynamics of conflict behaviour, showing the direction of movement of the system at any point.

In the discussion so far I have assumed that there are only two actors. But it is possible to extend the treatment to consider any number. Then, with respect to some variable representing attributes of the society or social decisions, the degree of conflict of interest could be taken as a weighted average of the differences between each actor's position (Axelrod 1970). Where the society tends to polarize, so that one group of actors takes one side of a conflict and another group takes another, the social conflict of interest increases. Where a society is less polarized, even if some actors have significant differences, societal conflict of interest is reduced.

Conflict behaviour, in so far as it is instrumental, aims to induce the other party to change its position. The initiator of the behaviour tries to make the other party alter its goals, move from a position that is damaging, or desist from conflict behaviour of its own. Of course, such behaviour can have both constructive and destructive results.

The theory sketched here has shown how changing environmental conditions leads to moves by social organizations, that can set up conflicts of interests between them. It has also suggested a means by which social organizations can divide into separate interest groups. In practice, of course, the formation of conflicts of interest and new political groups and socio-economic interests is a complex process, driven not only by the imperatives of material interests, but also by the politics of identity group formation and the way in which political actors construe themselves and their situation (Cedermann 1997: 32; Wendt 1999: 128–9). I need now to turn to consider how social organizations construe these interests, and how actors representing organizations formulate their goals. Without such an understanding, we cannot grasp the purposive as well as the reactive aspects of conflict.

Actors and interests

So far I have considered how conflicts of interest emerge and how actors intensify them by conflict behaviour in pursuit of their goals. But how are goals shaped? How do a party's existing interests, values and positions generate new goals in other domains? Are goals dictated by the necessity of material interests, or are they constructed socially through the will of the actors, representing understandings and values shaped by the wider culture?

To speak of a social group as having a goal involves a degree of abstraction. Generally economics restricts decision-makers to persons, or at least corporate persons, who can be said to have preferences. Groups clearly have members with different preferences and do not necessarily behave like persons. Nevertheless, social actors with many members do act in a purposeful way. Organizations have collective interests, goals and plans that differ from those of their members.

The way in which organizations, polities and other collective groups formulate such goals is the subject of politics. Organizations may be simple interest groups that act on the basis of those interests. But often interest groups are themselves organized into larger political coalitions, and comprise different sub-groups within themselves. The creation of social actors thus depends on an identification of interests, and this itself will usually involve the construction of an identity and also the formulation of collective interest on behalf of the organization.

Social actors are influenced in part by the interests and changes affecting their members, and in part by the way their decision-makers construe their interests and goals. Typically an existing leadership group construes collective interests and develops policies and plans in the name of the collective organization. This leadership group may change, or it may change its ideas, and this will alter the action that is taken.

The actions of all the members of the group influence the collective actions that are possible. Consider, for example, American farmers in the coastal colonies of America in the nineteenth century. Individual families pursued different goals as families. Some moved north, some moved south, some moved back to Europe, others had just arrived as immigrants from Europe. But the dominant movement was westwards, because people saw opportunities to make a better living where the land was cheap. This had a quality of a mass movement, propelled by a 'logic of large numbers'. We can say that the American farmers collectively developed an interest in westward expansion and that this interest arose in part from the geographical conditions they found and in part from their values (which were to be self-sufficient and to grow rich and to improve themselves). The representation of this interest as a political goal depended on it being taken up by political representatives and articulated by them.

How the political representatives formulate goals on behalf of their communities depends in part on the trends and challenges they face, and in part on their existing set of values and goals. Perceived interests reflect both objective circumstances and a group's perceptions of the meaning of these circumstances. Indeed, the very definition of a set of relevant circumstances is itself laden with meanings vested in the situation by the group and reflecting its sense of identity and its world-view. Goals and interests, then, are socially constructed (Wendt 1999: 114–15, 122–30). But there is a logic in how groups formulate their goals, which reflects their circumstances and those of their members. Actors can step out of their situation and do something novel and different. But even then their situation shapes what is feasible. As Marx said, men (and women) make history but not in conditions of their own choosing.

In many conflicts, interests are strongly determined by context, and a deterministic representation, in which goals are functions of existing interests and positions, has some plausibility. Social forces do channel and shape social action. However, the decisions and will of human actors are also crucial parts of the story. History cannot be explained convincingly as a clockwork pattern of social forces without taking account of how decision-makers interpret their interests and set their overall values and goals. We need, then, a cognitive theory of goal formulation, which allows for the setting of new goals in the context of developing social forces, taking into account the interplay between cultural, cognitive and political factors.

A cognitive theory of goal formation

One of the drawbacks of the deterministic vision of history is that it sees the future as driven by the past. Past trends determine future events. We have allowed that large social forces do have a kind of statistical determinism, which limit the scope for the entirely new. However, cultural evolution differs from natural evolution. Human agents are aware of their environment. We have views about where we want to go. Human groups are purposive. Our actions need to be explained with reference to teleology as well as by reference to past trends.

An important part of the theory of conflict must therefore explain how parties *formulate* their goals. We cannot adequately account for conflict as contradictions between social forces without taking account of this teleological aspect, because frequently incompatibilities arise

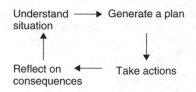

Figure 2.17   Kolb's model of reflective learning

over plans that have not yet been carried out, or over fears rather than over damage that has already been done. 'Contentious goals are infinitely various' (Kriesberg 1998: 78), but they are formulated deliberately to match an existing set of purposes, interest and values. Goal-seeking is thus a part of an overall teleological process which is characteristic of living things (Galtung 1996: 71).

Sommerhof's (1969: 184–5) general theory of teleological processes is suggestive here. He gives the example of an arm reaching out to grasp an object. The initiator of this event is the mental act of volition: 'I wish to grasp this object'. In order to execute this plan, a set of sub-goals has to be executed successfully. The upper arm has to be extended, the lower arm raised, the hand clenched and the thumb and fingers brought together in a co-ordinated way.

An essential feature of purposive, or goal-directed behaviour, is that it adapts to varying environmental conditions. An arm that simply extended in the same way, irrespective of the location of what it wanted to grasp, would not exhibit goal-directed characteristics. The essential feature of a teleological system is that it adjusts actions, and sub-goals, to perform the desired action in the context of a variable environment.

In a similar way social actors adopt linked sub-goals, and direct their movements according to an overall plan. Actors form goals in relation to their existing understandings of the situation, their pre-existing purposes and their experience. In turn they act on and reflect on those goals and modify goal-seeking behaviour accordingly.

A model of how this is done can be derived from Kolb's reflective learning cycle, shown in Figure 2.17. In a changing situation, actors 'understand' the situation by assessing their environment and their position, determining which aspects of their position are strengths and weaknesses, formulating plans for improvement, and so on. In a social situation, of course, this means also assessing the plans and positions of others. Goals are set accordingly and then evaluated. Building on the Kolb diagram, we can reformulate it as in Figure 2.18.

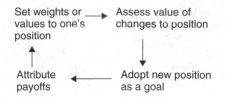

Figure 2.18   A model of adaptive learning

It is interesting to compare this with the model of adaptation proposed by Holland (1992, 1995). Holland develops schemata to explain how complex adaptive systems can formulate goals in environments where the rewards may be distantly related to the rules that lead towards them.

The problem is encapsulated by his example of a frog trying to catch a fly. The frog has no problem in doing this. It forms the volition that it wants to swallow a fly, its tongue shoots out and the fly is in its mouth. But designing a frog capable of performing this trick is a complicated task. The frog must be programmed to detect the fly, distinguish it from other moving objects that might be threats, anticipate the fly's direction, determine the angle to rotate its head and flick out the tongue at the right moment. Holland suggests that a way to model how evolution might accomplish this would be to allow selective retention of rules that combine together to formulate the plan. For example, the frog might consider the rule 'if small flying object detected, then move head 20 degrees'. Rules are tried out and then 'posted' on a message board. The combined rules govern the behaviour of the frog and successful rules are rewarded with the payoff of catching the fly.

The combination of rules in force at any moment depends on how well they have performed in the past. Holland proposes an allocation scheme (the 'bucket brigade') whereby successful rules pass on payoffs to one another, so that the value of individual rules to the whole result can be assessed. The rules present are rewarded after each success and their strength adjusted relative to other rules. Slight changes in the rules continue to be made (according to random mutations, assisted by genetic crossover) and these are selected according to their success.

Using a similar set of ideas for the formulation of goals, we can now get some sense of how an actor continually formulates and reformulates a set of goals as a social situation develops or as the environment changes. An actor, we assume, starts with a position in a social context and an existing set of goals. The actor's success or otherwise is reflected in some form of payoff, which is then used to re-allocate a set of weights to the goals. According to this process, strengths and weaknesses are assessed. The actor then formulates a new goal which carries it forward. Actors retain goals while the payoff they receive seems to justify them. They discard goals when they are no longer profitable. Actors will add new goals to existing goals, forming a tree of organized goals or decision rules. Axelrod (1976) and others have demonstrated that decision-makers do construct 'goal trees' in this way.

Under natural selection, adaptations are rewarded by payoffs from the environment. Successful adaptations are selected and allowed to breed. Under cultural evolution, it is the actors themselves who do the selecting. Actors pick their own goals and choose their own positions. The payoffs therefore come in part from their own valuations, as well as from the outcomes they achieve. In political contexts those who support a particular plan win political support in so far as they can persuade their group of the value of the plan. This will rest partly on their political success in carrying this plan forward relative to other programmes championed by alternative leaders, and partly on the success of the plan itself.

Cultural evolution is faster than natural evolution. It is not limited to the blind process of mutation and natural selection. It discriminates and it is purposive. When the geneticist Richard Dawkins created evolving 'morphs' in a computer by allowing them to mutate according to simple rules, he selected and bred the specimens he liked. In this way he rapidly generated life-like creatures. In social evolution, the actors select their goals and adopt patterns of behaviour by discarding old positions, moving on to new ones and integrating their goals into an overall purpose. Competition and conflict within groups over alternative plans further increase the rate of change.

In practice, of course, different members of any social group have different ideas about appropriate goals, and it is common for groups to comprise sub-groups which may compete for support for different plans. A plan that carries the group with it, or that can be successfully foisted on a group, becomes the group's plan. We do not require any concept of a 'group mind' here: it is sufficient that groups can hold collective intentions or collective beliefs or collective policies because their members accept or acquiesce in them (Gilbert 1992: 306–8).

But sub-groups may pursue different plans, and groups may differentiate on the basis of different plans for the future just as readily as over different interests in the present. Typically parties to conflict comprise sub-groups with different views about the appropriate gains. Plans may also reward sub-groups differentially. There is thus a basis for competition over plans between groups and a mechanism for new plans, championed by sub-groups, to appear. Often these new plans will be copied from existing ones but adapted and revised in some significant respect. When groups try out different plans their relative success creates a basis for individuals to choose which group to join. Hence the social mechanism of groups offering support for (or acquiescence in) different plans offers a social parallel to Holland's 'bucket brigade'.

This reflective model of goal formation is consistent with the view that groups' interests are not given but are socially created as a result of discussion, deliberation and political competition (Wendt 1999: 113–35). As Wendt points out:

> Often one of the most difficult tasks facing foreign policy decision-makers is figuring out what their interests *are*. This process does not typically consist of weighing competing interests on a 'grocer's scale' of intensity, or even of aggregating the exogenously given preferences of different individuals. It typically consists in complex and highly contested process of discussion, persuasion and framing of issues. In short, what goes on is collective deliberation about what their interests in a given situation should be. These deliberations do not take place in a vacuum, either domestic or international, but neither are they strictly determined by domestic or systemic structures. (128–9)

Ambiguous

Decision-makers choose their goals, under the influence of their cultural and social milieu and their immediate exigencies. The formulation of new goals thus reflects in part external circumstances, in part intragroup dynamics, and in part the values and cognitive processes of decision-makers. It is clearly a crucial step in the process of conflict emergence. If contentious goals are chosen, parties can make conflict much more likely. On the other hand if goals are chosen that take into account other groups and other interests, conflict may be more likely to be prevented or mitigated (Kriesberg: 1998; Bartos and Wehr 2002).

Let us take an example from the conflict leading to the American Civil War. A key choice of goals was the decision of people in the southern states to try to establish a slave state in Kansas, and the decision of northerners to ensure it was free. How did both sides in the conflict become committed to the goals of a Kansas organized to allow slavery, or not?

The political background here was one of increasing pressure on the Missouri Compromise and the gradual breakdown of the existing party system which straddled the North–South divide. The South had defeated the Wilmot Proviso of 1846, which had sought to ban the establishment of slavery in any territory annexed following the war with Mexico. The gold rush brought an inrush of free labour to California, making it politically impossible for slavery to get established there. The southern states were not prepared for slavery to be restricted to the existing areas, for then the southerners would lose their equal standing in the Union (Brogan 1986: 307). A further compromise, the Compromise of 1850, provided for California to be admitted as a free state, New Mexico and Utah to be admitted as territories with their inhabitants to settle whether they were free or slave, the slave trade in the District of Columbia to be abolished and a stricter Fugitive Slave Law to be enforced. The Democratic Party, under the leadership of Senator Douglas, then proposed a new programme to organize the Nebraska Territory, between Illinois and the Rockies, on the basis of popular sovereignty as in the Compromise of 1850; later it was divided into Nebraska and Kansas. The intention was to smooth the differences between northerners and southerners, for the area was considered unsuitable for slave plantations: while slavery would not be excluded, popular sovereignty was expected to make the territories free soil. In practice the proposal backfired. Douglas agreed to repeal the Missouri Compromise, and to the northerners it seemed that his measures meant that slavery could spread even to the North. The slave-holders in Missouri seized the opportunity to try to make neighbouring Kansas slave-holding. Their settlers collided with the stream of free farmers and homesteaders arriving from the old Northwest. The two sides organized rival governments and, to the chagrin of the northerners, the Missourians managed to install their own government first (helped by fraudulent elections), which the Democratic President Pierce recognized. An open conflict developed with small-scale fighting between the two factions.

This conflict was at the local level, between rival groups of settlers, in a relatively lawless, frontier environment. But public opinion and the interventions of leaders on both sides kept it at the forefront of national politics. The southern Democrats, who dominated the government at this stage, wanted to ensure their political dominance and they became committed to holding the position that the Missourians had taken in Kansas. This was reinforced by popular propaganda and a sense in the South that southern honour and the republic were threatened by the anti-slavery position of the North. The northerners, in contrast, became committed to the free soil position in Kansas, despite the distance of Kansas from the main centres of population. The old national parties, Whigs, and then Democrats, lost their support in the North. For a time the anti-immigrant, anti-Catholic Know-Nothing party supplanted them.

But after a time the Republican Party emerged as the main vehicle for organizing the northern sectional sentiment. The northerners were against the Kansas–Nebraska Act because they perceived it as extending slavery and threatening the position of the free people of the North. Their propagandists wrote about the North itself being enslaved by the South. They saw the struggle in Kansas as a battle in the larger struggle for the soul of the republic. They were enfuriated by the Missourians who invaded Kansas to vote in the local elections. They were outraged that President Pierce supported the pro-slavery government. And they linked 'bloody Kansas' with the assault by Brooks, a southern congressman, on Sumner, the anti-slavery Senator, and with what they saw as the assault of the 'slave power' on freedom and the free republic. In these ways the settlement of Kansas, either as a slave state, or as free, became a goal dividing the South and the Democrats from the North and the Republicans.

What lifted the dispute from a local competition for advantage in a particular state to a central battle of national politics, given the introduction of popular sovereignty, was the identification of Kansas as a crucial stake in the control of the Senate, and hence in the management of the larger conflict dividing the two sides. So the coming of popular sovereignty increased the payoffs to each side from the race to settle Kansas.

Figure 2.19 suggests the way in which the 'goal trees' of the two sides evolved over time. The initial goals of the parties, were, on the southern side, to maintain and improve the position of the Cotton Kingdom and hence to foster the wealth and status of southern society, especially its elite. The southerners also wanted to sustain the republic in their own image, as a society in which freedoms and property rights, including

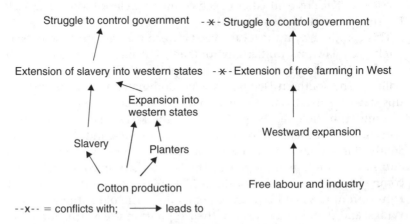

Figure 2.19   Goal trees of the ante-bellum North and the South

property in slaves, were respected, and the values of southern society preserved. On the northern side, the goal was to foster individual initiative and enterprise, to allow individuals to make their own living and prosper, to exploit the new territories for free farming. So preserving the freedoms of the republic, allowing western expansion were among the key goals of the north. As intermediate goals, the northerners and north-westerners were committed to western expansion and the organization of the west for free farming. They were also determined to preserve their position in the Union and avoid the domination of the Union by free states. And so the northerners through the Republican party adopted the goal of securing Kansas as a free state.

A model of the process of goal formation might be outlined as follows. An actor has an existing set of positions and goals. These can be organized as a cognitive map and represented in a matrix form (Axelrod 1972). The actor operates in an open environment, in which new issues and events arise both as a result of the actions of other actors and exogenous change. The actor evaluates these new events and adapts its goals to them either by forming new goals in relation to them and/or by discarding or rearranging existing goals.[13]

How does the actor relate the existing goals in its cognitive map to the new environment, to formulate new goals? One way of representing this is to link objects in the environment to existing sub-goals using IF–THEN rules. Let the object in the environment be the possible action: 'Organize the territory of Kansas'. Consider the South in 1852. This new issue has arisen as a result of the passage of the Kansas–Nebraska Act. The South already has as goals 'preserve slavery', 'extend slavery' and 'improve our position in the Senate'. The South can link the new issue to its existing goal tree by formulating the new rule: IF [we] 'Organize the territory of Kansas' [with certain conditions], THEN [we will] 'improve our position in the Senate'. In general, any new issue (I) can be linked to existing goals (G) under suitable conditions (C), with the function IF I [(and C)] THEN G. The goal of 'Organize the territory of Kansas [in a way which meets the goal of extending slavery]' is then linked to the existing goal tree.

In this way new goal formation and the evolution of a goal tree over time can be modelled. The simple IF–THEN rules offer a sparse logical relationship. A more complex syntax could allow for more complex meanings and relationships between goals. It is also possible to allot weights to different issues and sub-goals, according to their importance to the party's overall goals. In principle this procedure allows for the generation of new variables relating new issues to parties' existing interests and goals.

Summary

I shall now attempt to bring together the different aspects of the theory of emergent conflict. The evolutionary conflict theory set out in this chapter offers a way of conceiving of social organizations as existing in 'niches' on relevant variables of social development. Their welfare or fitness depends on how well they are adapted to their environment. If we take a point of maximum welfare or fitness as the 'goal' of the organization in a sub-environment, we can develop a welfare or viability or fitness function over a range of values of the environment, where fitness falls with distance from the goal. The goal on one variable is linked to goals on others, in a chain. Social, cognitive and cultural factors shape the goals, which are influenced, but not determined, by material interests.

The main steps in the development of the theory were to show that environmental change can damage the fitness of an organization, and when this results from change by another organization it constitutes a conflict of interest between them. Sub-groups can form as a response to different environmental pressures and they are the basis for differentiation of organizations. I showed how a conflict of interest between organizations can become an incompatibility. And I discussed how conflict behaviour between groups can amplify existing conflicts of interest and make competition ruinous.

The cognitive theory of goal formation suggests that conflict behaviour has to be seen as teleological, rather than reactive. Conflicts are clashes between adaptive plans. I described mechanisms by which actors can adjust their goals in response to payoffs. I indicated how parties can adopt new goals, by linking new possibilities in their environment to an existing cognitive map. Using IF–THEN links they can then formulate new goals as extensions to existing goal trees. At the same time old goals can be discarded and the whole system of goals can be reorganized (by adjusting weights between goals, changing the links between goals, and adopting or discarding goals) in accordance with the needs of the organization.

All this can be illustrated in a very simple model of a teleological conflict, which could apply to the Peloponnesian War, the American Civil War, or the potential conflict over global warming. This is depicted in Figure 2.20. Each party starts from a position on a separate variable that determines its material interests. In the case of the Athenians, for example, their population is becoming dependent on imported corn: the level of imported corn that is optimum at a particular moment in time is given by S_A in Figure 2.20. Given this interest, the Athenians seek a bigger fleet (e_2 on the top curve). The Spartans' interest is to secure their land allies in the Peloponnese against the risk of a Helot rising. So they prefer a smaller

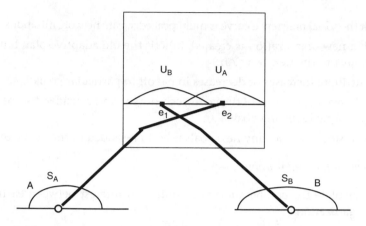

Figure 2.20 Conflict as striving and frustration

Athenian fleet (e_1 on the top curve). The striving for separate interests creates a conflict of interest on the common variable.[14]

Conflict parties are thus seen as teleological systems. Given existing interests, they formulate chains of goals (or adaptive plans), in the same sense that the arm in Sommerhof's example grasps for its object. In the process, they come into contact with other adaptive plans. This results in frustration, conflict of interest, and eventually a contradiction.

A procedure for calculating the development of conflict of interest can be set out in the form of a flow-chart, as in Box 2.1 below.

Box 2.1 A flow-chart for calculating emergent conflict

Initiation

Read the names of the initial variables
Read the names of the initial organizations
Read the initial positions of the organizations
Read the initial goal trees of the organizations

For each time period:

For each organization

Identify feasible moves for the organization that improve its position

Make the moves and calculate the resulting viability curve, given its goals and the values of the variables

If the social preference curve is multi-peaked, create new organizations

If a new organization is created, inherit the old adaptive plan but adjust to the new position

Attribute increases or decreases in payoff to particular goals

Change the weights of the goals accordingly, and consider discarding or reorganizing goals

Consider whether any new goals need to be added to the goal tree

For all the organizations

Calculate the co-operation and conflict of interest between each organization

Context

Introduce environmental changes
Introduce new variables as appropriate
Eliminate low viability organizations

From conflict of interest to overt conflict

The discussion so far has explored the conditions of emergent conflicts of interest. I have said little yet about how a conflict of interest in which the parties are damaging one another or frustrating each other's goals, turns into an overt and potentially violent conflict.

Most relationships between parties embody a mixture of conflict and co-operation. Some conflict issues can be dealt with by co-operative means. Others can be lived with, without being resolved. Co-operation on some issues balances conflict on others. Why, then, do some issues become so salient that parties are ready to fight over them?

In real conflicts a typical process is the early emergence of a conflict of interest over a relatively minor issue. This gradually intensifies as the parties put more and more energy into the conflict, and other goals polarize around the issue in conflict. Eventually the conflict becomes the most important issue to the parties and occupies their attention to the exclusion of other factors.

A number of political, social and psychological factors are involved in this intensification. First, the significance of the conflict of interest to the parties itself grows, to the point where it may appear ruinous and threaten the destruction of one of the parties. Second, polarization around the issue divides societies or states around the conflict, as other issues become linked to the core issue. Third, parties seek to influence each other's behaviour by threats, inducements, persuasion or coercion. Fourth, psychological processes are engaged, which distort parties' perceptions of one another and provoke mutual distrust, fear and hate. Fifth, political processes are critical as the conflict fractures an existing structure of parties and brings about political realignments, often along the lines of the conflict cleavage; intra-party competition intensifies and more extreme leaders come to power; and the struggle over the issues in conflict expands into a general struggle for power in the relevant political arena.

Increasing significance of the contested goals

I have described above a process whereby social or environmental change brings about changes in goals, and this is the fundamental factor in making them more significant. I have also suggested how actors attach different weights to different goals over time, as circumstances change. Changes in conditions make peripheral issues vital. For example, Kansas became a burning issue in antebellum America not because of the local significance of the contest for the state between slave-holders and free settlers, but because of its importance for the control of the Congress after the legislation of popular sovereignty.

At any time an organization will have a variety of goals. Some of these will be vital to its survival. Others will be more peripheral. There is some justification for regarding some interests as inherently more vital than others. Some material interests which are functionally significant for an economy, and without which it could not operate, have a reasonable claim to be described as vital interests. However, the crucial factor is how parties construe their own interests. If two bald men think a comb is worth a fight, there will be a fight, however much outsiders shake their heads.

There may be a number of reasons why parties may regard contested issues as more significant to them than observers might think they are. First of all, they may regard a low priority goal as being linked to higher priority goals, or potentially linked to them (even if an observer might doubt the validity of this link). Second, they may fear that any loss may potentially threaten larger stakes, such as their identity, their power or their reputation. A decision-making elite may fear losses on its watch, even if they are insignificant, if this could give domestic opponents ammunition to use against them. Third, parties may fear others even if the threat they pose is not significant.

All of these are ways in which parties can invest significance in an issue, and thus amplify its significance. A person seeking a particular goal, especially if they are thwarted, may strain with greater effort to secure the goal and in doing so their investment in the goal increases. Protagonists invest their will and identity in the contested goal, projecting their ego onto the goal. The threat to the goal can then become a threat to identity (McConnell 1995; Volkan et al. 1991; Mitchell 1981).

This process of linking goals together once a conflict of interest has begun is a typical part of conflict intensification. Once begun it has a momentum of its own and increasingly significant goals may be linked by one side to its threatened interests as conflict becomes more open and intense.

Polarization

Conflicts over specific issues tend to widen and draw in other issues. When the conflict becomes acute, this can lead to polarization of a whole society, or of a set of states, around the key conflict. The process of polarization is one in which the multiple parties and conflict cleavages gradually become aligned along the axis of the conflict.

The conflict leading to the American Civil War is a classic example. The conflict of interests had developed between the slave-owning South and the northern states, which were dominated by free labour. In the 1820s the conflict manifested itself in controversies over tariffs, states' rights and western expansion. But the sections were not yet clearly articulated as political interest groups, and the major political parties drew support from all the sections. The political leadership of the United States at this time was drawn from the Middle States, and they saw the Union's national interests as overriding sectional interests. A variety of conflicts of interest sometimes aligned the West with the Northeast, sometimes with the South. The West was economically dependent on the South, which bought its agricultural products. Northern financiers and ship-owners organized the cotton trade for the South. So although the slavery issue was, as Jefferson called it, 'a fire bell in the night', it did not immediately lead to national divisions. The parties accepted the Missouri Compromise as a means of managing the slavery issue until the 1840s.

By the 1840s, however, the differentiation of the sections into a cotton-growing slave society in the South and an urbanized, industrialized North had become more marked, and the conflict over slavery and over the extension of slavery to the west intensified. From the mid-1840s the sections became aligned into differing political interest groups, which regularly took opposing positions. The race for control over new states became a struggle for control of the Union.

Opinion on both sides hardened. Churches and political parties found it increasingly difficult to straddle the divide and the 1850s saw a decisive realignment of the political system on sectional lines. With the identification of the Democratic party with the slave power in the South, and of the new Republican party with the free labour interests of the North and Northwest, the polarization of American politics became intense. Finally, in the very last stages of the conflict, the middle states of the upper South could no longer avoid taking sides.

Threat and escalation

Issues become significant because of changes in environmental conditions and the perceptions of parties. They become polarized when they are linked with other issues and become the basis for political alignments. Finally they become a threat to survival when parties turn from competition over contested issues to direct attacks on one another.

A key element of this intensification is the making of *threats*. If a conflictant is suffering some losses as a result of another party's position or actions, he may use threats to induce the opponent to move from that position, to desist from the obnoxious actions or to comply with required actions. The threat raises the stakes, since if executed it would usually lead to deliberate damage to the interests of the other party or to direct hurt. In this way, a threat can translate a conflict of interest into a destructive conflict directly between parties.

The threat originates from the instrumental logic of goal-seeking: in order to secure my goal, I require you to conform to my wishes. But threats quickly take on a logic of their own. They lead to counter-threat and escalation. As a result parties can quickly proceed from an apparently calculated communication to a deeply irrational conclusion (Schelling 1960; Rapoport 1974, 1989; Ogley 1991; Howard 1999).

Psychological processes

Threats are closely linked with fears, which are linked in turn with parties' interacting goals. A party that fears being out-manoeuvred or exposed to losses in the future may respond by threatening to take damaging actions, and the threat then may induce counter-threats, which further poison the atmosphere. These threats do not necessarily have to be realistic to be politically important. For example, in 1856 the southern States feared that an anti-slavery North would subordinate the South to the North's interests and destroy its way of life. According to one New Orleans newspaper, 'If they should succeed in this contest ... they would repeal the fugitive slave law ... they would create insurrection and servile war in the South ... they would put the torch to our dwellings and the knife to our throats.' (Craven, *Coming of Civil War*, quoted in Collins 1981).

It did not matter whether such fears were well-founded. Real or imaginary, they had a powerful impact in aligning opinion in the conflict.

Delusions can play an important part in motivating conflict (McConnell 1995). Other psychological processes, including projection, splitting, stereotyping, displacement, selective perception, group-think, and so on, are well known in the literature (Mitchell 1981; Janis 1972; Volkan et al. 1991; Covington et al. 2002).

The struggle for power

Closely related to fear is the issue of power, for when a conflict becomes significant the possession of power becomes vital as it is seen as the key to resolving the conflict. So a serious conflict always develops into a struggle for power between the parties. In a civil contest it tends to becomes a struggle for control of the government. In an international contest, it becomes a struggle for power in the international system. This struggle readily leads to further polarization, as both sides seek allies.

The final stage, in which an open violent conflict breaks out, depends on the precise circumstances, the trigger causes. In the case of the American Civil War the states of the deep South decided to secede as soon as Lincoln was elected President in 1860, out of fear of the threat they perceived to their way of life from his election. However, the upper South remained in the Union, and awaited Lincoln's response to the secession before making a move. While the Democratic caretaker administration continued, Congress discussed further schemes for compromise and revisions of the constitution that would guarantee equal power to the South. The effect of these moves was to consolidate the support of the North and West for a defence of the Union against those who were seen to be wrecking it, either by secession or by upsetting the Constitution.

When the developing conflict becomes a crisis on the brink of violent conflict, there is often a 'funnelling' process, as wider issues in conflict are focused on particular points of contention, which thus become invested with a broader significance while having no great significance in themselves. The particular issues chosen as a test of strength may depend on individual decisions and circumstances. In the case of the American Civil War Lincoln chose not to enforce federal law against the seceding states in the deep South. He carefully avoided appointing federal officials collecting federal customs in the southern states, lest these should trigger war. But he did decide to insist on retaining control of the federal forts in the deep South, Fort Pickens and Fort Sumter. When he took this position Lincoln had believed the forts could be held for a long period. On taking office he learned that Fort Sumter needed to be re-supplied.[15]

The Confederate government refused to allow this and started the attack on the fort on 12 April 1861. Accordingly, it was the question of federal control of Fort Sumter that proved the trigger for the outbreak of the war. When Lincoln then called on the states to supply troops to suppress the insurgency, the second wave of secession began, led by Virginia and followed by most other states in the upper South and South West.

The threats involved in these events had all been well trailed beforehand. The North and West had made it clear that extension of slavery into western states would be resisted. If an anti-slavery movement captured federal power, Southern state leaders had threatened to secede. Northerners and westerners had made it clear that in order to defend the Union, they would not allow secession. So the sequence of threats and events leading to war had a remorseless logic, although at the same time the nature of the war that actually took place depended crucially on the sequence of events in 1860–61.

To recap, I have outlined how parties experience an emergent conflict of interest as a result either of environmental changes or of their making moves which put their interests in conflict. Subsequent moves bring the interests of the parties into more intense conflict and polarize the society along the lines of the conflict cleavage. As the conflict becomes increasingly salient the parties become acutely sensitive to their power balance. Their common institutions become an arena for conflict. At the same time the conflict turns from competition over issues to direct threats or hurts against the parties. At the point that the parties believe their survival is at stake, they see no alternative but to go to war.

From conflict of interest to structural conflict

At this point I wish to turn briefly to two other types of conflict that I will cover more briefly: structural conflicts and cultural conflicts. As Galtung argues (1996), both of them are significant if we are to identify positive conditions for peace and hence for peaceful change. I will confine myself here to sketching schematically the processes by which structural conflict and cultural conflicts emerge and indicating the links between them and the theory of emergent conflict above.

Social structures reproduce conflict when they embed relationships of dominance or inequality in roles and relationships. Examples of such 'structural conflicts' are the conflicts of interest between masters and slaves embedded in slave societies, between lords and peasants embedded in feudalism, or between castes in caste societies. Modern examples are the embedded conflicts of interest in the organization of contemporary global economies, which reproduce immensely wealthy metropolitan entrepots in some places, such as San Francisco, and immensely poor urban slums in others, such as Caracas. Most societies maintain and reproduce unequal relationships and conflicts of interest. In some cases, these may be so pervasive, deep-rooted, intractable, and apparently unchangeable, that they do not necessarily precipitate the development of overt conflicts. In others they may lead to political mobilization resulting both in movements for reform and violent revolutionary uprisings, violent repression and other forms of violent conflict.

Sociologists (Bartos and Wehr 2002: 38–41) distinguish *vertical differentiation* from *horizontal differentiation*. In principle the notion of conflict of interest extends readily to vertical differentiation, which can be identified on such variables as 'income', 'access to capital', and 'ownership of land'. One can then identify social interest groups and political actors or coalitions who mobilize these interests and express them as goals.

The emergence of a structural conflict of interest can be seen in quite simple social interactions. Anthropologists have examined how uneven development allows concentration of resources and how readily this leads to social stratification and the emergence of vertical structures, such as chiefdoms. Historians have examined the same process in literate societies. For example, Hicks (1969) offers a useful model of the processes involved in the formation of the lord-and-peasant system, which is typical of feudal societies; again this is a deliberately schematic outline. Bloch (1962) and other historians offer an explanation of the complex historical circumstances in which European and other feudal societies actually emerged.

In a simple, undifferentiated society farmers are responsible collectively for both production and security. They work the fields together; they fight together if they are threatened. But over a period of time it is likely to be more efficient for some people to specialize on food production and others on security. Perhaps the more important farmers come to take on special roles, as chiefs, and take a leadership function in emergencies. Having started down this road the two groups are likely gradually to specialize while becoming interdependent. The security specialists obtain food from the other farmers and the farmers obtain security from the security specialist. Since there are more farmers than security specialists, the security specialist can dictate the terms of the exchange. The security specialist evolves into a lord. The lords are then in a strong position to play the dominating role since their specialism gives them the means to coerce as well as protect. This structure is reproduced through following generations as people born into a stratified society occupy and reproduce stratified roles and the relationships.

Similar processes can be seen in apparently co-operative processes, such as the emergence of specialized traders, another process Hicks considers. Imagine, for instance, that a group of peasants are engaged in rudimentary agriculture. They come together for fairs or feasts, to barter and exchange their goods. In the process some well-placed individuals do relatively well in trade, and accumulate greater stocks than others. They are then in a position to withdraw from production and concentrate on trade. Once they have developed a stock and a place to sell it from, it will be natural for the other peasants to go to the trader rather than buy from each other. Gradually the remaining trading peasants will find themselves undercut and eased out by the trader, whose larger stocks give him the power to control the terms of trade. A conflict of interest does not necessarily develop: but the trader has opportunities to become richer, to set prices for goods and to dictate the terms of trades. In this way, again, a process of specialization leads to the emergence of vertical structure and may embed a structural conflict of interest.

It is relatively easy to see how apparently benign social changes can lead to this kind of structural change, sometimes in a wholly unintended way. For example, regions with well developed innovative sectors in information technology are gaining huge dividends from the growth in this market, while regions without such sectors face all the problems of dependency on new products with high relative prices, together with a relative price fall for their own products, which are in less demand.[16] In this way the market tends to funnel wealth in one direction and poverty in the other, in no less decisive a way than feudalism.

Cultural, identity and belief conflict

Conflicts of interest and structural conflicts are both cases where the interests of groups are damaged. But conflict can also be caused by hurts to the values that groups hold dear, or by incompatible beliefs, which may be seen as no less threatening than conflicts of interest. Perceived threats to religious beliefs and ethnic identity or political doctrines are just as likely to precipitate conflict as material hurts.

Cultural differences readily develop between groups and societies that are separated by distance, status, or language. Groups develop their own distinctive patterns of activity, meanings and division of roles, and any small group that is together for some time develops an identity of its own in this sense. As individuals also incorporate elements of a group identity into their own identity, this aspect of the group becomes very important to the individual. Changes that are perceived as a threat to the identity of the group are also felt to be threatening to the individual. Hence, for example, actions perceived to insult an ethnic group's identity or a religious group's beliefs may readily provoke overt conflict.

Of course, variety of beliefs, cultures and identities does not necessarily involve conflict and may indeed foster enrichment and offer potential for cultural dialogue, synthesis and creativity. But a number of types of change can foster conflict. Separate cultures tend to promote separate world-views and hence difficulties in understanding the motives and actions of others. There is therefore plenty of room for misinterpretation. Combining this factor with the tendency of in-groups to stereotype out-groups and to project onto them undesirable attributes, it is easy to see how readily difference can lead to suspicion and suspicion to hostility. When different cultures and identity groups come into contact there may be both intended and unintended impact on cultural traits or symbols of the other group. Sometimes quite trivial differences can become symbols of a cultural gulf as, for example, the controversy over *chadors* between France's white, secular majority and the Muslim minority (Ross 1993: 4–14).

We can represent a set of beliefs as a cognitive map, with beliefs linked together in an interconnected system. An evolving belief system can be seen in terms of a changing cognitive map, where new beliefs appear, old ones are discarded and new relationships between beliefs are developed (Axelrod 1976, Eden 1988). This belief system of course responds to a changing environment and, as it does so, pressures are set up for beliefs to change (since they have to correspond to their environment to be meaningful). Individuals, and societies as a whole, may hold beliefs that are inconsistent and this may lead to strains and dissonance within the society. However, when different communities or decision-makers hold inconsistent beliefs the belief system of one group may appear directly to threaten the belief system of another. Some of these threats can be real but misperceptions caused by different cultural interpretations of symbols, acts and gestures can create cultural conflict too.

Conflicts over identity, culture and belief can be seen to be closely linked to conflicts over interest and material conditions if we take the view that social organizations do not only organize a certain material environment, in which they must be viable, but also a cultural domain. All social organizations have a cultural dimension and they relate to their environment in terms of meanings, symbols and social codes as well as in terms of functions and interactions. Societies and social organizations are 'logico-meaningful' entities, as Sorokin insisted, and the cultural world is not divorced from or separate to the material world; rather, both infuse the other. So new organizations can emerge in cultural space, including the formation of new identities, new mentalities and new beliefs. Moreover, the change of an organization over time is exhibited characteristically in changing cultural forms (in Spengler's sense) as well as in social organization.

Conclusion

I have argued that, in order to develop a more satisfactory approach to conflict prevention, we need a better theory of emergent conflict. The evolutionary theory developed here shows how social or environmental change opens up conflicts of interest between organizations, how these can turn from small differences into contradictions, and how success or failure in adapting to change affects the viability of organizations. The theory allows for social differentiation and the creation of new organizations, and the extinction of those that are no longer viable. The cognitive model of goal formation suggests that conflict parties carry their goals with them and that they adapt these goals, taking on new ones and discarding old ones, in accordance with circumstances. I went on to develop a teleological model of conflict in which actors develop adaptive plans on the basis of their existing interests and these plans come into conflict. I suggest that such a theory, which brings together evolutionary processes and teleological processes, is necessary in order to embrace the phenomenon of emerging conflict.

The theory helps to explain the formation of overt relational conflicts, structural conflicts and cultural conflicts. A number of factors, cognitive, social, psychological and political, can translate conflicts of interest into overt conflicts, and in some circumstances into violent conflicts. However, I have argued that there is nothing deterministic about these processes. Organizations construe their own interests. The identification of processes that may lead to violence by the same token indicates points at which this process can be interrupted.

Conflicts are shaped not only by process but also by structure. The context of the conflict plays as vital a role in shaping outcomes as the process. The social context can be an aggravating factor, fuelling destructive conflict, or a constructive factor, channelling conflict into peaceful paths. The balance between the preventors and the causes of violent conflict is therefore a crucial determinant of peaceful change.

3
Co-operation and Conflict Transformation

In Chapter 1, I identified peaceful change with mutual development, mutual trust and co-operative behaviour. In Chapter 2, I outlined a theory of how conflicting interests emerge and develop into overt conflict. In this chapter I want to trace the process through which change is accommodated through co-operation and conflict transformation.

This implies a stronger process than the mere absence of conflict. Conflict is avoided when goals do not clash, coercion does not develop and people do not engage in destructive behaviour. Peaceful change in the weak sense can be achieved by the mere avoidance of these undesirable conditions. In the stronger sense, peaceful change implies the development and fulfilment of complementary goals, which is the essence of co-operation. In this chapter I consider first the nature of complementary goals, then the process of emergent co-operation among groups, then the question of co-ordination and specialization, coming to a view of conflict transformation which embraces changes in behaviour, changes in goals and changes in the identity of co-operating groups.

A harmony of goals exists when the goals different actors pursue are mutually supportive, or complementary. This is a more stringent condition than merely mutual compatibility or mutual dependence. If A and B hold goals G_A and G_B, G_A is compatible with G_B if G_B can be achieved as well as G_A ($G_A \cap G_B \neq \emptyset$). G_A is dependent on G_B if G_A can only be achieved if G_B has been achieved ($G_A \supset G_B$). G_B supports G_A if the achievement of G_B contributes to or supports the achievement of G_A ($G_B \rightarrow G_A$). So a harmony of goals between A and B exists if $G_B \rightarrow G_A$ and $G_A \rightarrow G_B$.

Thus there is absence of conflict when the goals of groups or states are not incompatible with one another. There is a positive harmony of interests when groups share goals or contribute to the achievement of each other's goals. Typically groups have mixed relationships, with elements of co-operation, conflict and indifference. There is rarely total harmony or total disharmony.

When the interests of social groups or states coincide, so that they are pursuing similar goals, there is a harmony of interests. When they do not, groups or states can either act in such a way as to deliberately harmonize their interests, through co-operation and conflict transformation. Or they can make no attempt to adjust their policies, which may lead to discord and political conflict (Keohane 1984).

We can talk about a process of harmonized development when actors adjust their positions and, if necessary, their goals and values in such a way that their goals are complementary. A family, for example, has to adjust arrangements and procedures to allow for change over time, but if the changing pattern of relationships is accommodated in a way such that the mutually supportive relationships persist, then the family remains in harmony. Similarly, a society accommodates change through harmonizing relationships among its members.

When groups are interdependent, their achievement of the goals depends on each other. But interdependence does not necessarily imply co-operation. It may lead to conflict or co-operation. Keohane and Nye (1986) identified 'complex interdependence' as a condition where parties were bound together in a web of mutually dependent relationships, so that whole groups of goals depend on the actions of other actors. In their definition, interdependence may involve mutual benefits or mutual costs. Even when there are mutual benefits, there is no guarantee that this will not precipitate conflict over the distribution of these benefits.

A society or a community is mutually interdependent, when the fulfilment of goals by any part of the community depends heavily on fulfilment of goals by others. A community can be said to be harmonious when its members' actions do contribute to the fulfilment of other members' goals and to their welfare, and to be harmonious with other communities when the same conditions apply to them. Following Galtung's (1996) and Curle's (1971) definitions of peace, peaceful development can therefore be defined as a process in which people help one another to fulfil their potential and contribute to one another's well-being.

We need not assume that peaceful development rests only on the possibility that independent actors have coincident or complementary goals during a process of social or environmental change. The actors have the power to construct peaceful relationships by acting in a mutually co-operative way. The utilitarian tradition in economics and political science tends to assume that actors operate only in their own self-interest, seeking to maximize their utility, defined in terms of individual revealed preferences. However, as Sen (1999, 2002: 225–44) points out, it is not necessary to adopt such a restrictive definition. Actors may pursue the welfare of others as well as of themselves – and arguably, most do so.

Political actors tend to have complex and mixed motives. People depend on others not only for the achievement of their material needs but also for recognition as part of a community, which in itself is a common goal worthy of collective action. There are social goods, as well as private goods, which individuals seek to obtain; and social goals as well as private goals. We are concerned both with our private interests and with the 'general good' of the community.

Social choices not only contribute to individual interests. They also communicate information to others. In this sense behaviour is expressive. It communicates meaning, affecting the perception and memories of others and thus the construction of relationships. For example, in a series of prisoner's dilemma games, the player who plays 'defect' not only gains a certain score in each round, but also communicates an intention about the relationship in which expectations of defection are established (Wendt 1999: 346). Similarly, a player who plays 'co-operate' communicates a different intention and this begins to constitute the basis of a social expectation. Actors who pursue their own interests but also understand one another's needs and act in a way that is sensitive to them are by so doing expressing something about their own values and the kind of relationship they expect to develop.

In most communities, there is a mixture of interests, some complementary, some conflictual. In most communities individuals do not take only their own interests into account. They identify themselves with a larger community and are then prepared to act in the interest of that larger group. This is, indeed, an elementary aspect of political co-operation, which requires acting together in some common interest. The co-operating group then constructs its own joint goals, to which the members subscribe. In this process the definition of interest and identity is transferred from one level to another: from individual to the group, or from groups to a larger group.

In the course of this process, individuals or groups may hold a mixture of private and public goals. They value public goods; but they value individual goods too. Conflict and co-operation within and between groups frequently co-exist, as individuals or groups seek to uphold their individual interests while also upholding those of the group.

Co-operation

Thus it is possible to identify three levels at which co-operation operates. The first is behavioural. Groups or individuals with separate goals agree to make moves that benefit the other; either because they expect reciprocation or because they value the benefit of the other. The second is through the adoption of goals. Co-operation occurs when individuals or groups adopt common goals or align their goals to one another. The third is at the level of identification. When groups or individuals identify a common interest, they begin a process of redefining themselves, and constructing an expectation of mutual benefit.

In terms of our evolutionary theory of conflict and co-operation, the first can be seen as a move by an actor to a position that benefits another group. The second can be seen as an alignment of goals, or of cognitive maps. The third can be seen as the integration of separate individuals or groups.

In terms of the evolutionary model of conflict advanced in the previous chapter, a co-operative process of accommodation takes place when party A moves its position on an environmental variable in a way that benefits another party B. A reciprocal process of accommodation takes place when both move to benefit the other. Since the benefits of co-operative behaviour may outweigh the benefits of self-interested behaviour, there are selective advantages in the evolution of co-operation.

Co-operative behaviour can be modelled in much the same way as conflict in the previous chapter, using the same framework of a set of dimensions representing behaviour or other social attributes, and goals or chains of goals connecting the interests of a party on one dimension given its position on another. For example, take the situation as represented in Figure 2.20. Here, instead of driving the other party into unviability as each strives for its own benefit, the organizations co-ordinate their actions or reframe their goals taking the goals of the other party into account. In Figure 2.20, A might move from S_A to another position from which its goal on e is closer to e_1, i.e. closer to B's interest, thus reducing the conflict of interest, in the expectation that B will reciprocate. Alternatively, A might alter his goal function, so that a position closer to e_1 replaces e_2 as the goal function from S_A.

Just as a conflict of interest may tend towards polarization and alignment of goals in conflicting patterns, so too co-operative activity can lead on to alignment of goals and ultimately towards integration. Actors that are able to co-operate through reciprocation, ensuring mutual benefits for each other, may begin to take each other's interests into account. Once they do so, they begin to co-ordinate their actions, and then it becomes natural to align goals. Finally, having adopted common goals and come to see joint benefits, they may be on the way towards acting together as a common group.

Co-operation is thus linked in important ways with the construction of actors' ideas of their own interests and ultimately their own identities. Wendt (1999: 333) distinguishes the 'simple learning' involved in actors learning to achieve their wants by reciprocation, without changing who they are or what they want, from the 'complex learning' involved when interaction leads to change in interests and identities.

In the process of learning to co-operate, actors may think of themselves and their interests in different ways. This is one way out of the paradoxes of collective rationality in prisoner's dilemma and co-ordination games. If Arnold and Bill are the prisoners, and they are not allowed to communicate, it is individually rational for each to confess, but collectively rational to stay silent. But let us invoke the existence of a Gang, of which Arnold and Bill are members, and which has other members outside the prison. Each prisoner then reasons that if he defects by confessing, the Gang will punish him when he gets out of prison. This changes the payoffs and makes staying silent a preferable strategy. So the mere existence of the Gang, without any communications being involved, can alter the behaviour of the prisoners. Moreover, if we remove the Gang, and simply consider that Arnold and Bill are able to think of themselves as a team, they are then able to reason as a team and reap the benefits of collective rationality rather than the losses of individual rationality.

Sugden (1993) developed the idea that 'thinking as a team' could explain how individuals overcome the barriers that individual rationality sets to collectively rational behaviour. As Bardsley (2001) puts it, people considering how to play in co-ordination or prisoner's dilemma games have the option of thinking in terms of 'what should *we* do', rather than 'what should *I* do'. Once this shift is made, even if the 'we' constitutes a group only for the duration of a one-shot game, one can consider answers in terms of collective rationality. Co-operators are prepared to 'think as a team', even if they do not yet have the identity of a team. Then the co-operators can approach games of co-ordination or prisoner's dilemma in the following way:

(1) It is common knowledge between [*players*] 1 and 2 that they are a team, and therefore that they both think as team members: there is common knowledge of collective rationality.

(2) Thinking as a team member involves being prepared to do one's part without having to anticipate the consequences of one's individual act.

(3) Because [the co-operation option] is clearly best for the team, both players deduce that [playing Co-operate] is their part and therefore play [Co-operate]. (Bardsley 184)

The process of becoming a team is obscure under the strict conditions required by early game theory, namely that there is no communication and individual rationality is exclusively in the individual's self-interest. But these assumptions are strained as representations of real life. If we drop them, it is reasonable to assume that individuals may be willing to act as though they were part of a team, in a situation where there is advantage in so doing. It is rational to think and act in a way that reaps the benefits of collective rationality when these outweigh those of individual rationality. Being willing to act as though one were part of a team then leads to the intention to co-operate. The act of co-operation then leads to the expression of oneself as part of a team.

Similarly Hollis (1977: 135–7) argues that 'expressive rationality' can be a remedy to the dilemmas of social action, when it is individually rational not to act in the collective interest. He cites the example of the Determined Voter, who turns out to vote on a wintry evening in a safe constituency. The Voter may reason that there is no instrumental rationality in enduring the discomfort involved, since any one vote cannot affect the outcome. Nevertheless, the act of voting can be rational because it expresses an identity as part of a community (in this case, the community of voting citizens) which the individual values. As Hollis puts it, the actor acquires real interests 'with those characters in which he is himself'. Thus, expressing himself as a voter, the individual acquires the interests of the group of voters. The individual develops a collective as well as an individual identity and thus comes to have interests as part of a particular collectivity. Through co-operative action, then, actors redefine the characters whose interests they invoke. This can come through voluntary action, in which individuals come together to forge collective interests ('Let us form a union together, to promote our collective interests'). Alternatively a social movement can mobilize a whole population by creating a sense of common identity ('Workers of the world, unite!').

The formation of a social group can then be seen as an extension of the formation of a team. It involves the creation of collective purposes, a collective identity and collective action. Gilbert (1992: 2) explores the question of 'what makes a collectivity out of a sum of living human beings', and finds it in the concept of a 'plural subject'. In her view, a condition of joint action is 'that each must make clear his willingness to accept a certain goal jointly with certain others' (1989, 199). 'Each must manifest willingness to constitute with the other a *plural subject* of the relevant goal' (1989: 199).

This does not require any metaphysical idea of a collective mental activity on the part of collective groups. It simply means that some people identify collective interests and plans for the group, and other people accept them, whether actively or passively, willingly or unwillingly. After all, social organizations do have interests and plans at a collective level. These are distinct from and often different in kind to the individual interests and plans of the group members.

The process of coming together as a social group, at any level, substitutes a collective actor for individual actors in some domain of social action, even though the individuals may continue to act as individuals in other domains. Conversely, a social group dissolves into individuals or subgroups when the group can no longer act collectively and subgroups pursue their own goals. These processes are integration and differentiation. In complex societies, of course, there are multiple domains of social action, multiple groups and cross-cutting identities, so that it may be possible to transform conflict and generate conflict or co-operation by making one type of identity more salient than another.

Although co-operation can come about between purely atomistic individuals, as when individuals or states tacitly co-operate for individual gain, it is arguable that a more significant form of co-operation takes place when the individuals form themselves into groups, which become the plural subjects of co-operative acts. Indeed, in large-scale societies, large groups act on behalf of smaller groups, which may themselves be made up of groups. The process of group formation is thus as important in co-operation as it is in conflict. It follows that theories that fail to treat actors and their interests as fluid and changeable cannot capture some of the essential elements of co-operation and conflict.

Seen in this light some of the examples of evolution of co-operation that Axelrod (1984) cites no longer look like pure reciprocation between atomistic individuals. For example, in the case of the trench warfare of 1914–18, the German and French soldiers who refrained from shooting at one another or deliberately shot wide may have seen each other as members of a temporary group constituted by being together in a similar predicament in the trenches. The soldiers on each side shared an interest in avoiding attacks on the other, since this would bring down attacks on themselves. They also shared a common problem in that their superior officers were ordering them to make pointless attacks. In this extreme situation the opposing soldiers were capable of coming together as plural subjects of a temporary new group, which had the objective of live and let live.

The formation of co-operative groups is a complex process. It normally requires signalling of co-operative intentions, but it may emerge in a self-organizing way. For example, people in the street trust others not to hurt them, even though they are passing strangers in close proximity. There is an 'emergent' safe space in which people are unlikely to be taken by surprise and attacked, because everyone is visible. Similarly medieval traders found advantage in promoting safe trade through securing markets, honouring promises, providing insurance, protecting themselves from interlopers, and so on. Guilds emerged to institutionalize these forms of co-operation. Similarly in international relations, a security community becomes safe, because people become used to dependable expectations of peaceful change. Emergent forms of co-operation such as these coalesce when the expectations of large groups of people converge, through shared cultural understandings or social mores.

Kant's conception of a perpetual peace through a universal civil association invokes the possibility of such an emergent process, as does Patomäki's notion of a peaceful public space. The formation of civil society is another example, when civic norms come to prevail, generating 'a rule governed society based on the consent of individuals' (Kaldor 2003: 585) rather than on domination or violent coercion.

Spontaneous emergent co-operation is not the only way that co-operative arrangements can emerge. They can also come about through negotiation. The negotiations that led to the Law of the Sea treaty were a good example of such a negotiated order for a domain where conflicts of interest were emerging, but that had not required previous regulation. A third way in which co-operation can come into being is through an imposed arrangement. For example, a hegemon may dictate what the arrangements will be, and others may then consent to his prescriptions (Keohane 1984). Somewhere between hegemony and a spontaneous emergence of co-operation is the process in which a leader leads with the consent of the led. And combinations of these processes are possible. Negotiated rules may be built on customary, spontaneously emerging arrangements. Emergent mores may come to have the force of imposed orders, as when socially generated norms socialize people into approved forms of behaviour.

In short, emergent co-operation comes about through the self-organizing, negotiated or imposed development of conventions or agreements which pattern behaviour in new ways. The signalling of an intention to co-operate and not defect in repeated prisoner's dilemmas is just such a convention. Groups align their behaviour and goals in such a way that co-operation becomes a dependable social expectation. They begin to co-ordinate their actions.

Co-operation and co-ordination

I have discussed co-operation as an emergent property of self-organizing systems, when units start to co-ordinate their actions. Complex systems also require a measure of co-ordination to sustain co-operation. This may be achieved by the units themselves, or by the formation of an agent, an institution or a rule responsible for co-ordination.

For example, consider two departments of a firm, each of which can set its own production levels. At a certain point, the production of each firm begins to impose externalities on the other. For example, the production of an upstream department pollutes the water supply of the river and so affects the downstream department's production. The downstream department silts up the river and so affects the upstream department's transport costs. If the departments set their production only in accordance with their own interests, they will both suffer from the externalities resulting from the other department's actions. If they co-ordinate their production levels, to take the externalities into account, they will each do better than if they did not (see Appendix). As the interdependence of the two departments grows, there will be increasing social benefits from co-ordination.

What is crucial here is how the departments set their goals. If the goal functions are related only to each department's own production, the departments end up damaging one another. If the goal functions are set to take account of the production of both departments, the production of the firm as a whole benefits. In firms, co-ordination is exercised hierarchically, through a manager. In self-organizing systems, the co-ordination function is exercised by the units themselves.

Any form of co-ordination that links separate goals is a form of joint goal, or a rule. Rules, conventions and norms play the same role as managers. By enabling co-ordination they manage potential conflicts over divergent interests and produce social benefits. Complex societies develop not only actors with complex chains of goals, but also complex social rules that regulate the actors. Such rules develop into institutions; indeed, institutions have been defined as 'persistent sets of rules (formal and informal) that prescribe behavioral roles, constrain activity and shape expectations' (Keohane 1989: 3).

Co-operation and public goods

An important element of co-operation is the establishment of collective goods arising from the co-operative relationship. These may be joint benefits that actors gain from co-operation, as when actors come together to achieve goals that they would not be able to achieve singly, or public goods, as when co-ordinated action leads to public benefit or creates a shared public space.

Public goods are important for co-operation because they give individuals incentives for pursuing social as well as individual benefits. People can hold goals about social welfare, public rules, values, and so on, which not only represent personal aspirations for themselves, but also for the kind of society in which they would like to live. These are 'milieu' goals, as opposed to 'possession goals' (Wolfers 1962). Similarly, states may pursue policies at an international level which are concerned with not only upholding their own interests, but also shaping the kind of international society they would like to form.

Amartya Sen (1984: 14–15) makes a similar point: 'Social demands on conduct in situations of interdependence can go well beyond modifying the preference ordering of a person (e.g. in a more "social" direction) and may involve systematic departures from the pursuit of one's preference orderings. The obligations towards others may not just take the form of giving weights to their interests (or goals) in one's own goals, but may also require that one's choice of actions not be naively tied to one's own goals (even moral goals) ... The question of rules of conduct as opposed to the contents of preference is not, of course, a new one in social analysis.'

Thus the aspiration for the kind of society one would like to live in, the need to co-operate with others in order to achieve it, and the need to establish social rules, all represent inducements for co-operation beyond the pursuit of self-interest. Forming rules, norms and values for the community is significant not only because they are constitutive of community, but also because they specify socially accepted ways of co-ordinating behaviour, taking decisions and resolving differences. Instead of contesting each issue as a conflict between the involved actors, we simply apply the socially accepted rules (Etzioni 1964). In this way accepted norms and social goals constitute a basis for the conduct of peaceful relationships and the prevention of conflict.

In Chapter 2, I discussed how conflicts over public goals (such as control over government policy) are a source of potentially serious conflict, intensifying conflicts of interest. In a similar way, co-operation over public goals, such as consent to agreed rules, shared norms or common institutions, gives us a basis for peaceful change.

Co-operation and specialization

An important form of co-operation is specialization of roles. In Chapter 2 I considered specialization and interdependence between peasant producers. In an undifferentiated society there is little specialization and most households produce some of each resource. The households are usually linked by kinship bonds and reciprocity, but there is no organized system for the co-ordination of different productive activities.

Then a process of specialization begins. This may have its origins in technological change, or organizational improvements, or an outside stimulus. It becomes more efficient for peasant households to concentrate on a smaller range of activities, and after some time distinct occupations emerge (fishermen, crop-farmers, woodsmen, gardeners). At the early stages needs not met by the household's own production are met by barter. There will be some system for exchanging goods (even if only gifts) in the undifferentiated society, and the barter system will be integrated into the culture of the peasant society and its kinship system. However, as the degree of specialization increases, and with it the volume of barter, the nature of the barter changes. Some exchanges of goods become indirect. A fisherman who needs timber may find it inconvenient to barter with the woodsman. Instead he will obtain his timber from an intermediate producer (a crop-farmer perhaps) who has previously bartered with the woodsman and has timber to spare. This new form of barter leads to the identification of standards of value different from the direct exchange of goods, and allows intermediate goods to have a value as a currency. It also means that goods are no longer required only to satisfy immediate needs. They become a primitive form of capital. The law of comparative advantage may mean that all parties benefit from the trade and are satisfied with it. Nevertheless, the cohesion of the undifferentiated society is strained, and the intermediaries with goods that can be used as capital have a motive to develop a sectional interest as traders, rather than conform to the pre-existing norms of reciprocity and barter for immediate needs. As specialization increases, intermediate producers will develop a stock of goods and will be able to rely more on bartering and less on production. At the same time, intermediaries who are more centrally placed in a bartering network, or in possession of more easily stored or more liquid goods, will tend to benefit. Peasant producers will find it easier to barter with them than with other peasants. So the intermediaries gradually give up their productive functions and concentrate on trade. In the process, they naturally come to have a privileged role in negotiating the terms of trade since they can stock goods, buy cheaply and sell dear. They gradually develop distinct interests as a specialist group, and these interests may come into conflict with those of the producers.

The emergence of the merchant further drives the process of specialization, as it benefits the producers to specialize in supplying what the market requires. This kind of process of course encapsulates co-operation, and creates mutual benefit and increased production, distribution and consumption of goods. But it does so in a way that sets up potential conflicts of interest over the benefits of specialization between different groups.

When the social benefits arising from co-operation are distributed in a way that is regarded as mutually beneficial, or at least as satisfactory, then specialization will tend to promote co-operation. When one side manages to take most of the social benefits, the process can lead to structural conflict. Similarly, when specialization leads to one-sided dependence, as in the case of the primary producer dependent on a single merchant, or the peasant dependent on the lord, specialization readily leads to exploitation. In more complex societies, however, where peasant farmers can trade their produce and are not dependent on a single merchant or a single landlord, a more complex pattern of interdependence may permit a wider sharing of the social benefits.

Conflict transformation

I have emphasized the importance of harmonization of interests in co-operation, and this is an important part of conflict transformation enterprise. Conflict transformation is concerned both with defusing the esclatory and destructive dynamics of conflict and with identifying co-operative and constructive channels for change.

The theoretical framework advanced in the previous chapter can be used to address not only emergent conflict but also the process of accommodation and harmonization of interests. Referring again to Axelrod's measure of conflict of interest, conflict is removed and interests are in harmony at the unit square, where both parties' interests find mutual benefit (Figure 2.1). If the parties change their positions or their goals in such a way that they move in the direction of decreasing their conflict of interest, then they are harmonizing their goals. This can be, but is usually not, a sudden flash of enlightenment, where an integrative solution is suddenly discovered. Typically it is a gradual process that takes place over time, as parties move their positions and goals, in a purposive way. It takes time for organizations to adjust to one another's interests, to find new ways of meeting their interests which are compatible or complementary with those of others. This may involve quite complex changes of position and interests.

Some simple illustrations of conflict transformation at an early stage of conflict may illustrate the general process. First we will consider how conflict transformation can come about in the Lords of Milan conflict. In Galtung's presentation, this has an integrative solution when both brothers achieve their aim. We considered the emergence of this conflict, and the competition between the old aristocracy and the parvenus. The presenting issue was who would control the revenue from the new trade. The underlying issue was over the relative economic strength and status of an established and a challenger group. This conflict too is open to a transformative resolution. For example, the aristocracy and the parvenus might intermarry and share the benefits of the new trade. The parvenus invest in land and the aristocrats in trade. This resolves their emergent conflict of interest and prevents it from developing into a conflict over power. It is the linkage between the two groups' goals that makes possible the transformation of the conflict.

Similarly, a possible co-operative approach to conflicts arising over global warming might be to meet the underlying needs of North and South for economic development by developing renewable energy and energy efficiency, and turning energy supply companies into providers of energy management services, with compensating commercial benefits and reduced costs from carbon emissions on both sides. This illustrates a general approach from conflict resolution which also applies to peaceful change. The process is to go down the goal tree and find the links that can be changed or substituted. Does a particular interest x have to be tied to position y? Could position z be an alternative way of meeting it? Can the underlying needs q and r be met in any other way? This is the approach to conflict resolution advocated by Burton (1994), Pruitt and Rubin (1986: 149), and other authors in this school. It is illustrated in Figure 3.1, based on Pruitt and Rubin's example of the conflict between the father and son, where the conflict is resolved by substituting an alternative goal (a4) to the top-level goal (a3), for example, to impress people by becoming a soccer star instead of by making noise on a motorbike, hence resolving the conflict with the father's wish for peace and quiet. Here a top level and an intermediate level goal are discarded and a new top level goal is adopted that is compatible with the top level goal of the other party.

The goal tree is often expressed in conflict resolution as a hierarchy of position, interests and needs (Ramsbotham et al. 1999). But the tree can be of any length. The conflict transformation technique, then, is to go

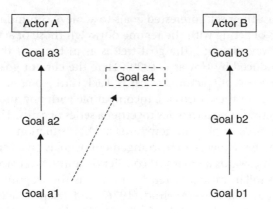

Figure 3.1 Resolving conflicts by substituting goals

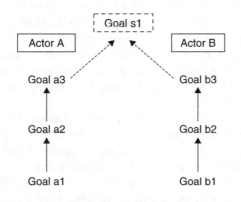

Figure 3.2 Resolving conflicts by adding shared goals

down the goal tree to the more fundamental goals, and up it to the positions expressed, and find a way to reconcile conflicts by discarding existing goals and substituting alternative top-level goals (or strategies).

Another means of conflict transformation is to find a top-level goal that both parties can accept, a superordinate goal that links or co-ordinates their goal trees. The creation of public goods is one means of creating a shared interest. This is illustrated in Figure 3.2.

The adjustments here are equivalent to Sommerhof's concept of directive correlation, with the subunits harmonizing their goals and activities to achieve the social objective. This is similar to the co-ordination of departments discussed above. The parties can then adjust their lower-level goals to meet the new superordinate or public goal. For example, members of a regime adjust their self-interested goals to achieve common goals, since the benefits of acting with the regime outweigh those of acting alone.

Another way of seeing the goal tree is as in terms of the card table model introduced by Howard (1999). Here the current goals and strategies of the actors are pictured as cards. Each card represents a goal, or a strategy. Some of these cards are incompatible with one another. Others are tied together. A goal tree ties together a series of cards. The actors can discard old cards or pick up new cards as their situation changes. Over time, a complex sequence of rearrangement of goals on all sides can lead the situation towards a polarized conflict or conflict transformation.

A third, similar, means of representation is the 'cognitive mapping' technique developed by Axelrod (1976) and Eden (1988). Cognitive mapping represents the beliefs of a decision-maker as a set of statements (or constructs) connected by directed graphs, with positive or negative links between pairs of beliefs. Eden has used the technique extensively to model changes of strategy in complex organizations. The technique is also used for modelling conflict between organizations (or between people in organizations). If the actors' goals are represented as such a graph, then changes in the links between goals, abandonment of some goals and adoption of others, can be used to model the emergence of conflict and its transformation.

This representation of conflict in terms of organizations, their positions on social and environmental variables and their goals is a framework for mapping the gradual change of actors, relationships, goals, issues, and contexts, that comprises conflict transformation (Väyrynen 1991; Ramsbotham et al. 2005; Lederach, 1995a, 1995b, 1997; Rupesinghe 1995; Mitchell 1981). In practice, complex conflicts usually involve multiple issues and multiple parties. The process of conflict transformation is usually slow and difficult to follow. A series of interactions and moves take place, over time, as the actors adjust their positions, as the environment changes, and as the actors alter their goals. The process is seen in complex negotiations, where new possibilities emerge in the course of discussions, different packages of options are tried out, adjustments in positions are made, sometimes voluntarily, sometimes under pressure. In peace processes and other complex negotiations, parties frequently put together attempted resolutions that reconcile some but not all of the competing goals, and may satisfy some but not all of the competing parties. Typically proposed solutions fall apart and have to be reconstructed differently, and sometimes changes in the situation or changes in the actors are required for new movement to be possible. But the parties learn what adjustments to their positions may be mutually acceptable. Under favourable circumstances, they continue to reconstruct and rearrange their positions to the point that an acceptable outcome is reached.

The process may involve one or several of the following steps:

1. Parties altering their behaviour, or their position on the environment (or with respect to the issues in conflict).
2. Parties altering their goals, or shifting their priorities between goals. The way in which goals are formulated is a crucial ingredient in constructive management of conflict. An important part of conflict transformation is both the reformulation of goals and the reperception of the importance of particular interests, and of the connections between interests.
3. Parties co-ordinating their behaviour.
4. Parties adopting joint goals.
5. Parties altering themselves, for example, by splitting or integrating, or through change in their constituencies and composition.
6. Parties altering their identities.
7. Parties transforming their relationships.

Conclusion

In practice conflict resolution is rarely achieved as an instant solution to an existing conflict. Rather, it should be seen as a process in a developing situation, where goal trees are forming and developing in response to a social change. What distinguishes a process of conflict transformation is the formation of links between different parties' goals, and the reorganization of those goals, in a way that harmonizes or reconciles the parties' needs. What shapes a process of destructive conflict is the expression of goals as vital self-interests and the pursuit of these goals even when they develop into contradictions with the goals of others. There are also intermediate outcomes, such as a bargaining outcome that improves the position for both parties, but where the benefits are unevenly distributed, so that new conflicts develop out of a co-operative relationship (Bowles 2004). Conflict transformation leading to conflict resolution should be seen, then, as a process of change and mutual adjustment of positions, interests and needs.

This process of adjustment of goals, or the formation of rules, norms or institutions to link goal trees, which gives actors in a society coherence and unity, is constitutive of social capacity. Its disappearance or breakdown through polarization and conflict is constitutive of conflict.

Appendix: Co-operation under externalities

To illustrate a potential conflict of interest that can be moderated by co-ordination, consider the case of two departments of a firm, which are interdependent. It is not difficult to show that if both set production and prices independently of each other, both are likely to be worse off than if they act in a co-ordinated way. It follows that co-ordination yields joint benefits.

Pondy (1969, 1970) gives an example of two firms, or departments in a firm, which impose externalities on each other.[1] These may be positive or negative: one department's products may feed into the output of the other, for example, by enabling more efficient production, or it may damage the output of the other, for example through pollution. Pondy offers the following simple equations for the profit of each department as:

$$\Pi_1 = p_1 y_1 - c_1 y_1^2 - e_1 y_2 \tag{1}$$

$$\Pi_2 = p_2 y_2 - c_2 y_2^2 - e_2 y_1 \tag{2}$$

where Π_1 and Π_2 are the profits of the first and second department, y_1 is the output of the first department, p_1 is the price of y_1, c_1 is the costs of y_1 (assuming a quadratic cost function) and e_1 is a coefficient representing the externality imposed by the second department on the first per unit of output.

Each department sets its output (y), either singly or in co-ordination with the other department, with a view to achieving some goal, which is a function of the profits of the two departments:

$$G_1 = f_1(\Pi_1, \Pi_2)$$

$$G_2 = f_2(\Pi_1, \Pi_2)$$

These goals may be either competitive or co-operative. Each department can strive to help or hurt the other, and help or hurt itself. For example, if department one sets its goals such that $dG_1/d\Pi_1 > 0$ and $dG_1/d\Pi_2 > 0$, department one seeks to act in both its own interest and that of the other department. If $dG_1/d\Pi_1 > 0$ and $dG_1/d\Pi_2 = 0$ then department one pursues self-interest without reference to its effects on department 2. If $dG_1/d\Pi_1 > 0$ and $dG_1/d\Pi_2 < 0$ then department one seeks gains at the expense of department two: it acts in a hostile or malign manner. Particular cases of goal functions are:

$$G_1 = \Pi_1 + \Pi_2 \tag{3}$$

$$G_2 = \Pi_1 + \Pi_2 \tag{4}$$

where both departments act as a team, striving to maximize the collective profit (for example the profit of the firm), and

$$G_1 = \Pi_1 - \Pi_2$$

$$G_2 = \Pi_2 - \Pi_1$$

a zero-sum conflict.

In the case of the profit functions given for the two departments in equations (1) and (2) above, it is easy to demonstrate that co-ordination outperforms self-interest if externalities are significant. Suppose each department sets its production to maximize its own profit, ignoring the effect of its output on the other department. In other words, it seeks to maximise G_1/Π_1. The optimal output $y_1{}^*$ is given by partially differentiating Π_1 with respect to y_1, yielding:

$$y_1{}^* = p_1/2c_1$$

Likewise for the other department,

$$y_2{}^* = p_2/2c_2$$

This results in profits for each department:

$$\Pi_1 = p_1{}^2/4c_1 - e_1 p_2/2c_2 \tag{5}$$

$$\Pi_2 = p_2{}^2/4c_2 - e_2 p_1/2c_1 \tag{6}$$

In the case of co-operative goals, the output levels are set by differentiating Π_1 and Π_2 partially with respect to $y_1 + y_2$ yielding:

$$y_1{}^* = (p_1 - e_2)/2c_1$$

$$y_2{}^* = (p_2 - e_1)/2c_2$$

resulting in profits as follows:

$$\Pi_1 = p_1(p_1 - e_2)/2c_1 - (p_1 - e_2)^2/4c_1 - e_1(p_2 - e_1)/2c_2 \tag{7}$$

$$\Pi_2 = p_2(p_2 - e_1)/2c_2 - (p_2 - e_1)^2/4c_2 - e_2(p_1 - e_2)/2c_1 \tag{8}$$

The sum of these two is greater than the sum of the two departments' profits in the self-interest case, by

$$e_1{}^2/4c_2 + e2^2/4c_1.$$

In the first case, each department's profits are reduced by the externalities imposed by the other department's production. In the second case, co-ordinated action enables each department to set production levels at the best joint level, taking account of the externalities each imposes on the other.

In the case of zero-sum conflict, the departments increase the environmental costs on one another:

$$y_1{}^* = (p_1 + e_2)/2c_1$$

$$y_2{}^* = (p_2 + e_1)/2c_2$$

and the joint profit is lower than in the self-interested case. Co-ordination therefore pays off when interdependent actors are affected by externalities arising from one another's decisions.

A similar argument can be applied to cases with more than two actors.

4
Conflict and Context

Peace and conflict researchers in the behaviouralist tradition deliberately stripped conflict of its context in order to analyse its generic features. By doing so they came up with rich dynamic models of conflict processes. But real conflicts are shaped by setting as well as by process. We have to consider not only the process-level dynamics, but also the contextual factors which exacerbate conflicts or mitigate them. We need to put the context back into conflict theory, while retaining a theoretical approach to the relationship between conflict dynamics and the conflict's environment. In this chapter I consider how the context shapes the conflict and vice versa. The aim is to understand how contextual factors condition the prospects for emergent conflicts and influence whether they escalate into violence, are peacefully resolved, or lead to other outcomes.

How contexts shape conflicts

All conflicts take place at a certain time in a certain place, and the temporal and spatial context shapes them in specific ways. Considering the temporal context first, any conflict situation can be related to trends at various time-scales: very long-term processes (such as a long-term change in a social or international system), intermediate processes (such as the formulation of a particular policy by a decision-maker) and short-term processes (such as decisions). In the case of wars, it is common to distinguish underlying or background causes, proximate and trigger causes of war. The First World War, for example, had as underlying causes the strength of nationalism in Europe, the competition for power between large, industrialized, militarized nation-states and the fears and frustrations that arose from them. The proximate causes were the policies pursued by the major states in the context of this competition: the German attempt to gain diplomatic and political influence commensurate with its economic power, the forward Austro-Hungarian policy in the Balkans, the German willingness to support it. The trigger cause was the assassination at Sarajevo. The context for conflict in Europe became more war-prone as the preventive diplomacy of the Concert system broke down, to be replaced first by Bismarck's relatively stable alliance system and later by the more polarized alliances of the Triple Entente and the Triple Alliance. These changes in the European order set the context for conflict, although the intricate moves that led up to the crisis in 1914 created the particular conflict that took place. In contrast, during the earlier Concert period, Europe was relatively free of inter-state conflict. Fear of renewed revolution, a common interest on the part of the major powers in preserving the status quo, and scope for expansion overseas led the major powers to co-operate in settling conflicts and avoiding major wars.

As well as being shaped by the times, conflicts take their character from their spatial and social settings. A conflict system is typically embedded in a surrounding social environment that shapes the conflict in significant ways. First, there may be direct causal influences from the context to the conflict – most obviously, when outsiders stir up a conflict or supply the protagonists with arms. Or factors outside the conflict system may causally affect the conflict, as when a change in the means of production throws class interests into conflict. Second, the context constitutes the conflict system, shaping the actors, influencing their goals, and patterning their relationships. The wider setting influences what the conflictants want, what kind of outcomes they are willing to consider, and what the meaning of the issues at stake are to them. And it sets precedents, creates reputations, and alters pecking orders, influencing that status of the protagonists in the wider society.

Many conflicts are themselves *nested* within other conflict formations (Dugan 1996). For example, a dispute over wages between a tea plantation owner and a tea picker in Sri Lanka is embedded in a larger conflict formation between landowners and landless peasants, which itself is embedded in the political and economic structures of the global commodity markets, where prices of tea are set in relation to other goods and services. Parties are frequently engaged in more than one conflict, and their choice of actions is not a response to one conflict alone but to their total situation. This was clearly the case in 1914 when a local conflict in Serbia was nested within a wider conflict between the central powers in the Balkans, itself nested within the general competition for power between the European states.

Context is not only reproduced in conflict, but in a sense, is *encapsulated* in it. Elements of the context may be accessible and open for transformation within the local context setting (Etzioni 1964). Gandhi's struggles with the authorities in South African and India were in part local, specific conflicts, but they also engaged with larger processes of domination. He showed that non-violent resistance could not only make gains in local campaigns, but also enable people to stand up to the colonial authorities and thereby gain their independence. His response transcended the local conflict by dealing with the broader conflict encapsulated in the local one.

The concept of an *order* is useful here, since social orders and international orders shape the nature of the interactions within them. For example, a feudal society patterns roles and relationships around the control of land, and reproduces relationships in which tenants are obliged to swear fealty to their lords and supply produce in return for their holdings. This society reproduces structural conflict between the lords and the peasants as well as creating the setting and conditions for direct conflicts over land between lords. In turn the recurrent conflicts over land and status and the protagonists' needs for protection and support reproduce the feudal social order. Under certain conditions the outcomes of conflicts may also recast the wider order – as when the wars of the knights led to military and technological developments (castles, mercenaries, centrally financed wars) that made the knights obsolete (Howard 1976).

The prognosis for a conflict is affected by the nature of the order, or the prevailing structural conditions, as much as by the process and dynamics of conflict and conflictants (Dukes 1999; Rubinstein 1999). The order shapes the character of conflicts, the conduct of parties, the culture that influences how they act. It determines the actors and the issues that are salient. It influences the methods of dispute settlement, and the means of action that protagonists choose (Luard 1986).

How does the prevailing order structure the pattern of conflicts within it? The background context constitutes the character of the major actors, the substance of their relationships, the distribution of assets between them, their aspirations and their goals.

Drawing on system theory, we conceive conflict as a subsystem and the wider context as its environment. Although the conflict subsystem may well be tightly coupled, the variables in the system are also influenced by the wider environment. The goals and values of the actors are shaped by the prevailing culture, the actors themselves (whether states, political parties or interest groups) are constituted by wider historical processes, the key behavioural and positional variables that form the arena for the conflict are usually linked to contextual variables, and the very incompatibilities that arise between goals and whether they can be transformed are also shaped by the context. In each conflict, whether it is the struggle for lordship over Milan, the competition for grazing rights in the Tragedy of the Commons, or conflicts between classes in societies undergoing changes in their mode of production, the manifest conflict is the tip of the iceberg to a set of deeper contextual factors that shape its course.

Contemporary internal conflicts, for example, are typically influenced by the social and national context, regional influences, and the broader international setting. These can be pictured as a set of widening circles around the conflict system (Figure 4.1). We can identify factors that cause and prevent conflicts at each of the five levels that affect contemporary conflicts: global, regional, state, the conflict-party level, and the individual/elite level (Ramsbotham et al. 2005). We need, then, to put theories of conflict into their context. Taking Galtung's triangle (Galtung 1969, 1996), we should contextualize 'Contradiction' by examining the processes by which interests and goals are shaped, 'Attitudes' by setting them in the context of prior relationships, and 'Behaviour', memory and interpretations of previous behaviour. The context includes the society's culture, governance arrangements, institutions, social roles and norms.

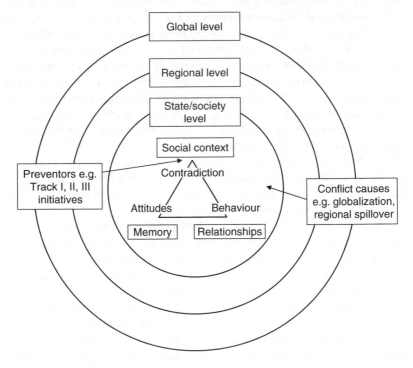

Figure 4.1   Conflict and context

Relationships involve the whole fabric of the society in which the conflict is taking place. Memories involve the socially constructed understanding of the situation, shaped by culture, discourse, learning and belief. These contextual factors are as important as the internal dynamics of the conflict, and they may either amplify or dampen the intensity and frequency of conflicts.

Amplifying and dampening conflicts

What determines whether the context tends to amplify or dampen particular conflicts? This is a very general question, but it is possible to draw general insights from anthropology, history, politics and international relations.

Consider two very different societies studied by anthropologists, the Dayak of Indonesia and the Semoi of Malaya. The Dayak were head-hunters who engaged in murderous raids on their neighbours as a means of fulfilling their society's code of honour. Participation in fighting was regarded as an initiation into adulthood. Those who succeed in fights were rewarded with status and seniority and took on decision-making powers, including decisions over the launching of new battles. In this way the social code reinforced and institutionalized aggressive violence. In contrast the Semoi Indians have a taboo against violence and actively intervene at an early stage to prevent interpersonal disputes from escalating. They hold individuals to account, mock expressions of aggression, and socialize children into conflict-avoiding habits. Their social code is so successful in inhibiting fighting that the Semoi are a warless society (Fabbro 1978).

Again, compare the international system in Europe in the late nineteenth century with the international system in Europe now. The nineteenth-century system was dominated by considerations of balance of power and lacked any overarching institutions. A dominating consideration in any particular conflict was the impact its outcome would have on the overall balance of power. Disputes might be picked, therefore, for demonstrative purposes, to show that a power was still great. The stakes in the immediate dispute were greatly magnified by the larger stakes in the international competition for power. This was a conflict-amplifying system. In contrast the international order in today's Europe is organized by an institution which has as a leading purpose the banishment of war from Europe's borders. The European countries perceive a common interest in European co-operation. They fear that failure to co-operate in particular areas may undermine the momentum of the enterprise. This is a conflict-dampening system.

A number of general features can be identified that distinguish conflict-generating from conflict dampening orders. First, the more sovereign, autonomous and unrelated the primary actors and the more their status and survival are based on their performance in conflicts, the more the system tends to be conflict-amplifying. As Buzan and Little argue (2000), the more 'raw' the international anarchy, the lower the interaction capacity, and the greater the security dilemmas for the constituent states. In contrast, the more an international society exists, with institutions, collective norms, procedures and shared expectations, the greater the scope for regulation of conflict. If the international society provides public goods and upholds public values, if there is a framework of common rules to which parties can be held to account, the more conflict among its members is likely to be channelled into political rather than military means. Of course, most international systems tend to be hybrid types, for example, with some states that may form shared values and institutions and others that reject these values and refuse to accept common norms. Such hybrids also tend to provoke conflict along the lines of cleavage between the different types.

The more the order resembles a closed system, in which autonomous actors have zero-sum interests, the more likely it is to be prone to conflict. When the only important consideration for actors is positional advantage or relative power, then the system is likely to provoke conflicts whenever positions change. Similarly, if social wealth and power depend on a sole fixed asset, such as the distribution of land, or the control of an oil production industry, conflict is more likely than in more diverse systems. In such situations any relative improvement for one actor can mean relative loss for another, and the actions of any actor carries high stakes for others. It is perhaps relatively small systems of a few powerful actors that are most prone to this kind of existential insecurity, but analogous processes take place within societies. In agrarian societies, for example, changes in the relative performance of different land-holders over time tend to set in force a process in which the successful accumulate more land and the unsuccessful lose it, resulting in a stratified landholding system and an unequal distribution of power and wealth between different classes (see Chapter 6). In contrast, the more open the system of wealth and status, and the more it offers opportunities for social mobility and new sources of income, the more it is likely that there will be opportunities for offsetting conflicts of interest and opening new avenues for advancement when existing ones are blocked.

In general, stratified and hierarchical social orders tend to be more capable of dampening direct conflicts than ones where there is a more horizontal distribution of power between similar actors, if these actors regard each other's policies as threats to the achievement of their own goals. This is because hierarchical systems have a mechanism for co-ordination and can impose common goals. This is why hegemonic international orders or autocratic political systems are sometimes surprisingly stable. As Keohane (1984) puts it, 'hegemonic leadership can help to create a pattern of order. Cooperation is not antithetical to hegemony; on the contrary, hegemony depends on a certain kind of asymmetrical cooperation, which successful hegemons support and maintain.'

Where there are conventions guiding co-operative behaviour, and norms around which states or domestic actors can legitimate their actions, conflicts are more likely to be prevented. In this case the role of a hierarchical co-ordinator is replaced by the agreed norms. The more these norms are accepted and followed, the more actors can trust that others can have dependable expectations of each other's behaviour, and hence of the basis for peaceful change. The more the prevailing order is seen to be legitimate and is accepted by its members, the more likely it is to be able to mitigate conflict. Where there are common public goods and 'authoritatively allocated values', then the wider context comes to resemble some of the qualities of a polity – as in a security community. In such an order, it is clear that actors will take the preferences of others into account, and act in ways that reflect the goals of others as well as of themselves.

Contextual changes and conflict transformation

Changes in the context of a conflict are sometimes the most significant factor in transforming conflict. How does this come about? We can identify transformations in the issues in conflict (including the positions that parties take, the vital interests that affect them and the goals they hold), changes in the information environment through which the actors perceive each other and understand the meaning and connections between events, changes in the relationships between the actors, changes in the actors themselves and changes in the structure of the conflict. Here I turn to consider how context makes conflict possible transformations of the issues, the actors and the structure.

Single issue conflicts are the simplest kind, and they may sometimes be resolvable without involving any change in the actors, the structure of the relationship or the context. More typically, issues in conflict are entangled with exogenous issues, which can alter the conflict system. For example, the potential for conflict between poor Egyptian farmers and the large landowners was eased by the rise in the price of oil and the subsequent growth of employment opportunities for Egyptian workers in oil-rich states. A land reform also took place but its scope was rather limited and it was an external, contingent change rather than a major change in the landed sector that enabled Egyptians to avoid a potential conflict.

Issue conflicts may be creatively resolved by redrawing the boundary between conflict and context. Fisher and Ury's story (1981) of the two readers in the library is a simple example. Their quarrel is over whether the window should be closed (to stop the draught) or open (to let in fresh air). The librarian resolves it by opening a window in a neighbouring room, letting in fresh air without a draught in the room. Another well-known example is the resolution of the Israeli–Egypt conflict at Camp David. The conflict was resolved by redefining it not as a tussle over territory, but as over territory and security. With US resources and security guarantees, it was possible to find a point at which both Israel's need for security and Egypt's for the restoration of its territory could be reconciled. Burton's (1969; 1987) idea of creative problem-solving is based on this kind of redefinition, and it is a common way of resolving many kinds of negotiation. The element of surprise in a successful resolution comes from the redefinition of the situation's boundaries.

Sometimes, indeed, this redrawing of the boundaries alters the wider order surrounding the conflict. The Thirty Years War became protracted and unresolvable when it was framed as a struggle between Protestant and Catholic forces in Europe. The shift to a new principle of 'cuius region, eius religio' not only resolved this conflict but also redrew the European order, ushering in the principle of sovereign territorial states.

The interests and goals of the actors emerge out of a constant interplay between actors and the wider context. How actors construe their interests is evidently socially conditioned. As Finnemore (1996) and Wendt (1999) argue, national interests are socially and culturally constructed. Therefore, when the international context changes, the setting for conflict is transformed. The end of the Cold War had a dramatic impact on many conflicts, including not only those in which the superpowers had been providing arms but also those, like Northern Ireland, apparently far from the East–West confrontation, because of its impact on how parties understood one another's interests.

A second way in which the context changes conflict is through the constitution of actors. The identity and character of actors is shaped by a larger context than the immediate conflict, but sets the framework for it. Who are the critical decision-making actors, and at what level of society do they operate? Are they sovereign entities? Do they act in a hierarchical relationship, or as partners? We have indicated earlier how important these questions are for the consideration of co-operation and conflict in the context of a prisoner's dilemma, where the Gang recasts the logic of individual rationality. The entry of new actors into a setting, or the change in the identity and character of actors, reshapes the context for conflict. Take the example of the landlord–peasant relationship. In the feudal society, this is circumscribed by customary obligations and responsibilities, but a structural conflict is endemic in the relationship. The entry of a trader alters the setting. It creates new relationships between the trader and the peasant and between the trader and the landlord. The trader provides credit and markets which may enrich some peasants, impoverish others and add to the capital stock of the landlord. It tends to alter the basis of the landlord–peasant relationship, from a personal to a market relationship. Of course this did not dissolve conflicts over land tenure but it did dissolve the main form of conflict built into the feudal structure.

A third way in which the context influences conflict is through structure. A change in context may render a conflict structure more, or less, unbalanced. We have seen this in the example of the landlord–peasant relationship. Marx envisaged that industrialization would concentrate surplus value in the hands of the capitalists and that this would inevitably strengthen their power and lead to conflicts with the impoverished workers. In the end, of course, despite Marx's visionary theory, industrialization did not lead to revolutionary conflicts within the major industrial countries. Despite the significant element of structural conflict in early and middle phases of industrialization, the benefits of economic growth raised the wages and living standards of the working people to the point where earlier social distinctions were blurred in the uniformity and wider access to opportunities of a mass industrial society. The bargains struck between the representatives of the working classes and the government, through which the working classes gained recognition of the rights of unions to organize in defence of working conditions, as well as the extension of the suffrage and of education, prevented social conflict from taking a revolutionary form in England, and laid the basis for a process of evolutionary change.

In some cases the sources of conflict are so powerfully driven by the wider context that conflicts are extremely likely to recur and be forced into a violent pattern. To take an extreme example, consider the feuds of Northern Albania, as brought to life by Kadaré in his novel *Broken Spring* (Kadaré 1990). If a breach occurs in the traditional code of honour, a young man is expected to lie in wait for a member of the enemy's family, and kill them by surprise. In turn this provokes a revenge killing from the victim's family. In one case a dispute over a bus ticket led to a cycle of killing that lasted generations. It is the cultural context, and not the trivial causes of the initial disputes, which influences the pattern of conflict.

In other settings, the coming of a common law and jurisdiction provides a basis for reversing this kind of cycle. Njal's Saga (Magnusson 1966) describes how the convening of an assembly that functions as a court and decision-making body started to banish the endemic feuding between households in medieval Iceland.

The wider context of the conflict can therefore be one that provokes, triggers and reinforces conflict, or one that turns conflict into constructive and non-violent directions, channelling and transforming conflict. The next chapter turns to focus more sharply on the characteristics of societies (and international society) that prevent conflict and foster peaceful change.

5
Preventors of War

Introduction

Over the last five centuries, two trends have affected war and peace. On the one hand, there has been a trend towards the intensification of war and its increasing destructiveness (Wright 1942; Tilly 1990). On the other hand, there has been a reduction in the frequency of international war and a very significant shift in its location. Europe has ceased to be the major war-zone. Parts of Africa, the Middle East and Asia have become war-zones instead (O'Laughlin 2004). Zones of peace have appeared in which armed conflict has almost fallen out of use (Mueller 1989; Kacowicz 1995; Adler and Barnett 1998; Kacowicz 1998; Lemke 2002).

Figure 5.1 shows the trends in armed conflicts since 1946. Internal armed conflicts have become a higher proportion of all armed conflicts and rose in number progressively until the early 1990s. The number of interstate wars showed no very clear trend in the period until the 1970s, but since then the incidence of interstate war has fallen sharply (Holsti 1996; Mack 2006). Since 1991, the incidence of intrastate war has fallen too (Gleditsch et al. 2002).[1]

The argument here is that preventing war is not a new task. War has been prevented before, many times. Some societies and regions have been free from the scourge of war for quite long periods. Even in societies and international systems which experience frequent wars, there are forces that tend to mitigate the incidence of wars and limit them to particular areas. The actual incidence of warfare can be seen as the outcome of a balance between the causes of war and structural factors that tend to prevent war. It is these 'preventors' and their effect on processes of emergent conflict that form the subject of this chapter.

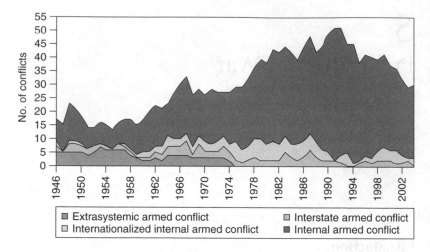

Figure 5.1   Active conflicts 1946–2004 by conflict type
Source: Uppsala University, Department for Peace and Conflict Research.
http://www.pcr.uu.se/research/UCDP/graphs1.htm

I will first cover the evidence for the development of war prevention in history, taking selected snapshots of particular places and periods to illustrate the theme. I then discuss the factors that have contributed to the recent decline in the incidence of international war. Finally I examine the evidence for structural prevention of civil wars.

War prevention in history

From the earliest times, conflict between human groups has been accompanied by efforts to prevent, regulate and limit conflict. Almost all societies have institutions and norms to keep the destructive potential of violence in check. These institutions, of course, are particular to the culture and conditions of different societies. One cannot expect that the same preventive factors will operate in all societies, nor that the same ones continue to operate as society changes. Indeed, the same institutions that regulate conflict and maintain the peace sometimes also precipitate and intensify warfare at times of deteriorating social order. Just as the causes of war change as societies develop (Howard 1976, 1983; Luard 1986) so do the means of limiting and preventing violence (Luard 1986).

Broadly, the story of interaction between preventors and causes may be organized into five phases:

(1) Societies without organized warfare. The earliest societies experienced fighting, raiding and small-scale murder, which was often extremely cruel. However, they lacked the specialization and resources to create permanent military forces and fortifications or to campaign far from home. Of those that have survived long enough into the modern era to have been studied by anthropologists some are entirely peaceful, others extremely violent. Trade and exogamy tended to mitigate and limit fighting.

(2) As societies grew more complex and stratified, military specialists appeared, weapons became more powerful and warfare more destructive. This led to a self-reinforcing military competition between societies, which encouraged the spread of war-fighting capacity. Institutions developed to support the financing and mobilization of professional warriors and the evolution of early states.

(3) A dynamic process of competition and aggregation between early states led in time to the formation of large empires. When these became enduring and stable, they created conditions for prevention of warfare inside their territories, although with enhanced capacity for large-scale war-making outside their borders. Empires waxed and waned and fought against the small kingdoms or barbarian tribes they found on their borders. Occasionally two large empires conducted a large-scale war, but usually empires enriched themselves by absorbing weaker entities on their periphery. Empires sometimes sustained a period of internal peace for centuries, but eventually collapsed, often with large-scale internal and external wars.

(4) The world of empires, or 'suzerain-systems', was eventually overthrown by the development and expansion of the European state-system from the fifteenth century and the rise of the European colonial empires (Bull and Watson 1984; Watson 1992). The main developments were the consolidation of military power and institutions in the state, and the disarmament of rival groups; intense warfare between states; and colonization of the periphery. Application of new technology led to sustained intensification of the destructiveness of war.

(5) In the twentieth century the international system of states which had grown out of this European framework began to develop into a global social and economic system, with the gradual absorption of

the sovereign national state into larger units of governance and the inception of some institutions of global governance. This was accompanied by the spread of internal peace from within states to the development of peace between large groups of states. At the same time, warfare and the institutions of war continued to develop, both as a means of disciplining challenges from outside the 'security community' and as insurance against the breakdown of the international order. The strongest state, the USA, effectively ran an arms race against itself. Hence the development of ever more baroque security systems, 'netwars', 'virtual wars', 'star wars' and the like.

Violence and prevention in early human history

Anthropologists have now dated the beginning of organized warfare to a period late in the Upper Paleolithic, around or after −10,000. Kelly (2003) suggests that the coming of war as an organized form of coercion between political communities was associated with an early social transformation – the development of segmentary rather than unsegmented societies. Segmentary societies are those that can be broken down into groups of various sizes: for example, a cluster of families makes a village, a cluster of villages makes a local community, and so on. Societies based on patrilineal kinship groups for example form a segmentary society, where every member can be identified as part of the group. The implication of this is that if one member of a segmentary group kills an outsider, the outsider can retaliate against any member of that group. In unsegmented societies, patrilineal and matrilineal descent groups are not recognized, and the political concept that any member of the group can be a legitimate target for retaliation does not develop.

Bands

For most of human history, people have been organized in small bands, usually practising hunter-gathering. There must have been strong pressures to avoid the use of weapons within these groups. Members would be very vulnerable to murderous acts within the group and so taboos on murder and damage to the person probably evolved at a very early stage. Indeed other primates developed social codes for reconciliation, avoiding conflict and limiting fighting (De Waal 1989).

Between bands occasions for conflict must have been limited by low population density and relatively infrequent contact. Nevertheless, raiding and skirmishing seem to have been common. But a key factor preventing and regulating such conflict emerged out of the needs of hunter-gathering bands to intermarry outside the local group, in order to preserve sufficient genetic diversity. Kinship relations therefore extended beyond the local band, and were a crucial part of regulating relations between bands. Whether men move to live with women in other groups, or stay in their own groups, for example, has been found to be a signifi- cant variable in explaining the incidence of violent conflict. On the whole, societies with patrilocal post-marital residence produce 'fraternal inter- est groups' of men living together. Such groups regularly resort to vio- lence to protect their interests in localized conflicts. On the other hand, societies with matrilocal post-marital residence do not have such frater- nal interest groups, and tend to have cross-cutting kinship ties, which encourage co-operation and peaceful resolution of conflict between neighbours. On the other hand, matrilocal ties allow alliances among several residence groups, making long-distance, external warfare more feasible. Although related groups do fight, on the whole intermarriage and kinship relations tend to regulate the pattern of warfare and foster co-operation and mutual obligations that tend to discourage fighting.

Kelly (2000: 133) suggests that 'warfare is typically rare to nonexistent within and between unsegmented foraging societies inhabiting environ- ments characterised by low resource density, diversity and predictability at densities below 0.2 persons per square mile'. Moreover, in societies that do develop warfare, that warfare is typically episodic (and not continuous, as Hobbes supposed). From the earliest times, there have been social mech- anisms to bring wars to a conclusion and to maintain peace in between wars.

Tribes and chieftaincies

With the coming of segmented societies grouped together in tribes, wars in the modern sense developed, with conflicts being used to impose the will of one group's leader on another, or to obtain or defend land, and to dominate another group or resist such domination. But relations between groups can also be moderated by exchange and political relations. It was quite common for mutual trade to create peaceful relations between groups, even in an environment where fighting was common (Ferguson 1990: 34), and quite complex patterns of long-term trade establish dis- tant political relationships between distant groups. Buzan and Little (2000) cite the *kula* ceremony, which developed between the islanders of the western Pacific, as a good example of this pacifying role of trade. It involved a circular, ritualized exchange of bracelets and necklaces to smooth the conditions for trade and limit the potential for conflict between the tribes.

The coming of agriculture required groups to be tied to particular pieces of land, and created stored goods that were valuable and needed protection. There is good archaeological evidence from Oaxaca, Mexico of a process of co-evolution of war and the state that must have been common. Flannery and Marcus (2003) traced the development of violence in the area by carbon-dating burnt wooden structures in the area. The first clear evidence of house-burning comes from −1540, a century after the first permanent village was established. The population was large enough to be divided into clans and lived in at least 18 separate villages. By −1300 there is evidence of a palisade, a sign of fortification. Within a few hundred years public buildings had developed and there is more evidence of raiding and the taking and sacrifice of prisoners. Later the villages moved to a more defensible site at Monte Albán and conquered a neighbouring town. The society had evolved into a state. Monte Albán went on to conquer neighbouring areas and became the first empire in Mesoamerica (Spencer 2003).

War prevention among early states

The existing evidence suggests that up until the neolithic age, and certainly during the phase of hunter-gathering bands, relations between groups were sometimes marked by fighting which could be as barbarous as any modern warfare, but that this fighting was also regulated by kinship and political relations between groups. The invention of the bow, the mace, the sling and the dagger at about −8000, the start of the neolithic age, represented a significant development in fighting technologies (Keegan 1994). The earliest towns that have been excavated (Jericho, with a population of two to three thousand in −7000, and Catal Huyuk with a population of five to seven thousand) were protected with walls and a moat, suggesting that warfare was a problem these first urban dwellers had to contend with. But four millennia later the early Sumerian cities were built without walls, and show no evidence of warfare (Keegan: 128). They were ruled by priest-kings and the evidence suggests that theocratic rule pacified the area. Later warrior rulers supplanted the priest-kings. Warfare between the cities and with outsiders became frequent between −3100 and −2700. Bronze weapons were developed and battles were recorded on clay tablets (Keegan: 133–4).

At the same time specialists in preventing war developed. The first heralds appeared – early diplomats who were granted a kind of diplomatic immunity. 'Peace chiefs' were generally more important and held more permanent positions than 'war chiefs' (for example, among the North American Indians).

Archaeologists made a significant discovery about the prevention of war in early Pharaonic Egypt when they discovered almost four hundred cuneiform tablets in Amarna, describing the relations between Egypt and neighbouring states in the Near East in the −14th century. The tablets set out a code of norms among states which possessed no common government, language, or religion, but nevertheless agreed to regulate the use of force between themselves (Cohen 1996).

In general then, while there has been a process of co-evolution between social organization and war (Otterbein 1973; Tilly 1990; Kelly 2003), there has at the same time been a less well-told process of co-evolution between social organization and war prevention.

Wars and war prevention in classical China

The epic story of the classical Chinese empire commands attention in any account of global war and peace. In terms of duration China has been much the most successful world civilization, surviving in a continuous form from the start of the Shang dynasty (−1766) to the collapse of the Qing Dynasty in 1911. For most of this long period the Chinese Empire represented the main system of governance in what the Chinese saw as the known civilized world. It was the centre of a system of suzerainty with outer barbarian chiefdoms and preserved a distinctive type of international and domestic political system. This long period of common rule contributed to China's relatively low frequency of warfare compared with the West (Wright 1942; Richardson 1960; Krus et al. 1998).

The Great Wall of China indicates both the vastness of the area over which the Empire's rule extended, and the effort to control a suzerain system. It was built incrementally, on the basis of previous walls built by the states of the Warring States period, and completed and extended by Qin Shi Huang Ti, the First Emperor. An essentially defensive structure, it served both to demarcate an area and to regulate relations with outsiders. The Chinese Empire proved more durable than the Roman Empire. Once it had reached its full extent it avoided further large-scale conquests, and relied on political means and bribes and essentially defensive military actions to regulate relations with outside powers. It sometimes broke apart, with attendant warfare, but was reunified. When China was occupied by outside powers, it absorbed them into its own civilization. It also succeeded in absorbing different belief systems; the syncretic tendency in Chinese thought enabled Taoism, Confucianism, Buddhism and even Islam to co-exist, so avoiding religious wars.

The remarkable feature of the Chinese Empire which served to hold it together and also to limit its expansion was the cohesive influence of the written Chinese language. Chinese characters were understood over a much larger area than were the various spoken languages and they retained their form and meanings over a much longer time period than spoken sounds, which change and alter over generations. The written language thus encodes a distinctive Chinese culture that has had extraordinary continuity. The Imperial officials, schooled in Confucian ideas, were its custodians. The system of civil service examinations, in theory open to all, though in practice dominated by the scholar-gentry, served to unify vastly different areas around a common system of governance and a common outlook on the world. It also provided a degree of social mobility, which channelled ambitions in a system-preserving rather than a system-disrupting direction. The rationale of Confucianism was to preserve order and harmony. It was the duty of the imperial officials to preserve harmony on behalf of the empire. Rebellions, wars with barbarians and similar symptoms of disorder were their responsibility.

An essential feature of this governing system was that it was largely civilian. The armed forces were secondary to the imperial bureaucracy. From a relatively early period, there was a market in land, restricting the potential for an independent feudal military class.

A record of the frequency of internal wars in Chinese history was collected by J.S. Lee (1931), and is quoted in Sorokin (1962). Lee calculated the occurrences of internecine wars by quinquennium from -221 to 1930. Lee found (in Sorokin's words)

> three long time periods of about 810 to 780 years: the first from 221 BC to AD 589, the second from 589 to 1386, the third from 1386 up to the present time. Each of these long periods begins with a flaring up of civil war which is quickly ended, and the country enters a long period of peace, marked by enormous technical and cultural achievements. After about the second half of the period of the curve it begins to rise, showing shorter periods of peace, and a greater and greater number of wars. One period ends and a new period begins with a general internecine war and anarchy with their satellites. (Sorokin: 357)

A significant factor underlying the dynamics of unification and disunification in Chinese history has been identified by Chi Ch'ao-Ting (1970). He identifies three 'key economic areas' each of which represents a distinct and relatively self-sufficient geographical region. The first Emperor managed to unite these three areas into one political unit. In subsequent periods, when these areas were integrated and effectively linked, particularly through public water-control works, the empire tended to be stable. When the integration of the three areas failed, the empire tended to become disunited.

These factors contributed to the very major differences between the course of Chinese and Western history. The Chinese empire was held together by a thinly spread but cohesive ruling class of gentry, scholars and literati, who gained their income from renting out land.[2] The ruling class lived in the towns, which had a well-developed local cash economy. The empire was very vulnerable to peasant revolts, which broke out frequently when taxes and rents became too high. These were the most common and most destructive form of warfare in Chinese history. In contrast the European area after the end of the Roman empire was politically disunited, and shaped by a long period in which feudal institutions were dominant. Long-distance trade was important to the economy and merchants and towns were able to find a degree of autonomy outside the lord-and-peasant system, which laid a basis for capital accumulation and expansion outside the agrarian economy. In contrast, the profits of Chinese traders were put back into the land tenure system, and large-scale expansion of trade was regulated and checked by the state. The political fragmentation of the European system led to a division between the Church and the State. As a result the shared Christian culture was not associated with politically unifying institutions and warfare between sovereign units became endemic.

The Chinese experience illustrates the central importance of a common state in preventing warfare – and its limitations. Political unification is clearly important as a means of preventing and ending wars within the unified territory. From different ends of the earth, Tudor England and Tokugawa Japan offer additional illustrations of this pattern.

Political unification in England and Japan

Like Shih Huang Ti in China, the Tudor dynasty in England and Hideyoshi in feudal Japan managed to curb internecine warfare by unifying their countries, ushering in long periods of internal peace. All used forceful methods to crush their opponents, but a system of governance and administration then developed which gradually gained legitimacy and acceptance. In England Henry VII's defeat of Richard III at Bosworth Field in 1485, and a succession of other challengers over the next ten years, led the way to 'the Tudor peace', a long period in which baronial challenges declined and the power of central government became established. This was underpinned by improvements in financing and administration, which increased the power of the Crown. Justices of the Peace enforced the law locally in the name of the Crown. In Japan Toyotomi Hideyoshi (1536–98) and his successor Tokugawa Ieyasu (1542–1616) brought a long period of peace to a society dominated by a warrior class. Remarkably, they secured a ban on the use of guns that lasted for two centuries. Hideyoshi crushed armed resistance and obliged the *daimyo* to send members of their families as hostages to Yedo. An extensive network of spies gave early warning of potential revolts.[3] Later, as in the Chinese and English cases, the new system of governance resulting from Hideyoshi's legacy was to bring a more accepted and legitimate system of internal peace, albeit one achieved by hegemonic means. A similar story of unification and consolidation can be told for many other states. Civil wars continued to break out, but the steady strengthening of the power of the state tended to reduce the risk of internal conflicts while increasing the scale of external wars. Once competing internal centres of military power had been disarmed and pacified, the next step was the establishment of institutions to regulate conflict (usually in a direction that was acceptable to the governing classes). Practices varied greatly from state to state, with some states relying on the authority of the rulers, and others on a more complex balance between the rights and responsibilities of the citizens and the regulatory powers of the state. The rule of law, a system of justice that offered redress without violence, parliamentary assemblies and the development of similar institutions made it possible to reach accommodations over disputes and divisions that would previously have been settled by recourse to arms.

European wars and war prevention since Westphalia

It is very clear from the records in ancient, medieval and modern times that the incidence of warfare has undergone large variations in time. Some regions, at some times, have been full of wars; others have had long periods of peace. By virtue of its fragmented political system and its rapid economic and military development, Europe became the site of the largest and most destructive interstate wars from the seventeenth to the twentieth centuries. After the treaty of Westphalia in 1648, wars gradually grew less frequent but more intense. A succession of brief periods of general war were followed by longer periods of general peace, occasionally interrupted by limited wars. Over time the general wars have got bigger, the periods without general wars have grown longer, and the limited wars are less frequent. Set against this there have been very long periods of sustained tension and preparation for war, when the outbreak of another large-scale war seemed possible, notably the Cold War which established the largest military confrontation, along the line dividing West from East Germany, that the world has ever known.

After each of the main wars, a peace settlement set up an international order, which was designed to regulate the issues and relationships that might threaten the prevailing order (Holsti 1991). These orders were not necessarily concerned with ruling out war. In the case of the post-Westphalia order, the intention was rather to put an end to the religious wars. In this it was effective. It created a minimal sense of a European community of interest, to which diplomats and statesmen were willing to refer, if not always to uphold. The Peace of Utrecht (1713), following the War of Spanish Succession, aimed to prevent the development of hegemonic empires in Europe, such as that of Louis XIV and Charles V before him. It too was relatively successful in this aim, and preserved a rough balance between the dynastic states until this was overthrown by the French Revolution. Like other treaties, the Peace of Utrecht secured the interests of the victors, and it served its purpose of hemming in French expansion. At the same time it aimed to set some bounds to competition between dynastic states by settling the main succession issues, neutralising Italy and establishing mutual guarantees. It scarcely limited the major state rivalries and war remained a frequent instrument of state power, with wars breaking out in Europe about once every three years. The Congress of Vienna (1815) ushered in a period of conference diplomacy, designed to avoid challenges to the existing order. It made for a century relatively free of general interstate warfare, although not without fierce competition outside Europe. Its principles were undermined by the growth of nationalism and the formation of new states, when Germany and Italy sought their place in the system of international powers. In the latter half of the century Bismarck's diplomatic system went some way towards restoring the Concert of Europe. The Great Powers, even when they were divided by the nature of their governments and their different interests, showed themselves capable of concerting together to preserve the status quo.

Peter Wallensteen (1984) arranges these successive orders into a sequence of what he calls 'universalist' and 'particularist' periods. The latter are periods when particular powers pursue policies unilaterally, without reference to other states, even if this disrupts existing international organizations and power relationships; the former are periods when states act in concert within some minimal multilateral framework of norms or rules. Wallensteen finds that during 'universalist' periods the major powers fought no wars with each other and engaged in only about half as many militarized disputes as in the 'particularist' periods. The number of wars between major and minor powers was also lower. There is evidence here that international diplomatic arrangements have been capable of preventing major power wars.

Each of these orders broke down when challenges to the status quo overwhelmed the international system, and especially when great powers were among the challengers. But the arrangements they constituted represented a primitive system of international governance. This has grown stronger over time. The League of Nations became a permanent international organization with the maintenance of international peace as its objective. The League Covenant indeed embodied principles of international conflict prevention for the first time. Article 10 pledged all member states to protect other members against aggression. Article 11 declared that any war or threat of war was a matter of concern to all member states. In articles 12 and 15 member states agreed to submit their disputes to arbitration. In article 16 any war disregarding these principles was declared to be a war against all the members. Despite the flaws in the League's concept and its inability to implement these principles in the conditions of the 1930s, this constituted a step towards an international system for regulating war. The United Nations took the principle further, explicitly stating in the Preamble that its purpose was to 'save succeeding generations from the scourge of war.'

Wars and movements against wars developed together (Hinsley 1963; Howard 1978; Luard 1986; Hinsley 1987; Howard 2000). On the one hand, the nineteenth century laid the basis for the terrible destruction of the twentieth through its nationalism, its Great Power competition, and the industrialization of warfare. On the other, it gave the impulse for international efforts to regulate wars. Although achieving an effective system was beyond the primitive systems of international governance in place, the first significant step was taken towards establishing some international machinery for war prevention. Another significant development took place in the nineteenth century: the emergence of what has become known as 'the liberal peace'.

The rise of the 'liberal peace'

The development of the 'liberal peace' in the nineteenth and twentieth centuries needs to be placed in the context of broader developments in the world's political economy. The rapid pace of industrial development and urbanization on the one hand led to a much tighter integration of national economies into the international trading system, and a greater mobility of capital around the world. On the other it also encouraged vigorous European competition for colonies and dramatically widened the gap between industrialized countries and the rest of the world. There was much competition also between and within states, and a large gap between the propertied elite and the working classes. Yet a solid bond of co-operation developed between the ruling groups of the liberal states who had most to gain from managing this system, in particular those in Britain and the United States. We do not have to believe, with Polanyi, that the gold standard underpinned the Concert of Europe, but it certainly helped to underpin the 'liberal peace'.

In the nineteenth century the United States and Britain patched up their former enmity and settled a range of territorial quarrels by negotiation. As a number of writers on peaceful change have pointed out, this was a remarkable case of a peaceful power transition (Crutwell 1937; Davidson and Sucharov 2001; Kupchan et al. 2001). Britain, at the height of its imperial and naval pre-eminence, ceded its position in the American hemisphere to the rising power, and came to recognize that its interests would be better served by a friendship with the United States than an enmity. This has been recognized as a remarkable case of a power transition achieved by peaceful change. After conceding to American claims over the Venezuela dispute in 1895–96,[4] the British government consciously opted for a new relationship. Territorial and fishing disputes in Alaska and Newfoundland were settled to the American advantage. In response the United States did not make difficulties over the Boer War. Churchill and others began to speak of the community of interests of the English-speaking peoples. Later, as the United States pondered whether to enter the First World War, the editor and journalist Walter Lippman coined the phrase 'Atlantic community' in making the case for American involvement.

It was co-operation in war, above all, which forged this liberal alliance, but in the aftermath, the Atlantic partners found a common cause in dictating the terms of the peace. President Woodrow Wilson aimed to build a new postwar order that would be 'safe for democracy'. Prime Minister Lloyd George wanted to preserve wartime unity and maintain American diplomatic engagement with Europe (Williams 1998). The refusal of Congress to sign the Versailles Treaty, which left the US outside the League, was a blow to these policies. Nevertheless, Atlantic ties remained strong. The League of Nations was able to prevent a number of disputes from escalating into violence, and Germany and Japan had democratic governments in the 1920s. This first wave of democratic expansion rolled back as the postwar settlement came under pressure and the reverberations of the Wall Street Crash toppled democratic governments and led to the world crisis of the 1930s and 1940s. But with the end of the Second World War, Roosevelt and his Allies again sought to establish a world order based on liberal principles. Roosevelt wanted a world safe for his 'four freedoms', based on 'the co-operation of free countries, working together in a friendly, civilized society'. The building blocks for a restored liberal peace would be the institution of democratic governments in the defeated countries, reconstruction aid to Europe, an open, expansion international economy, a liberal world trading system underpinned by the US dollar, and the establishment of the United Nations.

The statistical evidence from the quantitative research effort into the correlates of war has suggested three tendencies. First, the 'democratic peace' proposition suggests that pairs of democracies are statistically much less likely to fight one another than other states.[5] However, democracies are no less likely to engage in war than other types of states. Raknerud and Hegre (1997) showed that the apparent discrepancy between the behaviour of democracies in monads and dyads is accounted for by their tendency to join in coalition wars against autocracies. Democracy is only a preventor of interstate wars with other democratic states. Outside the borders of the 'liberal peace', it is a stimulus to wars.[6] Second, it is argued, though this is also contested, that trade tends to be associated with peace, in the sense that dyads which trade with one another tend on that account to experience less mutual militarized conflict (Schneider et al. 2003). Hegre (2003) suggest that this relationship is linked to development; more developed and more democratic dyads are less likely to experience war. Thirdly, it is argued that involvement in international organizations reduces the risk of war (Russett and Oneal 2001). These, of course, are all statistical findings and attributing cause is more difficult. The problem is not finding an explanation for the 'liberal peace', but rather cutting through the thicket of alternative explanations. Democratic dyads, economic interdependence, transnational transactions, strong states, and membership of common institutions, Cold War co-operation, a US-led international order – these are all possible factors: they are a complex of linked conditions contributing to the liberal peace (Adler 1998).

Rasmussen (2003) argues convincingly that these conditions did not develop by accident, but were constructed deliberately as part of a historical process. The close political relationships fostered between Britain and America formed the nucleus of an evolving set of political ties. As Rasmussen puts it, 'peace is not a fact, it is a policy'. The liberal peace was made because it suited the interests of the liberal states, who benefited from mutual trade, interdependence and avoidance of war between themselves. The victors of the world wars deliberately embedded liberal principles in the postwar orders (Williams 1998; Rasmussen 2003). The success of the liberal order then led to its expansion.

An important element in this process was the dynamic increase in the number of democracies following wars, and the resulting incorporation of new states into the 'liberal peace'. Democracies tended to win wars and defeated states then ousted autocracies and installed democracies. As a consequence there was a systematic growth in the number of liberal states and these states were incorporated in the Western-dominated liberal system. As Mitchell et al. (1999) argue, 'democratization tends to follow war, democratization decreases the systemic amount of war, and the substantive and pacific impact of democracy on war increases over time.'

Of course, democratization continues to be promoted also by peaceful means. Democracy promotion is now a conscious adjunct of development, peace-building and conflict prevention policy. As such it has been taken up by the major international institutions and is used as a condition of financial support by the international financial agencies. Democratization may indeed become an instrument of conflict prevention and conflict management when democratic institutions flourish in ways appropriate to local conditions. The danger is that it is applied only as a veneer, in response to external pressure, and used to legitimize one-party rule or the dominance of the largest ethnic group. Then democratization can be a factor that exacerbates conflicts.

The role of regional organizations

Mutual democracy and participation in the Western system of international institutions were not the only means of building 'security communities'. In Europe, the decisive initiative that consolidated the ending of centuries of internecine war was the development of the European Union. The reconciliation between France and Germany, implemented through the visionary agreements between Jean Monnet and Robert Schuman, constituted a dramatic change in European politics. Major issues between European states were now dealt with now by bargaining and negotiation, and the forward momentum of European integration, at least until the Maastricht Treaty in 1991, created the political space within which elites in Europe could fashion a close accommodation. The successive enlargements of Europe also assisted the transition of the peripheral member states into democracies and, especially after 1989, provided the basis for the peaceful integration of members of previously hostile military alliances. With the Copenhagen conditions for accession, and the promotion of EU models of human rights and governance, Europe became an active centre for the further consolidation and expansion of 'the liberal peace'. Yet this came at a cost. The intrusion of Western democratic models and market conditionality into eastern Europe proved disastrous in the case of former Yugoslavia, and the wars in Croatia, Bosnia and Kosovo were a searing reverse. As in the case of democratic peace, regional organizations could have mixed effects, preventing some conflicts, yet exacerbating others.

In other parts of the world, too, regional organizations appeared to be presiding over improving interstate relations. The Association of Southeast Asian Nations (ASEAN), for example, managed to apply the 'Asian way' of consensual politics and prevented interstate disputes among its members escalating, while preserving a strict policy of non-interference in member states' internal affairs. In Latin America, similarly, the Organization of American States (OAS) has presided over an unusually low level of interstate war, and has also encouraged a norm of non-intervention. These regional organizations have had less impact in managing internal conflicts, which have been severe in both regions. The Organization for Security and Co-operation in Europe (OSCE), in contrast, became an instrument for internal conflict management as well as confidence-building and conflict prevention between states which had been members of rival alliances. There are grounds for describing all these regions as additional zones of interstate peace.

The end of major power war?

Does this imply, as Muller et al. (1989) suggests, that wars between major powers have become obsolete? Certainly the destructiveness of waging modern warfare makes its costs prohibitive for modern industrial states. The coming of nuclear weapons and other weapons of mass destruction no doubt adds a further element of caution. Yet the rational, controlled policy-making that this requires sets standards that may not always be met. Political leaders have shown their proclivity for destructive and even suicidal policies in the past. The world, we now know, came remarkably close to war in the Cuba crisis. Given the incoherence of official doctrines of deterrence, we should be sceptical of its efficacy as a preventor of war. There are too many major conflicts of interest, too many unresolved disputes and deep divisions between human populations to be optimistic about the end of major power war. Weapons are unreliable instruments for preventing wars. Political and institutional arrangements are necessary.

Conclusion: prevention of international wars

To conclude, there is increasing evidence that prevention of international wars is taking place, within security communities, zones of peace, and the 'liberal peace' zone. The extension of international institutions, the development of international law, the widespread acceptance of international norms, all create standards of conduct and common values laying the basis for peaceful change. States have an increasing capacity for negotiating disputes and conflicts and arriving at acceptable outcomes without resort to force. Rosecrance's argument (1986) that the rise of the trade-state has offered states previously tempted by militarism an alternative route to world power is convincing. So is that of Keohane and Nye (1989) who, arguing from a theoretical point of view, suggested that under conditions of complex interdependence, states are likely to consult one another, develop coalitions between officials in different governments, act in predictable ways and avoid the use of force since this is both costly and inappropriate when the interests of states are interconnected across a multiple set of issue-areas. The statistical evidence from the research literature on international conflicts suggests that development, interdependence, joint-democracy and international organization are all interlinked elements of the explanation for 'the liberal peace'. We have argued here that policy has been important too. This has been a constructed peace. Yet it remains a fragile one. The 'liberal peace' is in many ways a huge achievement, especially in its European manifestation. If it can be extended to overcome the historic rivalry between Russia and the West, that would be a further dramatic achievement. Yet it remains a flawed peace. It is a peace at home combined with an easy willingness to use armed force abroad, a peace that protects the prosperity of millions of people at the expense of the destitution of other millions. Above all, it is fragile because the institutions at its core have developed around continued growth, mobile global finances, full employment, a large supply of oil, and expanding trade. If these conditions were to falter, the associations between economic development, democracy, trade and peace could turn out to be uncomfortable in reverse.

The evidence for structural prevention of conflict remains contested and tantalizing, and it is difficult to distinguish between competing explanations. The capacity of international society to manage its conflicts is growing, and in the aftermath of the Cold War a more benign international atmosphere has been positive for international conflict prevention. At the same time, the seriousness and divisiveness of long-term conflicts of interest is manifest, and there can be little confidence that the capacity is yet sufficient to manage the crises that are likely to be in store.

Structural prevention of civil wars

As Figure 5.1 shows, intrastate wars and intrastate wars attracting international intervention now account for the vast majority of armed conflicts. Over the last decade or two the conflict research community has turned its attention to identifying the sources and explaining the incidence and duration of civil wars. The main research question has been to identify the independent variables or combination of variables that best explain the incidence of civil war. Few of the studies set out to look explicitly for factors that prevent wars. Nevertheless, this literature suggests many useful insights on the nature of 'preventors' as well as the conditions of civil war.

Many of the findings of this literature are contested, but there is general agreement on the strongest factors associated with the onset of civil war. Civil wars are low probability events, which occur under a range of different circumstances in many countries. Few systems of governance have proven absolutely impervious to civil wars. Rich countries as well as poor ones are at risk of armed conflicts. Nevertheless, the statistics of civil war incidence indicate that there are circumstances that make civil war less likely than others.

Different authors have used a range of different statistical methods and different datasets, based on slightly different definitions of civil war, sometimes using different time periods and sometimes different groups of states. Some findings that are significant on one dataset appear insignificant when tested with another. There has been less convergence in the field that might have been expected. Recently researchers have attempted to carry out large numbers of runs with multiple datasets using different combinations of assumptions (Hegre and Sambanis 2006).

Sambanis (2002), in a review of the literature on civil wars, identified three factors that show significance in almost all studies. These are the time since a previous armed conflict, the (logged) size of population and GDP per capita, measured as the natural log of GDP per capita in constant dollars. There is a larger range of other variables on which there is less agreement.

Perhaps the strongest finding, on which all studies agree, is that previous civil wars predict to new civil wars, not surprisingly in view of the recurrent, protracted nature of much contemporary armed conflict. Another strong finding is the association between civil war and low average per capita income. Developing societies with low average per capita incomes are much more likely to suffer armed conflicts than developed societies with higher per capita incomes, and there is a strong statistical association across the range between per capita income and avoidance or occurrence of civil war. Another important variable is the size of the country – larger countries tend to experience more civil wars, although if one controlled for population size, wars per capita would fall with country size (Richardson 1960). Another important factor is political instability. Countries that have experienced a recent change of regime are more prone to civil war than those that have not, and 'anocracies', countries which have a transitional form of government between autocracy and democracy, with some elements of both systems, are more prone to civil wars than established autocracies or established democracies.

Exploring these factors in more detail, we turn now to consider the influence of democratic governance, development, governance, political institutions, human rights, and education as preventors of civil wars.

Democracy and democratization

The association between democratic governance and civil peace remains controversial. Some authors argue that democracies tend to be more peaceful internally than non-democracies. For example, Gurr argues that this effect of democratization is responsible for the reduction of internal wars since 1992 (Gurr 2000; Gurr et al. 2002). Elbadwi and Sambanis (2002) focus on the incidence of civil wars with more than a thousand deaths over the duration of the war between 1960 and 1999. They find that political rights are associated with the prevention of conflict and argue that political variables are more important than economic ones in explaining civil war and its prevention. Others argue that there is no connection between democracy and civil war. Collier and Hoeffler (2004b) separately tested a 'grievances' model, a 'greed' model and a combined model against a dataset of the prevalence of civil wars in five year periods between 1960 and 1999. They found that democracy was highly significant in the 'grievances' model; repression increased the risk of conflict. However, the 'greed' model, which concentrated on economic variables, performed better than the 'grievances' model. A combined model, which performed better than either separately, gained more power when democracy was excluded. This led Collier and Hoeffler to conclude that democracy was not significant overall.[7]

Another influential study that fails to find a significant preventive role for democracy is Fearon and Laitin (2003). They examined factors associated with the onset of civil wars, defined as conflicts with a threshold of 100 battle-deaths per year, between 1945 and 1999. They found that 'after controlling for per capita income (or other measures of state strength), neither political democracy, the presence of civil liberties, higher income inequality, nor discriminatory linguistic or religious policies' were strongly associated with lower odds of civil war. 'Given the right environmental conditions, insurgencies can thrive on the basis of small numbers of rebels without strong, widespread, freely-granted popular support rooted in grievances – hence even in democracies' (2003: 17). They found that conditions that favour insurgencies, in particular state weakness, poverty, large size and instability are a better predictor of civil war than grievances, lack of democracy or discrimination against minorities (2003: 31). As regards prevention they conclude that, while economic growth is associated with fewer civil wars, 'the causal mechanism is more likely well-financed and administratively competent government'. (2003: 32) In contrast, 'financially, organizationally, and politically weak central governments render insurgency more feasible and attractive' (2003: 3).

Hegre (2003) confirms the findings in a number of other studies that there is a U-shaped relationship between political regime and civil conflict.[8] Strong democracies and well-entrenched autocracies are both unlikely to experience civil wars. It is transitional regimes and 'anocracies' (regimes with a mixture of democratic and autocratic features) that are prone to armed conflicts. Gates et al. (2001) argue that this is because stable autocracies and stable democracies are institutionally self-consistent. They suggest that 'maintenance of a polity's institutional structure is in the interest of political elites, whether through autocratic or democratic control'. Hegre qualifies the U-shaped relationship by finding that 'democracy is correlated with civil peace only for developed countries, and only for countries with high levels of literacy'. His argument is that a developing autocracy will encounter pressures for change which may lead to the violent end of the system, while poor democracies are unstable and also lead to violence (Hegre 2004b).

This finding that semi-democracies have a higher level of war than either stable democracies or stable autocracies is rather ominous in a world in which democratization is in full swing, and is strongly encouraged by the major powers. There is evidence, however, that once a democracy has settled down, it tends to become rather stable. In the decade following the end of the Cold War, as Table 5.1 shows, 'old democracies' have had the least armed conflicts, and autocracies experienced the most wars of all regimes.

Autocracies have been under unprecedented pressure from globalization since the end of the Cold War. States espousing democratic values and market systems have dominated world politics. These states are applying the conditions for access to Western institutions and financial support. Thus, while closed autocratic regimes have been extremely effective in suppressing rebellions in the past, the international environment is more unfavourable for them now.

In summary, there is evidence that settled democracies, especially in developed countries, tend to avoid civil wars. Well-established autocracies also prevent rebellions, but this effect may be starting to wear off. However, in less developed countries and countries with recent changes in regime type, democracy tends to be associated with civil wars.

Table 5.1 Armed conflicts by regime type, 1989–99

Regime type	None	Minor	Intermediate	War	Total
Old democracies	19	2	2	2	25
New democracies	24	4	1	4	33
Transitional regimes	16	3	2	11	32
Autocracies	10	0	2	14	26
Total	69	9	7	31	116

Notes: Old Democracies are countries whose democratic political institutions were established before 1980 and that had not reverted to autocratic rule. New democracies are countries whose democratic institutions were established between 1980 and 1994 and that had not reverted to autocratic rule since 1980. Transitional regimes are countries with a mix of democratic and autocratic features plus countries that made a transition to democracy after the 1970s that subsequently failed. Autocracies are countries with autocratic institutions that did not attempt democratic transitions.

Armed conflicts are counted as contested incompatibilities involving the use of armed force and at least 25 battle-related deaths, with one of the parties being a government. Each country is coded by the largest internal armed conflict that occurred between 1989 and 1999. Minor armed conflicts are those with at least 25 battle-related deaths per year and fewer than 1000 battle-related deaths in the course of the conflict. Intermediate armed conflicts are those with at least 25 deaths per year and an accumulated total of at least 1000 battle-related deaths, but fewer than 1000 in any given year. Wars are armed conflicts with at least 1000 battle-related deaths per year. Calculated by the author from the Uppsala/PRIO dataset on armed conflicts (Gleditsch 2001) and the Polity database on regime types (Jaggers and Gurr 1995; Gleditsch et al. 2001).

It is the combination of democracy, political stability and development that appears to be effective in avoiding civil conflict.

Development

As noted above, economic development is one of the factors most widely identified with reduced incidence of conflict across the quantitative literature. Henderson and Singer (2000: 275–99), in a study of the onset of civil wars in post-colonial states in Africa, Asia and the Middle East, identify development, demilitarization and full decolonization as factors that tend to inhibit the inception of civil wars. Collier and Hoeffler (1998) and Hegre et al. (2001) confirm the widely accepted view that high levels of development reduce the risk of civil war. Many armed conflicts, not surprisingly, take place in countries with a low score on the UN Human Development Index, although many countries with middling scores and some countries with high scores also experience armed conflicts.[9] 'Development' reduces but does not eliminate the risk of internal wars.

Collier et al. (2003) argue that 'the key root cause of conflict is the failure of economic development. Countries with low, stagnant and unequally distributed per capita incomes that have remained dependent on primary commodities for their exports face dangerously high risks of prolonged conflict.' The risk of violent civil conflict is highest in the poorest countries, and it then diminishes in middle income countries and is much lower in high income countries. They find that 'doubling per capita income approximately halves the risk of rebellion' (2003: 58). OECD countries have an almost negligible risk of civil war. Similarly, Buhaug (2005), using the PRIO/Uppsala Armed Conflict Dataset, finds that increasing levels of income per capita significantly reduce the probability of conflict. Using the lower threshold of 25 battle-deaths in this dataset, the probability of onset of a civil conflict in a country was found to be 2.1% per year, assuming all independent variables in the study were at their median levels. Increasing GDP per capita to the 95th percentile reduced the probability of conflict by half.

Political stability and institutions

Collier et al. (2003) suggest that reform of political institutions can prevent conflicts in countries which are growing economically. It is almost a platitude that political stability is associated with conflict prevention, and instability shows up as a correlate of civil war in many studies (Hegre 2001).

Institutions

There is much evidence from the comparative literature that appropriate institutions tend to prevent violent conflict (Lipjhart 1977; Horowitz 1985; Sisk 1997; Harris and Reilly 1998). When they provide incentives and structures for co-operation and accommodation between elites, institutions tend to prevent conflict. In a striking finding, Reynal-Querol (2001) reports that there were no ethnic civil wars in countries with proportional representation. Using evidence from household surveys, Østby (2005a) has found evidence for an effect of political institutions on the conflict potential of horizontal inequalities. Based on a study of 61 developing countries between 1986 and 2003, Østby (2005b) found that socioeconomic horizontal inequalities are more likely to cause conflict in democratic and politically inclusive systems. This confirmed the findings from case studies of Stewart and O'Sullivan (1998). Policies that are politically and economically inclusive mitigate the risk of armed conflict when horizontal inequalities are present (Østby 2005b). Binningsbø (2005) found that power-sharing institutions, including proportional representation and territorial autonomy, were more likely to result in a durable peace in post-conflict societies. This finding was based on a study of 118 cases between 1985 and 2002. Buhaug (2005) suggests distinguishing between civil wars over territory and government. The former are conflicts over 'exit', the latter conflicts over 'voice' (Hirschman 1970). Buhaug argues that in mature democracies, civil wars tend to occur when certain groups wish to 'exit'. He finds, on the basis of a study of 214 civil conflicts since 1945, that 'institutional consistency is particularly effective at preventing conflicts over state apparatus'.

Quality of governance

There are strong theoretical and empirical grounds for believing that the quality of governance is significantly associated with the risk of conflict. Edward Azar (1990) saw the internal wars prevailing since the 1970s as constituted by interrelated failures of domestic governance, international development and local politics. He argued that the denial of human needs and profound failures in governance tend to lead to suppression of ethnic identities, militarized politics, and external intervention in support of one of the parties. Armed conflict in turn degrades governance, deforms institutions and destroys development. Hence, a protracted cycle of social conflict can set in, sometimes leading to complete state failure.

Conversely, an alternative and more benign cycle could prevent conflict through good governance, development, civil politics and helpful external policies. The World Bank has collected cross-national data on the quality of governance, based on expert perceptions. This data ranks countries according to six concepts related to good governance: voice and accountability, political stability, government effectiveness, regulatory burden, rule of law and control of corruption (Kaufman et al. 1999). Combining these indicators with Gurr's data on rebellions in a study of 113 countries, I found a clear association, as one would expect, between 'good governance' and prevention of violent rebellion. Table 5.2 shows the results. Seventy per cent of the countries ranked in the top third on quality of governance indicators experienced no violence in their minority conflicts, and only 5 per cent had large-scale violent minority conflicts. Of the countries ranked in the bottom third on quality of governance, only 37 per cent experienced no violence and 29 per cent experienced large-scale violence. The figures suggest that good governance, or some characteristics associated with its measure in these studies, helped to prevent violent ethnic conflict.[10]

Human rights

Human rights violations are a strong indicator of incipient conflict (Schmid 1997; Jongmann 2000), so it should not be surprising that good observance of human rights is a factor associated with avoidance of civil war. Schmid and Jongmann use abuse of human rights as an indicator

Table 5.2   Quality of governance and incidence of violent ethnic conflicts in 113 countries, 1995–98

	No violence	Small-scale violence	Large-scale violence
Top third of countries on governance indicators	26 (70%)	10 (27%)	2 (5%)
Middle third of countries on governance indicators	17 (45%)	16 (42%)	5 (13%)
Bottom third of countries on governance indicators	14 (37%)	12 (32%)	11 (29%)

Notes: Author's calculations based on Kaufmann et al. (2000: 10–13) and Minorities At Risk data. The findings represent 113 countries with data available in both sources. A composite indicator of quality of governance was based on the mean of each country's ranking on six governance indicators. Countries were grouped into three equal groups on this indicator. Figures for armed conflict are derived from the 'rebellion' variable in the Minorities At Risk dataset. MAR indicators were aggregated into no violent conflict, small-scale conflict (between 2 and 6 on the MAR scale, that is a local uprising to a small-scale guerrilla war) and major deadly conflicts.

of incipient conflict. Kosovo is a typical case where a sharp increase in human rights abuse signalled an escalation in the conflict. In contrast, a high level of observance of human rights tends to accompany democratic governance and high levels of development. Rummel and others argue that political freedoms as measured by the Freedom House data are associated with prevention of war. Data on human rights observance are not widely available through time on a country-year basis, so this indicator is not widely used in the quantitative literature.

Education

Collier and Hoeffler (2004b) found a negative association between male enrolment in secondary education and civil war. Besancon (2005) found that societies with a greater proportion of the population in higher education tended to have lower levels of violence in ethnic wars and genocides, though higher levels in revolutions. These findings are interesting but their statistical significance is outweighed by other factors.

Conclusion: prevention of civil wars

What can we conclude from this mass of complex and sometimes inconsistent results? This remains a fast-moving research field, and new results, methods and theories may modify the current picture. There have been few such clear-cut results in the civil war research as the interstate democratic peace-finding. Nevertheless, there are some reasonably clear results from across different studies. Higher income states, stable polities, internally consistent regimes, well-established and well-funded governments stand out as factors that mitigate the risk of civil war. There are intriguing suggestions from the quantitative literature about the significance of appropriate institutions, which the comparative literature emphasizes. Even in well-established democracies, political and democratic institutions retain many defects and require continued adaptation to accommodate change. The capacity to integrate diverse interests, to identify procedures that allow for the expression and negotiation of difference, and to create public goods and shared values are essential elements of the structural capacity to prevent civil wars.

Policy implications

There is a widespread appreciation in the international community of the value of structural conflict prevention in avoiding or mitigating armed conflicts. For example, the UN Secretary-General, in his 2001 *Report on the Prevention of Armed Conflict*, noted that conflict-sensitive development-led strategies 'can facilitate the creation of opportunities and the political, economic and social spaces within which indigenous actors can identify, develop and use the resources necessary to build a peaceful, equitable and just society'.[11]

Economists and policy-makers concerned with development are well aware of the negative effects of violent conflict on the prospects for development. For this reason the World Bank (2005) set up the Conflict Prevention and Reconstruction Team (CPR) in its Social Development Department. The CPR team issued a 'Conflict Analysis Framework' in April 2005. This attempts to identify the characteristics of a society that is 'resilient' to conflict. The concept of resilience is understood here as 'a situation where conflict issues are dealt with through political and social processes rather than through the employment of violence. It includes creating and supporting institutions in a country which allow for the management of conflict in a non-violent and inclusionary manner.[12]

Drawing on their findings, Collier and Hoeffler (2004) attempted to identify the policies most likely to be effective in managing conflicts. They strongly emphasized economic rather than political variables, suggesting that the three variables most strongly associated with civil war incidence are all economic. These are: low per capita income, negative economic growth, and dependence upon natural resource exports. They therefore suggest economic policies would be the most effective to prevent civil wars. They argue (Collier et al. 2003) that if a package of policy measures were introduced that obtained a sustained growth rate of 3 per cent per year in the poorest countries, shortened conflicts by a year and cut the rate of relapse into conflict, the global incidence of civil war could be halved.[13]

This emphasis on economic variables is perhaps overstated. The quantitative research literature and the comparative literature support the view that political and economic variables together are important for structural prevention of conflict. In particular, appropriate institutions can significantly reduce the risk of ethnic conflict. What is appropriate, however, is case-specific, and difficult to catch in large-N studies.

The decision of the UN to set up a new Peace-building Commission marks a significant step forward in the international commitment to mitigating the impact of conflict and avoiding its recurrence. Post-conflict peace-building is closely related to structural conflict prevention, and indeed they overlap, since peace-building aims to develop a durable peace and avoid the relapse into war. At the early stage of a conflict and in the recovery stage after a conflict, the preoccupations tend to be similar (Ramsbotham et al. 2005). Doyle and Sambanis (2000) note that the aim of peace-building is 'to foster the social, economic and political institutions and attitudes that will prevent these conflicts from turning violent. In effect, peace-building is the front line of preventive action.' They suggest that the success of peace-building turns on the local capacity for peace, the effectiveness of international support for peace-making, and the intrinsic level of hostility in the conflict situation.

Policies such as these link up the international order of the 'liberal peace' with the promotion of structural conflict prevention to avoid civil wars. There is a close link today between domestic and international peace. Both rely ultimately on the same international order. The further development of both civil peace and international peace will depend very much on whether this order has the capacity to become an acceptable, accountable and legitimate framework for world society as a whole, or whether it ultimately serves the interests only of the presently dominant powers. The international community has seen the value of promoting development, democracy, good governance and human rights as an instrument for managing conflicts. The requirements of conflict prevention in turn suggest an effort to promote development, democracy, good governance and human rights in the international community.

6
Land Reforms and Peaceful Change

Introduction

This chapter applies the theory of emergent conflict and peaceful change to conflicts that arise from changing access to land. Under what conditions do changes in land tenure tend to provoke violent conflict, and under what conditions do they foster peaceful change? Political mobilization theories suggest that land inequality develops into violent conflict when parties mobilize to exploit grievances and when state capacity for managing political conflict is weak. These asymmetric conflicts may be peacefully addressed when social movements balance power relations through non-violent political mobilization and negotiation. This chapter explores the evidence for an association between violent conflict and land inequality on the one hand and land reform on the other. It argues that there is no automatic relationship between conflict of interest, as measured by inequality, and violent conflict. It then explores land reform as a means of reducing the risk of armed conflicts. The chapter identifies a number of significant reforms carried out without violence and explores the case of Kerala in detail as an example of peaceful conflict transformation.

Land has always been an important source of wealth and power. Conflicts over access and control over land have been endemic in the agrarian societies of the past and still loom large in a world in which 45 per cent of the population make their living directly from the land (Prosterman and Hanstad 2000).

The twentieth century witnessed widespread efforts to address these conflicts through land reform. In many cases, these reforms were themselves a source of direct conflict. In others, the structural conflicts embedded in inequitable land tenure systems continued in a different form. In certain cases, land reforms have mitigated these structural conflicts without direct violence. This chapter aims to identify cases of peaceful land reform and explore the conditions for peaceful change in conflicts over land.

A review of the twentieth-century experience suggests that there is no single route to peaceful land reform. Land reform has taken place peacefully through social mobilization from below and government action from above, in reaction to foreign intervention and as a result of foreign intervention, with full compensation of the landowners and without. Nor are the conditions leading to peaceful reforms simply the opposite of those leading to violence. Rather, conflicts over land are dynamic processes whose path is influenced by the interactions between the protagonists and the local, regional and international context. The case study of land reform in Kerala presented here suggests that peaceful reform is best seen as a form of conflict transformation.

The first part of the chapter considers theoretical understandings of the relationships between land tenure and conflict. The second part examines the findings of research to date on the relationship between land inequality and violence. The third part explores the association between selected land reforms and violence in the twentieth century and identifies cases of peaceful change. While land reform has often been extremely costly in bloodshed (for example, collectivization in Russia and China), significant land reforms have been achieved without direct violence (for example in Taiwan, South Korea, Venezuela and India). The fourth part focuses on land reforms in India, contrasting Kerala with Bihar. The case study of Kerala shows that social mobilization, democratization and economic development outside the rural sector opened space for a largely peaceful transformation of Kerala's conflicts over land tenure and caste. These reforms did much to overcome the problem of absentee landlordism and insecure tenancies, even though residues of the old conflicts remained and new sources of conflict have appeared. The final part of the chapter considers what conclusions can be drawn for our understanding of the conditions for peaceful land reforms elsewhere.

The origins of inequality

Conflicts of interest over land arise as a result of the fundamental importance of land for economic welfare and power in agrarian societies. Income and access to credit are related to ownership of land. When the distribution of land is skewed in favour of large landowners, average social welfare is low and those with little or no land are poor. If they work for the larger landowners as tenants or labourers, the landlords can set the terms of rents and wages that determine their well-being. Where labour is plentiful and land scarce, the landowners have what Bowles (2004: 344–60) calls 'short-side power', which characterizes principal–agent relationships when markets do not clear and contracts are incomplete.

Eswaran and Kotwal (1986) and Bowles (2004: 350–60) show theoretically that continuous distributions of capital lead to a sorting of agents between different types of contracts. Agents form into classes whose members have similar interests and relationships with other classes. Combined with the evolution of institutions governing tenure and fluctuations in population and harvests, it is readily understandable that agrarian economies tend to generate uneven development and social stratification.

Structural conflicts of interest between agrarian groups may persist for many years without creating political conflicts. The conditions under which such conflicts are repressed, accommodated or turn into rebellion have been much studied by historians and historical sociologists. The view that agrarian grievances translate directly into insurrection seems unsustainable. As Skocpol (1979: 114–15) observes, to argue that 'peasants become revolutionary in reaction against exploitation ... [is] to turn a constant feature of the peasant condition into the explanatory variable'. Peasants are dispersed and difficult to mobilize – 'by themselves, the peasants have never been able to accomplish a revolution' (Moore 1967: 479). Political conflicts based on class originate when the political representatives of these groups champion incompatible policies, usually in alliance with other groups. Skocpol (1979) argues that a conjunction of conditions is necessary for a revolution, and that agrarian distress does not produce a revolution unless there is also a crisis in the state. This is typically triggered by international competition, which results in a breakdown of the state's coercive capacity at a time when the structural conditions are ripe for revolts against landlords.

Drawing on a range of theories, including those that stress grievances arising from deprivation of needs or relative deprivation (Gurr 2000, Azar 1990, Horowitz 1985, Stewart 2001), political mobilization (Tilly 1978, 2003; McAdam 1982), opportunity for rebellion (Berdal and Malone 2000; Collier and Hoeffler 2000b) and the capacity of social and political institutions to manage and adapt to social crises (Skocpol, 1979) I suggest the following general model of agrarian conflict. Threats to livelihood and well-being are created by inequality, landlessness, low human development, unemployment, or the extractive policies of rulers or landlords. These seed political conflicts if entrepreneurs or groups (representing the state, the propertied classes or the peasants) mobilize on the basis of them. However, grievances over land are typically only one set of issues involved in political conflicts and combine with other issues in locally specific ways. Political conflicts turn into violent conflicts when protagonists believe they will benefit from the use of violence, when the political system lacks the capacity to manage the conflict in other ways, and when the opportunity to launch an armed conflict exists. Conversely, conflicts of interest over land may be peacefully transformed when the political system has the capacity to manage conflict through political means, when protagonists believe they can pursue their aims without violence, when there are opportunities for peaceful mobilization and negotiation of the interests involved, and there is scope for political action to foster economic and social development.

Economic theory suggests that land reform can reverse uneven development. Using a general equilibrium model of an agrarian economy, Eswaran and Kotwal (1986) demonstrate that redistribution of land assets tends to decrease the inequality of income, reduce the level of poverty and improve overall social welfare (Figure 6.1). Land reform also tends to improve the condition of landless labourers as smaller, more intensively cultivated farms have a higher demand for labour and so

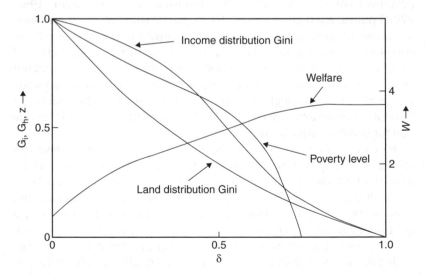

Figure 6.1   Impact of land reform on income distribution, welfare and poverty
Source: Eswaran and Kotwal (1986).

generate higher wages. A more even distribution of land assets tends to allow greater productivity, better access to credit, and better absorption of rural labour (Deininger 1999).

Where landowners control economic and political power, land reform may be difficult to carry out without violent revolution. However, peaceful change does sometimes occur. The theory of asymmetric conflict transformation proposed by Galtung and adapted by Curle (1971) suggests that an unbalanced relationship is transformed through a four-stage process. The first stage is raising awareness of structural conflict, which Galtung calls 'conscientization'. The second is a process of mobilization and confrontation, which addresses the power imbalance. The third is negotiation to agree the basis for a new relationship. The fourth is the development of new, more balanced relationships. Political parties have a key role here in mobilizing and representing the interests of the disadvantaged groups and carrying out changes either through the state or by negotiation with other parties, for example, by redistributing land or setting minimum wages. Land reform also creates beneficiaries who may become important supporters of new governments. Patomäki (1995, 2001) adds the idea of opening new political space to allow conflicts to be dealt with through exclusively political means. In Kerala, the coming of democracy transformed the rural power balance and opened new space for parties with mass support, offsetting the peasants' lack of economic and political power in their local communities. Modernization and democratization opened new sources of economic development and wider access to power, which helped to overcome zero-sum conflicts over a fixed amount of land. This echoes Väyrynen's (1991) suggestion that conflict transformation is a complex and gradual process of systemic change in which new actors, relationships, institutions and social structures emerge, dissolving the original conflict formation.

Land inequality and conflict

The relationship between unequal access to land and violent conflict has been widely canvassed in the literature on development economics and on the political economy of civil wars. Russett (1964) found evidence of a correlation between land ginis and violent political deaths in a study of 47 countries. Prosterman and Riedinger (1987: 25–8) found that 15 of the 22 countries in which they estimated landless people constituted more than a quarter of the total population had experienced revolutions or protracted conflicts. Conflicts over land have been a significant contributory factor in civil wars, including those in Angola,

Bolivia, Cambodia, China, Colombia, Cuba, El Salvador, Guatemala, Mexico, Nepal, Nicaragua, the Philippines, Russia and Vietnam. Murshed and Gates (2005) found a striking correlation between land ginis and violent conflict within provinces in Nepal. Where inequalities over land ownership are related to ethnic differences, the resulting 'horizontal inequalities' between groups frequently contribute to violent conflict, as in Algeria, Rwanda, Burundi and Zimbabwe (Stewart 2001).

Latin America, Africa and South Asia have been the regions most strongly afflicted by armed conflicts. They are also areas of high rural poverty and dependence on agriculture. De Soysa et al. (1999: 15) argue that in the post-cold war period, 'most of the armed conflict, whether domestic or international, is concentrated in regions heavily dependent on agriculture', and they suggest that demands for land redistribution, migration into agricultural areas, environmental stress and food riots are among the causes of violence. They point out that 'only five out of 63 states that exhibit a low dependence on agriculture have suffered armed conflict after the Cold War'.

Midlarsky (1988) argues that there is a relationship between 'patterned inequality' and political violence. Boix (2004: 24) also suggests a significant relationship between land inequality, agricultural economy and civil war. Others cast doubt on the postulated relationship between land inequality and civil war. Muller and Seligson (1987) found only a weak correlation ($r = 0.24$) between land ginis in 1970 weighted by agricultural population and political violence in the period 1973–77. They found that when income inequality is controlled for, the correlation suggested by Prosterman and Riedinger (1987) between landlessness and political violence is insignificant. Using a cross-national comparison of data on inequality and violent political conflict from 1968–77, they argue that income inequality is more important than inequality of land assets, and suggest that land inequality and landlessness operate indirectly through their impact on incomes (Muller and Seligson 1989). Moore et al. (1996) review land reform and political violence in Cuba, the Philippines and Chile. They conclude that there is no strong association between economic inequality and political conflict and that contingent effects influence whether violence breaks out.

The lack of good cross-national data on land ownership affects all these studies. The FAO data on concentration of land ownership are based on operational holdings. These are likely to understate the inequality of land ownership. The lack of reliable data on land ownership also makes it difficult to estimate landlessness. Even in India, where the National Sample Survey has carried out sophisticated annual surveys aimed at gathering information about rural poverty and landholding, a clear picture of the extent of landlessness is difficult to obtain (Cain 1983).

Lichbach (1989) and Cramer (2005) review the apparently contradict-ory findings of the studies on the inequality-violence nexus. They sug-gest that contrasting theoretical perspectives and empirical difficulties in defining and specifying both the independent variable of inequality and the dependent variable of violent conflict account for the diversity of findings. Daudelin (2003) suggests that the links between land and violence are very context specific and land policy is 'only exceptionally a critical factor of conflict'.

Fearon and Laitin (2003) find no significant association between inequality and civil war onset. Studies in which onset is the dependent variable tend to highlight opportunities for insurgencies to occur. In contrast, studies that relate inequality to ongoing forms of political vio-lence, especially those with a lower threshold than war, find stronger associations. For example, Besancon (2005) showed that, disaggregating civil wars by type, there is an association between inequality and the amount of revolutionary violence under way.

Let us examine whether a significant relationship exists between armed conflicts and the proportion of the population in the agricultural work-force and the proportion of family farms. A study was carried out of 105 developing countries between 1960 and 2000, based on the FAO/ILO classification of developing countries. I used FAO/ILO data on the pro-portion of the economically active population employed in agriculture as a measure of the agrarian basis of the economy (FAO 2004) and Vanhanen's (1997) index of family farms as an indicator of the propor-tion of farms not reliant on hired-in agricultural labour. I combined these with independent variables other studies have shown to be signifi-cantly associated with civil wars, namely, population size, GDP, ethnic fractionalization and political instability. The data on civil wars is taken from Fearon and Latin (2003). A civil war is defined here as an armed conflict between a government and a rebel group involving at least 1000 deaths overall and at least 100 per year, with at least 100 killed on each side. I used the intensity of revolutionary violence (deaths/year) from the State Failure dataset (Marshall, Gurr and Harff 2002). I carried out logistic regressions of the independent variables on three alternative dependent variables: the onset of civil war, whether a civil war was under way, and the amount of revolutionary violence. Table 6.1 presents the results. It shows that neither the proportion of agricultural workers in the workforce nor the number of family farms is significantly associ-ated with civil wars. I also found no significant association between

Table 6.1   Logistic regression of agricultural labour on non-family farms and other variables on civil war onset, civil wars under way and revolutionary violence

	Civil war onset	Civil war under way	Revolutionary violence
Agworkers on nff[1]	−1.835	−2.603	−1.472
P > z	(0.14)	(0.000)	(0.000)
Ln population	0.208	0.581	0.239
P > z	(0.14)	(0.000)	(0.000)
GDP/cap (lagged)	−0.352	−0.428	−0.184
P > z	(0.009)	(0.000)	(0.005)
Ethnic frac.	0.327	0.630	0.876
P > z	(0.487)	(0.001)	(0.002)
Instability	0.602	0.470	1.009
P > z	(0.031)	(0.000)	(0.000)
N. obs.	3005	3005	2407

Note: 1 Proportion of total population in agricultural work; 'Agworkers on nff' is the proportion of total population in agricultural work multiplied by the proportion of non-family farms.

income inequality and civil wars. There was a significant association between ongoing civil wars and revolutionary violence and the multiple of the proportion of agricultural workers in the workforce and the proportion of non-family farms, a construction that might be taken as an indirect measure of landlessness. However, the sign of the coefficient was the opposite of what might have expected if the relationship between inequality and violence is positive: higher values of the multiple (that is, higher dependence on agricultural labour combined with a higher proportion of non-family farms) appeared to reduce the odds of ongoing civil wars and revolutionary violence. It was not significant for the onset of civil wars.

The evidence suggests that there is no convincing relationship between rural inequality and the onset of collective violence, taking developing countries all together. How is this to be explained? First, the relationship between inequality of land ownership and violence is clearly not directly causal, since many countries with unequal land ownership are either politically stable or at least free of political violence. Unequal land ownership is a persistent background condition that cannot adequately explain the onset of violent episodes unless the proximate conditions of political mobilization and weak governance and the immediate trigger conditions of motive and opportunity are taken into account. Moreover, as I argue below, actors have choices over how they respond to this background condition, and non-violent mobilization may be favoured under certain conditions.

Second, a strong correlation should not be expected because the conflict data include many armed conflicts that have little or nothing to do with land issues. Stronger associations might be found if conflicts were classified by whether they involve agrarian issues, but this raises difficult questions of attribution.

Third, the relationship between agrarian distress and violence may vary over place and time. In certain societies, such as the Latin American countries with hacienda-based agriculture, peasant grievances provided a fertile ground for revolutionary movements, which resulted in large-scale violence inflicted by governments and anti-government forces. In the 1980s and 1990s ethnic conflicts and peripheral insurgencies, partly inspired by agrarian issues but also by nationalism became more common. Fearon (2004) calls these 'sons of the soil' wars. More recently, as opportunities for employment in the agricultural sector have diminished, there has been a significant flow of the rural population to urban slums. This may be shifting the location and issues of violence from the countryside into the towns.

Nevertheless, there is plentiful evidence that agrarian distress, in combination with other factors, has been a significant factor in particular conflicts. Certainly the structural conflicts between landowners and peasants were pronounced in the twentieth century and remain so in many developing countries. Although the evidence for an association between inequality and violence is not strong, it is worth investigating whether land reforms tended to mitigate or increase violence in the past, a significant consideration as policy-makers are seeking to revive land reform as a means to reduce poverty and increase rural welfare (Deininger 2003).

Land reforms

The twentieth century witnessed a wide range of efforts to introduce land reform (Binswanger et al. 1995). These varied in the extent and speed of redistribution, and in the degree to which they involved violent or peaceful means. When land reforms occurred, they tended to follow wars (for example, Japan, Taiwan, South Korea, eastern Europe), revolutionary upheavals (Mexico, Bolivia, Cuba, Nicaragua, Ethiopia) or decolonization (Kenya, Mozambique, Vietnam, Zimbabwe). But in some cases they took place without direct violence (Kerala and West Bengal in India, Venezuela, Egypt, Taiwan, Tanzania).

Binswanger et al. (1995) argues that since land reform is associated with the transfer of rents from landlords to tenants, it tends to be associated with revolts, revolutions and conquests. He notes that attempts to reform land ownership without political upheaval (as in Brazil, Costa Rica, Honduras) have not transferred much land. Similarly Griffin et al. (2000) observe that land reform almost always requires a prior war, revolutionary change or the threat of revolutionary change elsewhere. Nevertheless, democratic transitions can also create the potential for land reform, as in the Philippines after Marcos and South Africa after the fall of apartheid. A number of countries and international development agencies are also experimenting with less sweeping forms of land reform.

Land reforms can be divided into several types. The classic 'land to the tiller' reforms redistribute land (with or without compensation) from landlords to small peasants, tenant farmers and the landless. Tenancy reforms do not redistribute the land but alter the terms of land tenure, for example, by making tenancies more secure. Collectivization and decollectivization take land in or out of state control. Market-based or 'negotiated land reform' provides incentives for transfers from willing sellers to willing buyers. Another type with significant potential is the transfer of small plots of land to the landless, enabling them to build houses and obtain credit. In all cases, land reforms constitute only a part of a larger process of economic development. They are more likely to succeed if they are supported by training, marketing, credit and other measures, as part of a comprehensive strategy for rural development (Griffin et al. 2000: 27).

Land reform processes can be judged by two criteria relevant to peaceful outcomes. First, do they avoid violent conflict, and if so how? And secondly, do they achieve outcomes that are regarded as just and that raise the level of social welfare?

In principle the first question can be addressed by relating past land reforms to data on violent conflicts. An assessment is not straightforward because many factors besides land relations affect the incidence of violent conflict. Attributing a particular violent event to a change in the land tenure system is a matter of judgement even in single cases (Moore et al., 1996). Nevertheless, observation of the incidence of armed conflicts before, during and after land reforms gives a picture of some common patterns and helps to identify land reforms achieved without violence.

Table 6.2 gives details of the most significant land reforms for the period 1945–2000, together with estimates of the percentage of agricultural land redistributed, the proportion of rural households who were beneficiaries, and whether armed conflicts occurred five years prior to the start

131

Table 6.2   Significant land reforms, 1945–2000

	Land reform period	Per cent agricultural land redistributed	Beneficiaries as per cent of rural household	Peaceful in prior 5 yrs	Peaceful during land reform	Peaceful in following 5 yrs
Africa						
Ethiopia	1974–75			×	×	×
Kenya	1961–70	2	2	×	√	√
South Africa	1994–99			×	√	√
Tanzania	1963–; 1983; 1995			√	√	√
Zimbabwe	1980–87	12	3	×	√	√
Middle East						
Algeria	1963–66; 1974–78; 1980–94	6	22	×	×	×
Egypt	1952–78	15	10	×	×	√
Iran	1962–71	22	23	√	√	×
Iraq	1958–	60	56	×	×	×
Syria	1958, 1963, 1980	25	11	√	×	×
Asia						
China	1946–1950s;	100	100	×	×	√
China	1978–			√	√	√
India	varies by state; 2000–	3	4	√	√	√
Indonesia	1960–70			×	×	×
Japan	1946–49	33	61	×	√	√
Korea N.	1945–46			×	×	×
Korea S.	1948–58	27	46	×	×	√
Nepal	1959–60			√	×	×
Pakistan	1959–70s	4	3	×	×	√
Philippines	1940–85	11	24	×	×	×
Sri Lanka	1972–75	10	22	×	×	√
Taiwan	1949–53	27	63	×	√	√
Vietnam N	1953–60			×	×	×
Vietnam S	1970–			×	×	×
Latin America						
Bolivia	1953–70	32	48	×	×	√

(*Continued*)

Table 6.2   *(Continued)*

	Land reform period	Per cent agricultural land redistributed	Beneficiaries as per cent of rural household	Peaceful in prior 5 yrs	Peaceful during land reform	Peaceful in following 5 yrs
Brazil	1964–94	11	5	√	√	√
Chile	1970–73	60	13	√	√	×
Costa Rica	1960s			√	√	√
Colombia	1936–			√	√	×
Cuba	1959–	95	100	×	×	×
Ecuador	1954–74	5		√	√	√
El Salvador	1932–89	28	17	√	×	×
Guatemala	1944–54			√	×	×
Mexico	1915–76	14	68	×	√	√
Nicaragua	1978–87	47	57	√	×	×
Peru	1969–79	28	31	×	√	×
Venezuela	1960s; 1998–			√	×	√

√ No armed conflicts   × Armed conflicts occurred

of the reforms, during the period of reforms, or in the five years after the land reforms. The list of land reforms reflects the main cases cited in the land reform literature (Binswanger et al. 1995, King 1977, Christodoulou 1990, Deininger 2003, El-Ghonemy 1990, Prosterman and Riedinger, 1987, Tuma 1965, Thiesenhusen 1989). A number of interesting land reforms are neglected because they were of significance only in a particular community and were either not widespread in impact or sustained over time (for example, Manley's 1972–76 land reform in Jamaica). All countries implement laws, taxes and policies affecting land distribution and land tenure institutions, and there is no uncontested definition of what should count as land reform (Lipton and Ravallion 1995). Nor are all land reforms redistributive: in a number of cases land reform has tended to benefit existing landholders, or has been intended to suppress support for revolutionary groups rather than to reduce inequalities. The armed conflict data comes from the updated version of the dataset prepared by

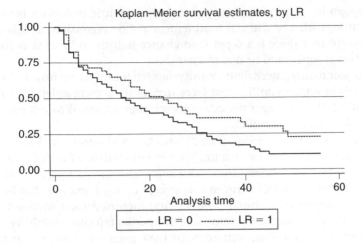

Figure 6.2 Duration of peace periods in countries with prior land reform (LR = 1) compared with those without (LR = 0)

Gleditsch et al. (2002). This includes armed conflicts in which government forces were involved with a threshold of at least 25 battle-deaths per year. The data on land redistribution and beneficiaries is from El-Ghonemy (1990) and Deininger (2003).

The table shows that almost two-thirds of these cases of land reform followed armed conflicts in the previous five years. Half of all the cases coincided with the waging of an armed conflict in the country. This confirms the observations made in the literature, that sweeping land reforms are frequently accompanied by revolutions or follow wars.

Does land reform tend to pacify conflict in the period after it has been carried out? In order to explore this question we carried out an analysis on all the periods without armed conflict for 105 developing countries. There were 259 such peace periods between 1946 and 2002, of varying lengths. These were analysed using survival analysis, with the failure event denoted by the onset of an armed conflict or censored at the end of the time period (2002). We investigated whether peace periods during or after land reforms were likely to be longer or shorter than peace periods occurring without land reforms. Figure 6.2 shows the probability of a peace period breaking down over time for the periods during or after land reform and those without. It shows that the introduction of land reforms tended to increase the length of the subsequent peace period and reduce the probability of armed conflict. Countries with land reforms had a higher probability of experiencing long periods at peace, although for short periods of peace there was little difference between countries with and without land reform. A Cox regression on this data indicated that there is a 6 per cent chance that the difference between the two groups could be due to chance.

To summarize, twentieth-century land reforms frequently followed periods of armed conflict and were frequently accompanied by armed conflicts. Over a longer period, however, they appeared to mitigate the risk of subsequent conflict.

We now turn to the question of whether land reforms led to overall improvements in social welfare. We present evidence for Kerala in the case study that follows. Here we simply cite El-Ghomeny's findings (1990) that countries with more sweeping land reforms tended to achieve higher agricultural productivity, increased rural incomes and reduced rural poverty. In countries with partial reforms benefiting only part of the population, welfare gains have been more uneven or have not been achieved. Of course, land reform is only one of a range of other factors that have also affected rural welfare.

Peaceful land reforms

Table 6.2 includes cases of land reform that have been carried out without violence. Several groups can be identified. First, the postwar land reform processes in Japan, Korea, and Taiwan. These were carried out under US influence, in the context of the wartime defeat of Japan, and they had the intention of forestalling potential communist movements. Although imposed under external influence, they found considerable support and constituted remarkable examples of transformation, in which the old landed oligarchs gave up their land to smaller farmers, releasing significant gains in economic productivity and overall welfare. The landlords were compensated, but the cost of the compensation was met from more efficient use of the land. In the Japanese case, the land reforms built on earlier peasant movements and were implemented by joint committees of landlords and peasants. In the Taiwanese case, the new KMT government introduced a wide-ranging land reform. These improved conditions for tenants, redistributed public lands formerly owned by Japanese corporations, and set land ceilings, with compulsory purchase of land in excess of the ceilings. The former landowners were compensated with bonds and industrial shares, and although some were impoverished, many became successful in the financial and industrial sectors. The reforms, together with public investment in agriculture, contributed to a significant improvement in welfare. Poverty was reduced, the number of tenant farmers fell from 40 per cent to 17 per cent, and agricultural growth took off, averaging 5 per cent per year between 1952 and 1964. This underpinned the economic transformation of Taiwan.

Although the land reform itself was carried out peacefully, the KMT had ruled Taiwan by martial law in the early years and carried out a violent repression against the Taiwanese elite following the 28 February incident in 1947. The context for the land reform in Taiwan was the desire to avoid communism in Taiwan, the granting of large-scale US aid in 1951, and the advice of the US land reform expert Wolf Ladejinsky, who also shaped the reforms in Japan and South Korea.

A second group involves social movements that campaigned for land reform, and managed to carry it out by making political gains, which carried the reform programme into government through parliamentary elections. Here two significant examples are those of Kerala, which is discussed in detail below, and West Bengal. Both contributed to significant improvements in social welfare in broadly-based development programmes.

Allende's reform programme in Chile was also carried out through parliamentary means, but the external and internal opposition contributed to the military coup of 1973. The new junta reversed the land reforms, returning the land taken by the state to its former owners or to new entrepreneurs.

A third group of countries are those that have experienced de-collectivization after or during rule by communist governments. Cases in this group include the de-collectivization of agriculture in Hungary, Poland and Czechoslovakia, in China after 1978, in Vietnam after 1980 and in Albania after 1991. In these cases the willingness of the government to abandon collective production, for ideological and economic reasons, has coincided with the wishes of the agricultural families and workers to own their own land. Moreover, the return of the land to private ownership has led to higher productivity, creating welfare benefits for society in general. For example, in China, decollectivization led to a growth in production of 80 per cent in a decade. Nevertheless, the manner of de-collectivization, and the question of who should benefit, has raised significant social issues and created new social cleavages.

Three cases can be picked out to illustrate the range of peaceful transitions. Venezuela's land reform programme in the 1960s has been described as 'the most extensive non-violent Latin American land reform' (King 1977: 147) – although it coincided with a minor conflict over government. It was promoted through an activist peasant movement, whose leadership came to power, and aimed to expropriate uncultivated land and estates let through intermediaries. Venezuela's oil wealth enabled the government to compensate the landowners at market value rates, and the boom also eased agrarian distress by enabling the agricultural population to be absorbed in the towns and in the industrial sector. The aim was to benefit all the landless families, and although the implementation of the reform fell short of this aim, some 4.6 million hectares of mainly public land were redistributed to 120 000 peasant families. Living conditions for the peasants did improve, but many of the beneficiaries received poor or inadequate land with limited access to markets, credit and extension support. As a result many sold their properties. The long-term redistributive effect of the reform was therefore limited, yet Venezuela enjoyed political stability in the countryside for many years after the 1960 reforms.

In 1998 President Chavez came to power with a programme to renew land reform. The aim has been to mitigate Venezuela's distorted development, improve conditions for the poor, enhance food security and biodiversity and reinvigorate the rural sector. The policy includes rural and urban land reform and a Women's Bank and is taken as a model land reform in some quarters.

The new policy aims to break up the large latifundias and redistribute land to the landless without compensation unless the existing owners can prove title. It also sets up co-operatives with marketing arrangements and micro-credits. The policy aims to protect the indigenous peoples and establish their legal rights. The urban land reform regularizes migration into cities and shanty towns, by giving the migrants title to land and setting up urban farms, producer co-operatives and micro-credit schemes. The large amount of land in public ownership, which increased following the bank collapses of the 1990s, has again allowed the government to subsidize land reform from public resources.

In some areas the rural land reform has aroused strong resistance from landowners, and some peasant leaders have been killed. The armed conflict in neighbouring Colombia is also spilling over into Venezuela, with guerrillas seizing land by force and landowners protecting themselves through private militias. The government's propaganda, which invokes the slogans of the Venezuelan revolution, risks polarizing social relations. The land reforms have mainly benefited Chavez's supporters. There is a risk, therefore, that this reform may provoke a violent backlash, although so far the reform has been carried out by largely peaceful means.

A second case is the Egyptian land reform followed Nasser's revolution of 1952. At that time land ownership was highly unequal, with the top 7 per cent of owners owning two thirds of the cultivable land. Most of the farms were small and tenancy was high. Rents were very high and the small owners, tenants and labourers were all poor, resulting in low productivity and little investment. The social system was highly stratified with master–servant relationships dominant and little social mobility. The landlords, who had dominated the pre-1952 parliament, opposed reform and the government tended to support them, allowing them to buy most of the public lands sold.

On the eve of the reform, land prices climbed to about six times the real value of land, and similarly rents soared. The economic consequences were disastrous for the peasants who responded with sporadic riots and attacks on local landlords from 1952. The government's defeat in the war over Palestine and subsequent inflation and unemployment led to a sharp social and political crisis. In this setting, after repeated government crises, Nasser came to power with a nationalist, populist programme that included land reform. The main aim of the reform was to break the power of the great landlords and to gain political support for the regime from the peasantry. The reform provided for land ceilings of 200 *feddans* per owner. Owners with larger farms were required to transfer lands above the ceiling to tenants, receiving compensation in government bonds fixed at ten times the annual rent. The beneficiaries were required to pay for their land in instalments and the reform law encouraged producer co-operatives.

The reform was imposed despite efforts by the landlords to obstruct the passing of the law. However, the land redistribution that took place did not have a massive impact on the concentration of land. The landlords surrendered the less good land and sold off other good lands before the reform came into effect. Even after the reform 5 per cent of the landlords owned half of the land. The main effects were to redistribute income and regulate rents, and the tenants were significant beneficiaries. Despite this the peasants still had only very low incomes. Among the landlords some suffered heavily, others suffered little, and the government was careful to avoid damaging the middle-class landlords who still owned significant holdings. Under 900 000 *feddans* were redistributed, out of 6 million.

El-Ghonemy (1990) gives Gini figures for inequality of income distribution in rural areas. The Gini of income distribution fell from 0.858 in 1949/50 to 0.37 in 1958/9 and 0.27 in 1964/5, though it later rose a little to 0.348 in 1974/5 and 0.337 in 1981/2. The percentage of rural population below the poverty line fell steadily from more than half in 1950 to less than one-fifth in 1982. However, the fall in rural poverty cannot be wholly attributed to land reform, given the limited scale of redistribution of land, the low share of agriculture in the overall economy and the slow growth of agricultural output, which failed to keep pace with population growth. Rather, rural poverty fell because real wages rose, non-farm economic activities grew, free education increased access to non-agricultural employment, and food subsidies gave the poor access to necessities. The construction boom after the 1970s also created jobs. Broad economic development and opportunities outside agriculture and outside Egypt helped to lift the rural population out of poverty.

The third case, which we will explore in more detail, is the land reform in Kerala.

The Kerala case

Kerala is quite unique in many respects. Its settlement pattern, its high level of social development despite a low economic base, and the proliferation of mass and class organizations mark it out from the rest of India. It is internationally recognized for its achievements in women's education and health, which have contributed to fertility levels comparable with developed countries. It has remarkable social indicators for a state with low average incomes (around $350/year). Life expectancy is high, literacy is 100% and access to education and health care is universal.

India offers a good basis for comparisons since different state governments have pursued different policies on land reform with strikingly divergent outcomes. West Bengal and Kerala have had communist governments in power in a democratic political system. Both achieved striking reforms. In Bihar, by contrast, the landlords have retained their control of the land and caste remains the basis for landholding and agricultural labour. The Naxalite conflict developed as a struggle between militias employed by the landlords and ideologically inspired revolutionaries who mobilize on behalf of the landless and the low castes. This protracted armed conflict has trapped Bihar in a cycle of under-development. It remains the poorest and least developed of all the Indian states (Chandran and Joseph 2002).

Kerala's transformation is all the more remarkable given the caste oppression and landlessness that characterized the princely states of Travancore and Cochin and the British Indian District of Malabar before they were united to form the state. The British colonial administration had given statutory protection to the landlords in Malabar, severing the customary links the landlords had with the intermediary and cultivating classes. Landlords were able to evict tenants and raise rents without check, so that Malabar gained 'the unenviable reputation of being the most rack-rented place on the face of the earth' (Herring 1983). The religious-communal divisions are significant (present-day Kerala is 60 per cent Hindu, 20 per cent Muslim, 20 per cent Christian). In 1921 the Moplah revolt of Muslims against the Hindu landlords was suppressed with 10 000 deaths. The 'evils of landlordism seemed to have persisted all over the region', but Malabar was a particular centre of conflict (Oommen 1971: 37).

The acute land problem in Kerala reflected the wider situation in India before independence. The growth in the rural population in the nineteenth century had led to a fragmented pattern of land ownership and rapid growth in the number of landless labourers. The customary relations between landlord and tenant were breaking down and a new class of absentee landlords, the *zamindars*, had emerged as intermediaries. They were able to extract more and more from the tenants, by bidding up rents and increasing fees for renewal of leases and mortgages for use of grazing land and river water. The peasants increasingly fell into debt and the money-lenders were able to charge exorbitant interest rates for providing the loans the peasants needed to get from one harvest to the next. The British Raj, without interfering directly in the structure of land tenure, favoured the landlords. Impoverishment and insecurity increased and serious famines developed.

In Kerala the high-caste Namboodiris owned most of the land but let it to another caste, the Nair, who managed it. In turn the Nair leased the land to other castes who worked it. The tenants had to pay the landlords a significant share of the crop in rent, although non-payment and arrears appear to have been common. As the population grew the landlords demanded higher rents and evictions became increasingly common.

A response to this situation arose out of popular reaction against landlordism, supported by Gandhian and socialist activists. Low-caste groups set up a Caste Improvement Association, and activists, with popular support, set up trade unions and a communist party. A key achievement of these social movements was the setting up of educational institutes and the creation of libraries in the villages. The high level of literacy led to a vernacular newspaper industry and a rise in social and political consciousness. There were successful strikes and confrontations in the 1940s. Kerala's activists participated in the struggle for independence, and afterwards, in the first state elections in 1957, a communist government was elected (Nossiter 1982).

The establishment of democracy in India gave the peasants and agricultural labourers a form of power, through their votes, that they had lacked in the old rural society. At the same time the balance between the communist government in the state and the Congress government of India forced the communists to rely on constitutional means. The communist party of India (CPI) believed its objectives could not 'be realised by a peaceful, parliamentary way' but 'only through a revolution, through the overthrow of the present Indian State'. Moscow, however, insisted on co-operation with Nehru's state (Nossiter 1982: 105). Accordingly the land reform was introduced by constitutional means, and when the first communist-led government lost its majority, its passage was delayed for ten years.

The first land reform bill, introduced in 1957 when the CPI had a majority of only two seats, was deliberately moderate and cautious. The reforms aimed to reduce the inequality in Kerala's society by tackling the issue of absentee landlords, abolishing intermediaries, giving tenants security of tenure and fair rents, and enabling them to acquire ownership of their plots. The reforms also aimed to place a ceiling on the size of land-holdings, and redistribute surplus land to the homeless. Large plantations and religious institutions were exempt. The landlords were to be compensated, and the reformers sought to avoid obstruction from the courts and the bureaucracy by entrusting implementation and dispute resolution to local land tribunals (Nossiter 1982: 149). The government consulted widely before passing the bill and accepted many amendments. The resulting bill was a compromise between the claims of the landlords for compensation and the desire of the communists to free the peasants from landlordism.

When the communist ministry fell the successor Congress ministry further watered down the reforms. Nevertheless, the issue remained high on the agenda of Kerala politics thanks to the mobilization of the peasantry and the workers. Even parties of the right committed themselves to policies of redistribution. A consensus developed across the political spectrum on the desirability of land reform. After a period of political instability and central rule, a Marxist government was returned to power in 1967 and finally passed a renamed bill in 1969. The implementation of the reform was carried out by a centrist coalition in the 1970s. By this time, an unofficial land reform was already going on. The pressure for reform over two decades and the militancy of the agrarian movement created an atmosphere in which many landlords decided to sell their land to tenants, often at low prices, rather than risk its confiscation by the state.

The land reforms had three main components. First, they provided security of tenure. The government took over the rights of the *Janmi* (landlords) and intermediaries over tenanted land, cancelling arrears of rent and preventing evictions, and gave the land to the tillers. Secondly, the *Kudikidappukarans* or 'hutment-dwellers', an important group which traditionally had the right to live in a hut on the land where they worked, were given ownership rights of their homesteads. The government subsidized half the purchase price and the hutment-dwellers paid the rest in instalments. Third, a ceiling was imposed on land-holdings and surplus land was to be redistributed to the landless.

In practice implementation of the reforms was slow. The landlords successfully opposed some of the measures in the courts. To overcome this, the Congress government introduced national legislation to secure the reforms. Tenants were not always willing to pay to become owners. Some hoped to escape paying rents.

In 1969 the Kerala government tried to abolish the remaining land-lord rights, but in practice new owners, many of them former tenants, stepped in to take the place of the old high-caste owners. So, although the caste basis of landholding together with the semi-feudal tenure system was broken, a different kind of ranked social order survived. As E.M.S. Namboodiripad, the leader of the reform process in the late 1950s, said, the feudal system was replaced by 'landlordism of another type', in which the power of the new owners was based on wage labour and rural trade. The new owners resisted redistribution of surplus lands and the majority of agricultural workers remained landless, although their wages rose.

Overall, however, the reforms transferred about 40 per cent of the total operated farmland to the tenants. The number of households owning some land doubled from 43 per cent in 1966 to 86 per cent in 1982.

Many former landlords, mainly Brahmins, moved into education and emerged as teachers and professionals, which redeemed them from their parasitic status and integrated them more productively in the economy. Moreover, many of the leaders of the communist party were high-caste Nairs, and opposition from the Syrian Christians was avoided through concessions on education and the exemption of the plantations. Above all, the landlords could no longer defend their interest on a particularistic basis, but had to operate through political parties, which were influenced by the public consensus in favour of reform. As a result, when the 1969 Act was passed, opposition to land reform had subsided considerably and the landlords had become resigned to the inevitability of change. While the new owners resisted further redistribution, there was general support for measures to improve the situation of the agricultural workers and in 1974 they were given permanency of employment, minimum wages, a reduction in hours of work and other benefits. An old-age pension was introduced in the 1980s.

The Kerala case is striking because a significant reform of land tenure took place in a democratic setting, under a communist government, without significant direct violence. What explains the lack of violence? A number of factors appear to have been involved.

First, the reforms were staged over several years and several pieces of legislation. Even when enacted, implementation was rather slow and in the end the aims of the reformers were not wholly achieved. There was time for accommodation and adjustment. The reform was not so abrupt as to cause immediate and sharp polarization.

Second, the government compensated the landlords. Although the *Janmi* lost their status and privilege as feudal landlords, social changes in Kerala were opening alternative means of advancement. The fact that the large landlords were absentees eased the process of reform. By taking over their rights as landlords, the government brought about a major change while retaining its democratic legitimacy. At the same time, its political alliances with the tenants and the homesteaders secured it strong political support. The high level of wages that resulted from the reforms gave the labourers a much better position than they had had before the reforms, and a better position than in many other parts of India.

Third, the land reforms created a new class of owner-cultivators, many of whom employed labour to work for them. This class benefited from the land reform and became the key figures in the new agrarian power structure. They also became a significant source of political support for the government and the reforms.

Fourth, broader changes in Kerala's society and economy created new openings for social mobility, and made subsistence agriculture a less central feature of the economy. Cash crops grew more important, and opportunities in new industries and in the towns allowed some migration out of the rural areas.

Fifth, the association of caste with landholding began to disappear.

Sixth, crucially, the political system offered alternative channels for expressing and moderating claims. By giving a vote to those who were formerly members of low castes or landless labourers, it opened new political space for the transformation of the old rural conflicts. The political parties began to take over some of the role of the caste system in regulating and channelling social conflict. As Oommen says (1971: 67), the leadership of the rural areas passed from the traditional landed aristocracy 'to political and social leaders of a different category'.

Seventh, a key element of the process was the mobilization of the population, through education, social movements, the struggle for independence and the political parties. This led to the expectation that the state would support redistribution. The state's ability to achieve structural reform was directly related to its responsiveness to social mobilization for structural change. The state was both a vehicle for achieving social change and an agency capable of mediating peacefully between different interests.

Heller (2000a) has argued that 'under certain conditions state and society can become enmeshed in patterns of interaction that have positive sum outcomes'. The Kerala experience illustrates a form of democratic deepening in which 'the formal, effective and substantive dimensions of democracy become mutually reinforcing' (Heller: 2000b). Certainly Kerala's vibrant civil society made an important contribution to its peaceful transition. Its protest culture and its social movements were inspired by Gandhi's campaigns. It was this combination of a constitutional process, the opening of new political space through democratization, the creation of new opportunities for social mobility outside agriculture, and a process of 'conscientization', confrontation and negotiation championed by social movements and political parties inspired by non-violence that laid the basis for Kerala's peaceful structural change.

Of course, the land reforms have not brought social conflicts in Kerala to an end. In recent decades the penetration of Kerala's agriculture by international agribusiness has created new issues. Falling prices for agricultural commodities and a shift towards less labour-intensive crops have created pressure to revise the limits on land-ownership introduced by the reforms. The introduction of contract farming, it is feared, may reintroduce some of the old conditions of tenancy and absentee landowners. Ramachandran Pillai argues in the Communist Party of India newspaper that 'the gains made by the land reforms in Kerala will be destroyed'. In response the State Agriculture Minister, K.R. Gowrie, who was a minister in the Namboodiripad ministry that introduced the reform legislation, has promised that the State government 'will not do anything which is detrimental to the gains Kerala made through land reform', although the government is prepared to consider changes in its land policy that do not threaten farmers or agricultural workers (Krishnakumar, 2004).

Conclusions

The theory that uneven distribution of land assets leads to sorting into classes and the exercise of 'short-sided power' by large landowners is amply confirmed in the twentieth-century experience. Attempts to overcome these conditions have taken different forms and varied in their effectiveness. The evidence on land inequality and conflict suggests that there is no necessary connection between inequality and violent conflict. Unequal conditions may be one of the conditions which foster violent repressions waged by governments or violent rebellions by parties representing peasant groups, but this depends on the way in which political actors mobilize their support, the capacity of the state to control its territory and the capacity of the political system to manage challenges through institutional channels. Although the relationship between inequality and violent conflict is controversial, the burden of evidence suggests the lack of a strong association between inequality and violence. The findings that a high agricultural population and low family farms may be associated with a reduced risk of a war being under way suggests that the very poor are not in a position to fight, although no significant association was found with the onset of civil war. This confirms the findings of other studies which report a stronger association between indicators of rural underdevelopment and inequality with long-duration measures of political violence than onsets of civil war. The equivalence problem may explain these mixed results. In future work it may be fruitful to code the conflict data by the salience of agrarian grievances. There is also a need for more data and analysis on political mobilization of agrarian discontent and its role in wider political coalition building.

The twentieth-century experience does not suggest that land reform has been a peaceful alternative to conflicts over land. The majority of significant land reforms have followed a revolution, a war, decolonization or some similar transition in the political system. A significant proportion of land reforms were also accompanied by some degree of political violence. However, this study suggests that in the period after the land reform, violent conflicts are less likely and peace periods are longer than in countries without land reform.

Nevertheless, I identified a significant number of cases of peaceful land reform, some of which have raised social welfare and contributed to development. These cases took place in a variety of settings and contexts. I do not suggest there is a single road to peaceful land reform. However, in line with the theories of conflict transformation, Kerala indicates the importance of education, empowerment, social mobilization and negotiation, embedded within a broader process of social development. Among the conditions for peaceful land reform, this suggests, are:

1. Political support for land reforms from a legitimate government
2. Social movements that mobilize in support of the change
3. The establishment of effective and legitimate rural institutions that represent rural groups and provide local channels for negotiation
4. Sufficient compensation for the landowners, or the development of alternative prospects that offset the losses in status and wealth
5. Structural changes (such as urbanization and industrialization) that reduce the significance of landed relationships as a basis for power

wealth and status and open up other avenues for social mobility and power
6. Acquiescence in a process of change that is regarded as inevitable and that is publicly accepted as legitimate
7. The linking of land reforms with wider social and economic development.

Land reforms have been easier to carry out where absentee landlords own land that is operated by tenant families, and these families take over the ownership of land that they previously operated (Binswanger et al. 1995). In haciendas, where tenants have a small house-plot for subsistence but work mainly on the landlord's farm, 'stroke of a pen' transfers from owner to tiller are much more difficult to achieve.

Recent initiatives in land reform have tended to embrace less sweeping measures, which may achieve significant benefits but tend to be slow to reach the bulk of the rural population. Negotiated land reform on the 'willing buyer, willing seller' principle is supported by international development programmes and of its nature avoids major conflict. Redistribution of very small plots and house-plots to the landless is a valuable programme that is unlikely to be politically contentious, because it does not necessarily threaten vested interests.

Land reform remains a key issue in developing societies but it is not the only, nor perhaps the most important, means of development and poverty reduction. The cases we have reviewed suggest that wider social and economic developments and rising incomes are at least as important in bringing about change. Where land reforms have been partial, as in Egypt, Costa Rica and Venezuela, rising incomes appear to have been more significant in avoiding conflict than land reform. Given the strong finding from conflict research that countries with higher per capita income are less likely to experience armed conflicts, raising incomes and general development may also be at least as effective a means as land reform of reducing the risk of conflict. Nevertheless, in countries with very uneven land distribution, land reform remains an important component of economic development. It may have to take new forms as international agribusiness takes a growing share of production in developing countries, presenting new challenges. The situations in South Africa, Brazil and India, and in the developing countries in general, suggest the continuing importance of finding effective and peaceful means of land reform.

7
Emergent Conflict over Climate Change

Introduction

This chapter applies the theoretical considerations of the first part of this book to one of the most important environmental and security issues of the early twenty-first century. Ever since the industrial revolution fossil fuel burning and other human activities have increased the concentration of carbon dioxide and other greenhouse gases in the atmosphere. There is now a scientific consensus that anthropogenic emissions are contributing to global warming. The warming to date is already having a clear impact on human well-being and the survival of other species. It is also clear that the issue has opened conflicts of interests between different groups within states, between states, and across generations.

This is a conflict in which we are all involved, since we all contribute to greenhouse emissions and we are all affected by climate change. But some contribute more than others to the pollution and some are more vulnerable than others to its effects. The Saudi government, for example, relies on revenues from fossil fuels for its political survival. The Association of Small Island States (AOSIS) represents people in low-lying countries who face an existential threat from the rising sea. These groups have a clear conflict of interest. More generally, the North has historically contributed most to carbon emissions, while the South is most vulnerable to its effects. Constraining future emissions will place the development paths of North and South in conflict, if they remain on a fossil fuel-intensive development path. There are also diverging interests within the North and within the South. For example, EU member states are more dependent on imported energy and more willing to consider restriction based on agreed targets, while the United States and Australia are large fossil fuel producers who perceive the costs of switching to a low fossil fuel economy as very high and currently reject agreed targets. Similarly the interests of fossil-fuel producing developing countries such as China and India differ from those of the non-oil producing countries of Africa which are vulnerable to changing rainfall and desertification. Producers and consumers, urban and rural dwellers, the rich and the poor all have differing interests. International co-operation is essential to develop an effective response but the differences of interest will make such co-operation difficult.

The impact of climate change

The first awareness of the possible impact of human activities on the climate dates back to the end of the nineteenth century when the Swedish scientist Svante Arrenhius calculated that doubling the concentration of carbon dioxide in the atmosphere would increase the average temperature of the earth by 5 to 6 °C. In the 1970s and 1980s a consensus developed in the scientific community that warming was taking place and that urgent international action was necessary. The Intergovernmental Panel on Climate Change (IPCC), which brought together the world's leading climatologists, reported in 1992 that 'emissions resulting from human activities are substantially increasing the atmospheric concentrations of the greenhouse gases ... These increases will enhance the greenhouse effect, resulting on average in an additional warming of the Earth's surface.' It would require 'immediate reductions in emissions from human activities of over 60 per cent to stabilize their concentrations at today's levels.'

By the year 2000 the level of CO_2 in the atmosphere had risen to over 370 ppm, a 30 per cent increase over the pre-industrial concentration of 280 ppm. The average surface temperature has increased by 0.6 °C over the same period. Predicting future trends is difficult because the future level of human activity, the carbon intensity of future economic development and the dynamics of the planetary climate are all very uncertain. In order to encompass a range of possibilities, the IPCC calculated a set of scenarios, ranging from worst cases in which the concentration of carbon dioxide rises by 220 per cent to 970 ppm and best cases in which it rises by 75 per cent to 540 ppm. This would imply rises in global temperature of between 1.4 °C and 5.8 °C by the year 2100.[1]

These changes in average temperature mask greater variations locally. Continental interiors would warm by 2.2 °C to 6.6 °C and the poles would warm more than lower latitudes. The warming in the Arctic would be from 3.6 °C to 11.4 °C.

The likely effects of these changes on sea levels, weather, rainfall patterns and plant and animal life have been widely canvassed. The British government report, 'Avoiding Dangerous Climate Change', suggested that a temperature rise of 2 °C might be a threshold (Schellnhuber 2006). Above this risks increase 'very substantially' with 'potentially large numbers of extinctions' and 'major increases in hunger and water shortage risks ... particularly in developing countries.' There are fears that the higher temperature ranges could lead to 'tipping points' where positive feedbacks are engaged. For example, drying and burning of forests could transform them from a 'sink' to a 'source' of carbon, and melting of the permafrost could release large amounts of methane.

Implications for conflict

The consequences will be variable for different communities. Some will benefit over the short term, as the climate improves in cold areas. Others will suffer as crops are affected, water supplies are diminished and extreme weather and storm surges intensify. A study of the effects on agriculture in developing countries in 2050, drawing on two models of climate change, one from the UK Meteorology Office, the other from the Goddard Institute of Space Sciences, suggested that larger farmers in Asia and medium and large farmers in Latin America might benefit, as a result of rising prices, while poor farmers and all farmers in Africa would suffer. Urban dwellers would also suffer with poorer people standing to lose more than the urban rich (Winters et al. 1999).

There is also likely to be conflict of interest over the response because of the uneven pattern of existing emissions, the unknown paths of countries' economic development in the future and the implications these have for agreeing on restraints. A clear line divides the developed countries, which have much higher CO_2 emissions per capita, from the developing countries, which have much larger populations. In 2000 a little over one-fifth of world population in the developed countries and the east European 'economies in transition' (USA, Japan, western and eastern Europe, Russia, Canada, Australia and New Zealand) emitted 65 per cent of world CO_2, while almost four-fifths of the world's population living in the developing countries emitted the remaining 35 per cent (Grubb 2003). The developed countries have been responsible for most of the carbon emissions to date, while the developing countries are more vulnerable to their effects.

If the South follows the North's historical pattern of development and goes through a fossil-fuel intensive phase of industrialization, as major developing countries such as India and China are starting to do, the carbon emissions of the developing countries will overtake those of the North. This is expected to occur by 2030 on current trends.

Because CO_2 remains in the atmosphere for a long time, global temperature will be raised for a long time as a result of higher emissions. What is the maximum level that is 'safe'? Although any increase may have undesirable effects, a case can be made for 450 ppm as a maximum 'safe' level of carbon dioxide in the atmosphere (Athanasiou and Baer 2002). This would increase global mean surface temperature by about 2 °C above the pre-industrial level. If this is to be achieved, sharp reductions by both the North and the South are necessary. The annual carbon emissions required to achieve an atmospheric concentration of CO_2 of 450 ppm fall steadily by about 60 per cent from 2000 to 2100, while the annual CO_2 emissions of North and South under the IPCC's A1 'balanced' scenario rise until 2050, reaching levels almost double their 2000 value in 2050 before falling back (Athanasiou and Baer 2002: 61). If the South industrializes along the same lines that the North took, even if the North's carbon emissions are stabilized, the resulting global emissions will continue to rise, taking atmospheric CO_2 well above the 450 ppm level. If carbon limits are accepted, they define a bargaining space within which the North and South are constrained. If either the North or the South takes up more than its limits within this constraint, it does so at the expense of the other. If they fail to observe the constraints, the climate damage will be at the expense of all. This makes it clear that the parties have at least a potential conflict of interest. For some, indeed, it is already existential conflict of interest.

Whether this conflict of interest has the potential for violence in the future has been a subject of popular debate. There is a widespread perception in policy circles that it could have. Sir Nicholas Stern, for example, who advises the British government on the economics of climate change, noted that climate change 'will create the potential for conflict and population movement, which will put pressure on the developed as well as the developing world'. Homer-Dixon (1991; Homer-Dixon 1994, 2001), Brauch (2002), Baechler (1999) and others have argued that climate change is likely to lead to violent conflict. Homer-Dixon (1991: 134) offers a three-phase model of the possible causal pathways in which environmental pressures and violent conflict are mediated by social and political structures. Others are sceptical of causal associations. Environmental scarcity frequently does not lead to violent conflict and in recent decades, indicators of environmental scarcity are poorly correlated with the incidence of armed conflict (Gleditsch 2001). Efforts to investigate whether environmental issues are directly and causally linked with violence may be misplaced since, as Peluso and Watts argue (2001), it is the social and political response to environmental change (and in some cases the political creation of environmental scarcities) rather than environmental change in itself that is the source of potential violent conflict – a point with which few of these authors would disagree. There have been many disputes over rivers and water resources, for example, but relatively few have been violent. Usually states have been able to reach agreements to share them (Lonergan 2001) – sometimes on rather unequal terms. Of course this does not rule out the possibility of wars over water in the future.

The argument being made here is not that climate change represents an immediate source of armed conflict. Rather, it is that this is a major environmental change that is already putting the interests of different groups into conflict. How this conflict of interests will develop remains to be seen. It clearly has the capacity to add to uneven development, exclusion and marginalization. It could potentially contribute to polarization between groups of countries with conflicting interests, and possibly to violence within and between them, in association with other sources of conflict. Alternatively it could be transformed through negotiations and co-operative action. This chapter aims to explore both the forms this emergent conflict could take and the conditions for co-operative action to transform it.

The North–South conflict

As a first step towards characterizing the conflicts of interest involved, I shall take two deliberately artificial and simplified representations of the conflict.

First, consider the conflict of interest between OPEC and the Association of Small Island States (AOSIS). This is a one-sided conflict where the viability of one of the actors depends on a variable under the control of the other (see Figure 7.1). Assume that we can quantify the utility of the actors under different levels of carbon emissions. Here carbon emissions (which rise with time) are measured along the horizontal axis, and the parties' utility along the vertical axis. As oil consumption and carbon emissions rise, the payoffs to the oil exporters increase, but a point is reached where the island states find conditions more and more difficult as the rising sea level takes effect. At every point OPEC prefers the business-as-usual option of expanding output over the alternative of restraint. At every point AOSIS prefers restraint. Since by assumption OPEC acts in its own self-interest and AOSIS has no power of decision, the situation is steadily driven to a less and less favourable outcome for AOSIS, and finally to its extinction.

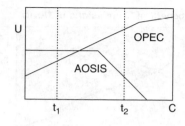

Figure 7.1   Global warming: the one-sided conflict

Now let us consider a two-sided conflict, in which the North and the South both control their own level of carbon emissions, and both affect each other in doing so. It is unrealistic, of course, to portray the North and the South as actors or even as groups having homogeneous interests. Nevertheless we can gain some insights by making a first analysis as though this were simply a North–South conflict. Figure 7.2 shows schematic cost–benefit curves associated with the level of carbon emissions from North and South. At first both parties benefit from the economic activities associated with carbon emissions. As large-scale industrialization takes place first in the North, the North obtains most of the benefits and imposes most of the costs of climate change on the South. However, as the South begins its own industrialization, it also experiences benefits while imposing increasing costs on the North. At some point the environmental disbenefits grow so large that both North and South suffer from further carbon emissions. Now, both parties have a choice between 'business-as-usual' strategies and restraint. At what point, if any, will the parties limit their emissions in order to avoid the pollution disbenefits? Assuming that each party acts in its own self-interest, it will only introduce restraint when its own perceived marginal costs from pollution exceed its marginal benefits from the activities generating carbon emissions. So the parties adopt restraint only when their own cost–benefit curves start to turn downwards. However, if they co-ordinate their actions, seeking to maximize joint benefits and minimize joint costs, restraint is adopted much earlier. The logic is the same as the example of the two firms imposing externalities on each other, considered in the appendix to Chapter 3.

This demonstrates that, in this simple model, a co-operative approach is collectively rational. But is it also individually rational for each actor? If the two agree to make side-payments, then there will be some distribution of side-payments which is also individually rational. However, it may not be easy to arrive at an agreement to split the benefits (and

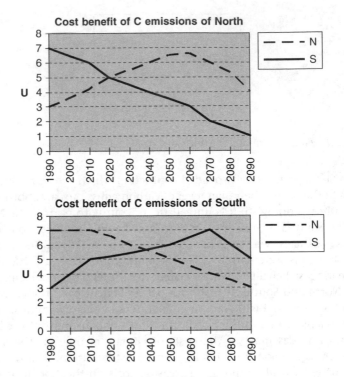

Figure 7.2   Global warming: the two-sided conflict

disbenefits) of co-operation. This depends on the course of bargaining and negotiations.

Let us now consider a slightly more realistic model, still based on the developing conflict of interest between North and South. The previous model assumed that actors would get signals from the environment as to the payoffs from their actions as they made them. In the case of climate change one of the difficulties is that the payoffs for present actions will only be known a long time in the future. We can therefore imagine North and South making bargaining offers to each other about possible restraint measures, and weighing up the value of these offers in relation to their expectation of the total emissions and their costs. The parties have to decide between 'business-as-usual' and proposals for restraint associated with proposed divisions of the resulting carbon emissions between them before the true costs are known.

How does this bargaining work? The characteristic of bargaining situations is that both sides have something to gain from a bargain, but there is a 'threat point' at which no bargain is agreed. Nash offered a solution to the bargaining problem that identifies a collectively rational, unique, Pareto-optimal outcome, but this depends on knowledge of both parties' preferences over the range of possible outcomes and, as Bowles (2004: 178) points out, never results in a bargaining breakdown. Zeuthen (1930) and Rubinstein (1982) proposed theories based on alternating offers by the bargainers, which come closer to the actual process, but again their proposals are designed to reach a solution and never break down. A more plausible model may be based on the evolutionary game theory approach. Here the parties propose offers for restraint which allocate different endowments of allowed carbon emissions to each party. Each party weighs the offers on the table, on the basis of their own preferences (which need not be revealed) and attaches a weight, or a payoff, to the offer.[2] This is done on the basis of rules of the form: if the total carbon limit is not greater than x, and our endowment of permitted carbon emissions is not lower than y, then accept the offer. Both parties make a number of offers and vary the rules, rewarding rules that are successful and eliminating rules that fail to reach agreement. After a number of rounds the bargaining ends. If the parties' rules have converged on the same offer then they make an agreement. Otherwise, the bargaining fails.

This model goes beyond the 'blind' behaviour of the parties reacting to each other's moves to include a teleological element. It also allows for a change of goals over time, in the light of changing circumstances.[3] The rules are analogous to goals the parties test out and the bargaining process offers a means of ascribing payoffs to alternatives before the final outcomes are known. In principle the method can be extended to multiple parties and to more complex combinations of rules.

Complex rules can also represent principles, or norms, which often play an important part in negotiation theory, but are poorly represented in bargaining theory. The UN Framework Convention on Climate Change was successful because it set out key principles that proved acceptable to all. The first principle, which said that the developed countries must lead the way, encapsulated the framework. 'Parties should protect the climate system for the benefit of present and future generations of humankind, on the basis of equity and in accordance with their common but differentiated responsibilities and respective capabilities. Accordingly, the developed country Parties should take the lead in combating climate change and the adverse effects thereof.' Such principles later have to be translated into commitments that can be implemented and monitored, but the choice between principles such as 'equal per capita limits' and 'equal proportional cuts' is crucial for framing the detail of the bargaining.

Conflict analysis of the climate negotiations

Turning from models to analysis of the negotiations to date, and prospects for the coming years, a more nuanced approach of the cross-cutting conflicts of interest between numerous parties is clearly required. There is a strong element of conflict of interest between the North and South but intra-North and intra-South conflicts are of equal importance.[4]

The climate negotiations opened in 1991 with a number of preparatory meetings leading to the Framework Convention on Climate Change. It was already clear in the preparatory meetings that participants were deeply divided. The US and OPEC resisted calls for binding reductions in carbon emissions, whereas other developed countries, especially the Europeans, wanted quantified targets included in the Convention. The developing countries resisted emissions targets for themselves but demanded new financial aid and technology transfer from the developed countries, which the latter resisted. In the end the Convention was limited to a framework of principles, leaving the details to later implementation meetings. It was adopted at Rio in 1992 and came into force in 1994. 185 governments and the EU signed it over the following ten years. This almost universal endorsement raised hopes that an effective regime might be formed. Government representatives subsequently met in annual Conferences of Parties (COP) to discuss the implementation of the Convention. The first stage was the effort to agree binding commitments among the industrialized countries.

The AOSIS countries had proposed that the industrialized countries should make reductions in their emissions of greenhouse gases of 20 per cent by 2005. This gained support from Germany, and although the G77 initially opposed the proposal, because of the objections of OPEC members, India led a breakaway group that endorsed the proposal. OPEC then swung around to support the proposal to avoid losing its position in the G77. With this coalition of European and G77 support, the US administration under President Clinton decided to accept the plans. Clinton, however, faced strong opposition in the US Congress. In 1997 the Senate unanimously passed the Byrd–Hagel Resolution, which said that the US should not be a signatory to any protocol that exempted the developing countries from mandatory emissions reductions, or that seriously harmed the US economy. Tied in this way Clinton sought to gain developing country participation. Argentina and Kazakhstan declared that they were willing to accept voluntary limits on carbon emissions, but the G77 countries objected to breaching the principle in the Framework Convention. Thus, although Vice-President Gore signed the

Kyoto Protocol on behalf of the administration, President Clinton was unable to secure its ratification by the Senate.

The Protocol, which was negotiated in December 1977, committed the Annex A developed countries to 5.2 per cent reductions in their 1990 emissions of greenhouse gases, to be achieved by 2012. The Protocol was based on hard bargaining between the developed countries and did not require cuts from all of them. The EU agreed to make a collective cut of 8 per cent, but some countries, such as the UK and Germany, accepted larger cuts and others were allowed increases. This led other OECD countries to claim they needed to increase their emissions too. The Protocol's mechanisms for trading of carbon emissions between states that had accepted emissions reduction targets, which had been inserted at the last moment, were also a source of disagreements. The developing countries saw emissions trading as a means for developed countries to evade their commitments and feared that they would be left out of the financial benefits of a trading regime. The Clean Development Mechanism, which provided for developed countries to claim credits from emissions saved through energy efficiency, renewables or forestry projects in developing countries was expected to raise much less money. The developing countries expected that emissions trading would 'turn greenhouse gases into commodities, locking in existing North–South inequities in the use of the atmosphere and natural resources and opening up many new and harmful profit-making opportunities for TNCs' (Gupta 2001: 72).

By 2000 it was unclear whether there would be sufficient international support to ratify the Kyoto Protocol. It needed 55 countries, representing 55 per cent of the 1990 carbon emissions, to come into force. The EU and the US bargained further over conditions for US entry, with the US demanding recognition of its 'managed lands' as carbon sinks, which would substantially ease the pressure of the Kyoto targets. Japan, Canada and Australia backed this proposal. The EU resisted at first, but its unity broke as several members with large forest resources saw the benefits of accepting 'sinks' in the regime. Nevertheless, despite the EU compromise at Marrakech on carbon sinks, President Bush decided in 2001 that the US would withdraw from Kyoto. Russia prevaricated for a long time, finally deciding to ratify Kyoto in 2005, after the EU supported its bid for membership of the WTO.

US withdrawal, though not unexpected, was a body blow to the Kyoto regime. It put in question the value of the developed countries' reductions since, even if the Kyoto targets were met, the reductions in carbon emissions would now make only a limited dent in the world's growth of carbon emissions. Moreover, the US withdrawal threatened to undermine the carbon emissions trading system, since there was now a considerable supply of excess carbon credits (mainly in eastern Europe and Russia) but much less demand for them than had been expected. US withdrawal also undermined commitment among other industrialized countries. Australia followed the US in refusing to ratify the Kyoto Protocol, and Canada, which was failing to meet its Kyoto targets, elected a government opposed to Kyoto in 2006. Japan ratified the Treaty in 2002, but its business sector regards the energy efficiency of the Japanese economy as already high, and the marginal costs of further abatement higher in Japan than elsewhere. Especially in the light of the lower energy efficiency of the US economy and US non-participation, this has weakened Japanese support for the regime. Only the EU retains its original commitment to and support for Kyoto, which has given it a leadership role. The EU still hopes that it will be possible to bring the US back into the regime. Yet the EU, too, is struggling to meet its Kyoto targets.

So the North has been seriously divided over its responses and remains so. In July 2005 the US set up an Asia Pacific Partnership for Clean Development and Climate, which also includes China, Australia, Japan, India, South Korea. Its aim is to reduce greenhouse emissions through voluntary partnerships and technology transfers.

The South, too, became more divided in the course of the negotiations. The AOSIS countries retain their demands for urgent action and for support for adaptation, but, as the G77 has become more divided they have lost influence. Africa and Least Developed Countries (LDCs) retain their demands for financial help, but this is not yet forthcoming on any significant scale. China still has a leading position in the group, but its rapid development and size make it distinctive. Chinese policymakers believe that China deserves credit for its population policies and its success in cutting energy consumption per unit of GDP by 50 per cent since 1980. The Chinese government therefore believes it is already making strenuous contributions towards the problem and it is not obliged to take on mandatory emissions reductions until it has become a rich country. Similarly India is developing its own renewable energy sector and seeking to improve energy efficiency, but objects to several aspects of the Kyoto regime. The Advanced Developing Countries (ADCs), which are now middle-income countries, take the line that they will only consider participating if all developed countries are committed to reductions, and if these reductions are being accomplished. The OPEC countries retain their concern that strong abatement measures would damage their main source of revenue, lowering both demand for oil and the oil price. However, the shift to higher oil prices may moderate this concern.

The group is also vulnerable and concerned by the prospect of climate change. They see prospects in carbon sequestration, cleaner fossil fuel use technologies, and conversion of fossil fuels to hydrogen. OPEC countries are concerned that Western governments, rather than OPEC, derive many of the benefits of oil consumption in taxation. OPEC still takes a leading role in speaking for the G77 in climate negotiations.

As is clear from this account a complex pattern of groupings has emerged in the course of climate change negotiations, with clear lines of difference appearing between different states and communities. These differences are affected by whether they are industrial or developing economies, whether they are large fossil-fuel producers or energy importers, and by their degree of vulnerability to the effects of climate change. It is not only states, of course, but energy companies, other industrial groups, agricultural interests, financial interests, the scientific community, non-governmental organizations and many others who are involved.

The energy question

The role of the energy industries and of energy policy in general is fundamental. In the major fossil-fuel producing and exporting countries, oil, coal and gas companies have become major sectors of the national economy. They enjoy close connections with government leaders and have an important influence on government planning over energy decisions. This is a reciprocal relationship. The central role of energy in modern industrial societies makes governments dependent on energy companies for advice and planning. The energy companies also need to work closely with government to establish a stable framework for their planning decisions. In the United States, for example, the oil companies have been traditionally close to the administration, particularly during the Bush presidencies. But coal too is politically influential, especially in 'swing' states such as West Virginia, from where Senator Byrd has been a vocal opponent of the Kyoto Protocol. In Russia, the giant Gazprom, previously a state industry, remains close to national decision-making. The influence of these companies and state energy planning organs over long-term investments in the energy sector is crucial. Other industries such as the car industry, aviation and energy-intensive sectors like iron and steel similarly shape future demand through their present decisions.

The climate change issue cannot be divorced from questions of energy policy. The arrival of 'peak oil' sets the context for both national and international decisions. Whether we have already passed or are about to pass the time when demand for oil exceeds the supply from low-cost,

readily available sources, the tightening world oil market has major implications. On the one hand, the higher price of oil, which drives up other
energy prices, should encourage energy efficiency, renewables and non-
carbon-intensive means of providing energy-based services. On the other,
the greater concern for energy security is prompting an international
scramble for control of oil reserves. Falling domestic production in the
US and Europe combines with increased projected demand for oil, so
that US and EU dependence on imported oil is growing rapidly. The
same is true of China as its demand for energy soars to keep pace with
the country's modernization; it became the world's second largest oil
importer in 2005. The US responded by seeking to bolster its domestic
production, including in areas of wilderness such as Alaska, intensifying
its hold over Gulf oil supplies, reinforcing its alliance with Saudi Arabia
and the other Gulf sheikdoms, encouraging them to expand their production capacity, developing new pipelines to the Caspian oil fields, and
seeking to diversify supplies by increasing production in Latin America,
Africa and elsewhere (Klare 2005). Strong US support for the Saudi ruling
family has been a pivotal part of this policy, and this gives weight to the
views of the oil companies and the Saudi government on carbon abatement policy. While the climate talks are discussing means to reduce carbon output, the burden of US energy policy in recent years has been to
find means to secure energy supplies, and to expand access to oil and
other forms of energy in order to fuel the economy's growth.

The growing conflict of interests between states over the security of
their oil and other energy supplies is a much more immediate security
concern than the long-term conflicts of interest over climate change. 'By
any estimation, Middle East oil production will remain central to world
oil security', stated Vice President Dick Cheney's *National Energy Report*
in 2001. 'The Gulf will be a primary focus of US international energy
policy.' It has also become a primary focus of US security policy and a
base for US Central Command. Besides the US, the EU, Japan and China
are all dependent on increasing oil imports. The developing competition
over access to oil and gas in the Gulf, the Caspian, the Caucasus and other
parts of the world is setting the stage for a new landscape in international affairs, and shapes the prospects for co-operation in climate
change policy. The political instability in most of the regions that are
sources of oil is leading most of the consumer countries to consider
investing in new and more diverse sources of supply. This seems likely to
have a negative impact on climate policy. Meanwhile the international
interest in these oil supply regions is tending to make them even more
politically unstable.

The energy situation is not the only contextual factor affecting the conflict of interest over climate change. Other questions high on the international agenda shape the prospects too. For example, the development of the world trading system and trends in the world economy (whether towards further globalization, or greater regionalization) will also affect the prospects for co-operation.

The post-Kyoto negotiations

The purpose of the Kyoto Protocol was not to arrive at a comprehensive response to climate change, but to take the first step by setting up an international regime operating within the UN Framework Convention. The next round of negotiations will be more challenging as it will have to secure deeper cuts and wider participation.

One natural approach to framing the problem is to identify a target level of maximum permissible carbon emissions, taking into account the very long time (approximately 100 years) that additional carbon remains in the atmosphere. The resulting emissions are then allocated between different groups of countries on the basis of agreed targets, which would be negotiated in the post-Kyoto talks.

For many environmentalists, a level of zero additional carbon emissions is the desired target, and people have begun to build zero-emissions houses and to experiment with zero-emissions lifestyles. In the near-term, however, reduction rather than elimination is the practical target. The extent of reductions is a trade-off between environmental impact and the political and economic effort societies are willing to make. The IPCC's Third Assessment Report projected the relationship between emissions of carbon dioxide and other greenhouse gases and global temperature changes within a range of 'climate sensitivity', which is uncertain. This means that there is a band of possible values for global temperature around a given pathway of carbon emissions.

Athanasiou and Baer (2002) argue for 450 ppm as a maximum limit, compared with 370 ppm now and 275 ppm in pre-industrial times, with a view to keeping the increase in global temperature within 2 °C. Hare and Meinshausen (2004) take the same view. 'Current estimates of the climate sensitivity suggest that only by stabilizing anthropogenic radiative forcing at levels below CO_2 equivalent concentrations of 450 ppm, the risk of overshooting the 2 °C target can be termed "unlikely".'

The EU has adopted a target of a maximum temperature increase over the pre-industrial average of 2 °C, but the EU view is that this allows for 550 ppm of carbon dioxide. Scenarios prepared for the EU also explore a higher limit of 650 ppm. Were there to be no restraint, the level of CO_2 in the atmosphere could rise to 900 ppm by 2100, which would result in an increase of global temperatures of more than 5 °C. These levels of temperature increase can be translated into likely levels of damage, using the IPCC's Third Assessment Report and more recent assessments. These suggest a higher risk from large-scale discontinuities, a large increase in extreme climate events, risks to many unique and threatened ecosystems, and negative aggregate impacts in most regions.

In making decisions about the appropriate pathway, decision-makers will be advised by economists, who attempt to weigh up the costs of the damage likely to be suffered by their country (and the world in general) against the perceived costs (in economic and political terms) of abatement actions. These calculations are difficult because of the long time scales involved and the high level of uncertainty.

Efforts to use cost–benefit analysis to work out appropriate global actions run into the problem of what discount rates to apply. Economists have engaged in a vigorous debate over whether to apply normal project discounting, on the grounds that capital invested in carbon abatement could be invested elsewhere in the economy and so should be discounted in the same way as any other investment, or lower or zero discount rates because of the long time periods involved. High discount rates tend to minimize the weight of long-term damage and inflate the short-term costs of mitigation actions. Zero discount rates are kinder to future generations. There are also arguments about how and whether to prioritize measures to abate the uncertain risks of climate change in the light of the existing needs of poverty, disease and stunted development.[5] In practice, decisions will not be taken at the global level. Governments will take different approaches to the discounting decisions and to the analysis of costs and benefits.[6]

There are considerable uncertainties and disagreements too over the costs of carbon abatement. These vary across individual end-uses of energy, economic sectors and countries. Opportunities for reducing carbon intensity are likely to be cheaper in developing countries than in developed countries. For example, cited costs of carbon abatement in the US economy vary across a five-fold range in different models. If economic activity has to be forgone in order to achieve carbon reduction, the costs can be massive. If carbon emissions are reduced by energy efficiency improvements that pay for themselves over a short period, the costs may be negative. These uncertainties add to the contentiousness of policy-making since it is easy to find either very high or very low abatement costs to support different cases.

Table 7.1   Estimates for global damage arising from climate change

Concentration of carbon dioxide in the atmosphere (ppm)	Total emissions of carbon dioxide (GtC)	T (average global temperature increase in °C)	Damage (as % of Gross World Product)
450	365–735	1.7371	0.274436
550	590–1135	2.460867	1.012163
650	735–1370	3.063387	1.905995
750	820–1500	3.579514	2.873741
1000	905–1620	4.617108	5.383492

As a basis for discussion I shall take the figures for carbon damage given in Table 7.1. The temperature figures are calculated from a formula linking temperature, radiative forcing, climate sensitivity and carbon dioxide concentration (Hare and Meinshausen 2004: 12). The damage figures are derived from a formula given by Nordhaus and Boyer (2000) for damage as a percentage of Gross World Product.[7] The regional distribution of damage is much more difficult to calculate, since it depends both on regional projections in the global climate models and the vulnerability of different societies is variable.

I take a conservative estimate of the abatement costs derived from the report by Criqui et al. (2003) for the EU.[8] This calculates the costs of achieving stabilization at 550 ppm and 650 ppm in terms of the percentage of GDP different regions would be investing in abatement by 2025 to meet these targets under a range of different scenarios for the post-Kyoto regime. Some of these scenarios involve 'per capita convergence', with all countries participating and converging to equal per capita emissions, either by the year 2050 or 2100. Others involve 'multi-stage' abatements, with an increasing participation of countries in accordance with their development. The multi-stage scenarios, which the EU currently favours, build on the Kyoto framework by excluding the poorer countries from commitments but expecting developing countries to take on reduction targets as they pass thresholds of economic development and carbon emissions per capita.[9] There are three stages for the non-Annex 1 countries: a first stage in which they are not required to meet carbon abatement targets; a second stage, when they are required to meet carbon intensity targets; and a third stage where they are required to meet absolute carbon reduction targets. Table 7.2 gives the costs as a percentage of GDP in 2025 for two scenarios and for concentrations of atmospheric CO_2, 550 ppm and 650 ppm. Costs are not presented for 450 ppm, but these would be higher than the 550 ppm figures. The costs include

Table 7.2   Efforts to meet carbon abatement targets by region in 2025, expressed as a percentage of GDP

	CO_2 concentration			
	550 ppm. PCC* 2100	550 ppm. MS*	650 ppm. PCC* 2100	650 ppm. MS*
EU	0.89	1.81	0.11	0.27
US	0.18	3.04	0.00	0.38
Canada	1.88	3.35	0.41	0.62
CIS & Eastern Europe	1.41	4.69	0.07	0.57
Australia, NZ	1.10	2.65	0.23	0.46
Japan	0.99	1.78	0.11	0.25
Latin America	1.54	0.72	0.14	0.06
Africa	1.58	−2.12	0.02	−0.30
Middle East	2.58	2.38	0.45	0.38
India	0.89	−0.49	0.10	−0.22
Other South Asia	−1.23	−1.36	−0.57	−0.16
China	0.8	−1.79	0.16	−0.13
Other East Asia	1.99	1.27	0.36	−0.02

Notes: PCC: Per Capita Convergence; MS: Multi-Stage.
Source: Criqui et al. 2003.

estimates of domestic abatement costs together with the costs of purchasing carbon emissions credits from others.

This enables us to get a rough idea of how different regions may look at the prospects of different scenarios. On the assumption that regions would favour abatement scenarios in which their costs were lower than the likely damage, it is clear from these figures that all regions would benefit from at least some scenarios of carbon abatement, but that lower levels of abatement would secure more widespread backing than higher levels, if conservative costings and national cost–benefit frameworks based on costs in the medium-term future (2025) were to prevail. For example, both the Per Capita Convergence and the Multi-Stage Abatement Scenarios are much less costly than the likely economic damage in the 650 ppm versions. In the 550 ppm versions, the Multi-Stage Scenario is relatively expensive for developed countries and also for the Middle East and other East Asian countries, but gives net benefits for many developing countries. The Per Capita Convergence scenario is less costly than the damage levels for the EU, US and Japan but more costly for Canada, the CIS countries and Australia and New Zealand. The costs for developing countries are also mixed, with some benefiting and others not.

If side-payments were allowed, these figures suggest that the Per Capita Convergence scenario could achieve 550 ppm stabilization without undue strain on any region. In other words, if the regions co-ordinated their behaviour, as in the simple models discussed above, they would achieve stabilization of CO_2 at a lower level than if each optimized on a self-interested basis. However, if each region were to seek to negotiate a scenario in which its own interests would be best protected, it would be difficult to find any consensus. On these figures the Middle East would not accept the 550 ppm scenarios, without compensation. For the developing countries, the Multi-Stage Abatement Scenario is a better option than the Per Capita Convergence option, while for the developed countries, the opposite is the case.

The implications are that a successful negotiation should be possible, though there will be hard-fought bargaining. There are overarching common interests suggesting that, given collective rationality, an agreed stabilization path is feasible. But most scenarios will have winners and losers at the national level, and this conclusion is even starker if we investigate matters at the sub-national level where political lobbies are actually formed. The clearest illustration of the consequences for the energy industries comes from contrasting the expected energy mix in a 'business-as-usual' scenario with the mix in a scenario that stabilizes carbon emissions, such as the 550 ppm. The reduction in coal use relative to 'business-as-usual' would be 70 per cent by 2050, and the reductions in oil and natural gas would be 50 and 45 per cent (Criqui et al. 2003). This makes the difference between rapid growth and gradual decline for these huge industries.

It is clear that the future behaviour of the climate regime depends heavily on how political elites frame decisions about long-term factors that are inherently uncertain. Here a range of factors will enter decision-making besides the rational calculation of costs and benefits. For some, national economic interests will be paramount, but for some constituencies, vulnerability to climate change will be a crucial consideration and others will be motivated by the 'milieu goal' of sustaining the natural environment and avoiding damage to all human populations. Both international and domestic politics will shape the course of events.

We can anticipate several possible scenarios:

(1) *Kyoto abandoned.* In the first, the US retains its objection to targets, and other non-EU industrialized countries join it in promoting a voluntary approach to carbon mitigation. It is difficult to see how developing countries would be willing to come into a regime for agreed reductions in these circumstances, and the remaining members with Kyoto commitments would have a difficult choice to make between clinging to Kyoto, in the knowledge that the regime was likely to be partial and of limited effectiveness, or abandoning it. In this scenario policy-makers fail to signal that a serious switch of energy policy is imminent, and the

market in carbon credits fails to take off. The industrialized countries would remain aligned around the 'business-as-usual' scenario and might invest heavily domestically in adaptation to climate change. Conflicts over energy security might become serious, and this would be the most likely source of violent conflict. The poorer countries would be left to deal with its consequences using their own resources. There would be a deepening asymmetric conflict along North–South lines.

(2) *Kyoto maintained with US isolation.* In this scenario the Kyoto regime would survive and gradually gain members, with a developing carbon market and a thriving low-carbon energy sector developing under its protection. The US and some other non-EU industrialized countries would remain outside but would participate in aspects of the new trade in low-carbon technologies. In this scenario the interests of the Europeans and the US may diverge and the Europeans may develop more distinctive policies towards their main energy suppliers in Russia and the Middle East. This could be followed by US re-engagement, or it could be part of a drift towards regional blocs, in which disputes over trade, energy security, climate and other issues might come together. This scenario of regional fragmentation might also involve a danger of violent conflict between regions, possibly over energy issues, although the reduced demand may help to mitigate the risk.

(3) *Kyoto developed or replaced by a new regime.* A third scenario would see the US either returning to Kyoto or renegotiating a new regime with existing members, possibly with a different design.[10] This may be linked with assurances that major developing countries, including China, would enter the new regime, which may have thresholds and per capita elements, as in the Multi-Stage scenario, to meet the position of the developing countries. In this scenario a carbon market may take off and a sustained international effort to develop and promulgate low-carbon technologies and socio-economic systems may get under way. Developing country participation may be gradual, but this could be accommodated in a flexible regime. The major risk in this scenario would be that the commitments taken on would aim for comprehensiveness at the expense of vigorous cuts, so that climate damage could still be significant, especially if climate sensitivity turns out to be high. There would still be a risk of violent conflicts over energy security but these could be much reduced by lower demand for energy and a reorientation of the energy business towards low-carbon opportunities.

A conflict transformation approach

A proactive move towards the post-fossil fuel economy would help to transform the emergent conflicts over climate change and energy security.

Instead of resisting it, this approach would encourage the economic, social and technical innovations that can reduce the carbon intensity of economic development and of people's lifestyles. In outline the transformation required is for developed countries to radically reduce their carbon emissions, sharply reducing carbon intensity of all economic activities. This will involve an acceleration of the existing historical trends towards lower carbon intensity. Such a transition is likely to be self-sustaining when it is under way, as costs will fall rapidly and new systems (like mass transit systems using lightweight vehicles) will replace the inefficient ones we have inherited from the era of cheap oil. The scope for cost-effective improvements in energy efficiency remains very large; once innovations have been developed to enable economies to 'mine' this potential source of wealth, it is likely that both carbon emissions and costs will fall together.

It will also be necessary to enable the developing countries to jump from low-efficiency, low-emissions economies to high-efficiency, low-emissions economies without going through the 'dirty' high-emissions phase that has been experienced by industrializing economies to date. Given the scope for technical improvement in the new capital stock that will be deployed and the scope for technological transfer, this is eminently practical. But to place renewable sources of energy and energy efficient improvements on a level playing field with fossil fuels, lifetime costing will have to be adopted, and this will be difficult for economies with low supplies of capital. Innovations like carbon credits can help here, together with diversification into new energy businesses by existing energy companies.

The oil-exporting countries will retain their importance, since oil will remain vital as a fuel, lubricant and chemical feedstock for the foreseeable future. The key to its effective use is not to waste it in unnecessary applications, such as space heating, electricity generation and propulsion of heavy automobiles. There may be scope for the oil exporters to follow the example of the Californian utilities and become suppliers of energy services, providing an energy service rather than simply a fuel.

The basic viability of this approach is founded in its economic rationality. As fossil fuels become less expensive and more environmentally costly, alternative sources of supply are becoming more economic, and efficient use of energy is becoming even more economic than it already is. Efficient energy technologies and non-carbon-based sources of energy share the characteristic that they are relatively costly to install but cheaper to run than fossil-based sources over their lifetime. The institutional challenge is to find ways to reflect these 'lifetime economics' in the rules that govern ordinary markets. Growing government support for energy efficiency and renewable sources of energy are signs that the case for investments in this direction is accepted.

Other forms of social innovation are developing besides direct investments in the energy sector and in energy efficient machines. Western economies as a whole are moving away from dependence on the more energy-intensive industries as new materials, miniaturization and the shift towards an information society change the basis of the economy. The example of China's modernization and its recent success in reducing its own carbon intensity shows that developing countries are also capable of moving rapidly in this direction.

Such a transformation would require changes of goal and changes of identity. The possible shift from oil companies to energy companies, and possibly to energy service companies, has been mentioned. Is it possible also to anticipate changes, for example, in the Saudi goal tree? At present this would perhaps prioritize the maintenance of the regime and development of the economy, supported by maximizing government revenue, maintaining a high flow of revenue from oil, pumping sufficient cheap oil to meet world demand, relying on security guarantees from the US and maintaining access to US decision-makers at the highest level. However, the regime faces threats to its survival, linked to its close association with the US. Could the Saudi government shift towards a policy emphasizing economic development built on support for other energy services besides oil, including 'clean coal' and energy-efficient oil-conversion technologies? Is a triangular trade possible between the oil-consuming countries, the oil-exporting countries and the developing countries, with oil flowing in one direction, carbon credits in another and low-carbon investments in a third?

Conclusion

The world's growing demand for energy is reaching a limit. Like the expansion of American states into the West in the nineteenth century, this limit creates conflicts of interest. Whether the complex conflicts of interest surrounding carbon emissions are likely directly to fuel violence is unclear. The post-Kyoto negotiations are a critical point. If the opportunity is lost to make a concerted effort to overcome the world's dependence on fossil fuels, the consequences both for the climate and for energy security are grim. We have seen that, as in other conflicts of interest, the links between issues are crucial. Climate change on its own may not be the most likely source of violence, but competition for oil and gas are already a factor in armed conflicts. The two are linked by the policies being taken to invest in the future energy supply and demand. Ignoring climate change and investing heavily in new sources of energy supply will lead into a world of greater energy insecurity, stronger conflicts of interest between regions, and potential conflict. A proactive response to climate change, through accelerating the transition away from fossil fuels, offers a means to transform this conflict.

8
Conclusions: Peaceful Change and Political Community

As the evidence considered in this book suggests, the prevention of wars depends on the capacity of communities to adapt to change peaceably and to regulate their conflicts by peaceful means. In order to do this people and groups have to find ways to reconcile their conflicting interests. This is a central problem in political life, both within states and in the international community. The difficulty in addressing it lies in the fact that there is a permanent conflict of interests between groups, and these interests change over time, so any particular set of social arrangements and institutions will meet the interests of some groups and fail to meet the interests of others.

E.H. Carr directed his critique of utopianism against the view that there is a natural harmony of interests in society. 'We must reject as inadequate and misleading the attempt to base international morality on the alleged harmony of interests which identifies the interest of the whole community of nations with the interest of each individual member of it.' (1939: 60). On the contrary, different groups have diverse interests that change over time. Emergent conflict between these interests is inevitable. 'To establish methods of peaceful change', as Carr observed, 'is therefore the fundamental problem of international morality and of international politics'. (1939: 222).

Although groups have differing interests, they also have common interests, and these are usually mixed. People are interdependent and they must therefore find ways of managing their different interests to make life possible. The main way they do so is by setting up communities that adopt rules, norms, relationships, laws, procedures, habits and institutions for regulating these conflicts. Through these means communities attempt to manage their internal conflicts, and when they do not suffice new political communities sometimes have to be formed. The United Nations, for example, was brought into being to 'be a centre for harmonizing the actions of nations in the attainment of [their] common ends' (UN Charter, Article 1.4). There is therefore a close relationship between the question of peaceful change and the nature of political community.

The problem of 'peaceful change' is closely linked with conflict transformation, if this is taken to apply to the emergence of conflict formations which arise as a result of social change. I have argued that conflict theory, which offers a remarkable set of concepts for understanding contemporary conflicts but tends to assume fixed actors with fixed goals, needs to be extended to cover emergent conflicts, and especially to deal with the changing interests of groups as societies change. I presented a framework for such a theory, from the stage of the first appearance of a conflict of interest, up to the development of contradictions, polarization and violent conflict. I have emphasized that such conflicts are not only driven by external changes in material circumstances, outside the control of the actors concerned, but also by the changing goals of the actors, and I have sketched a basis for a cognitive theory of conflict that allows for conflict arising from forward-looking, purposive adaptive plans, as well as from reactions to material changes. Such a teleological understanding of conflict is necessary if we are to properly understand conflicts such as the events that led to the Peloponnesian War and the American Civil War. It also suggests the possibility of alternative pathways, if different adaptive plans had been adopted. People do not act in circumstances of their own choosing, but they do have a choice over how they are to act.

Drawing on this idea of adaptive plans, an attempt has been made to sketch the basis for a theory of conflict transformation which similarly involves adaptive change. By negotiating over their interests, by changing goals and adopting common goals, and by making moves that harmonize with those of other actors, conflict formations can be gradually transformed.

These theoretical considerations make it possible to suggest some of the conditions for peaceful change. An important contributory factor, I have argued, is whether and how actors take account of each other's interests. The rational interest model in which actors take account of their own interests alone does not correspond well with observation,[1] and there is evidence that actors pay attention to 'milieu' goals as well as their own. Where actors can communicate and have sufficient flexibility to co-ordinate their actions and plan together, there is scope for co-operation. In particular I identified the capacity to 'think as a team' as a means of overcoming collective action dilemmas. Co-operation (and conflict) shapes the way actors think about their interests and even their identities. Thus co-operation can lead not only to a form of reciprocation which is in the actor's own interests, but to the acquisition of common interests with the other. Ultimately this can lead to the formation of a new collective actor with common goals. In this case the co-operative management of a conflict reshapes its social context and starts to construct a community of interest among the actors, which could, in time, become a community.

Conditions for peaceful change

Contrasts between roughly comparable processes of social change, conducted with and without violent conflict, suggest insights into the conditions of peaceful change. This book has only begun to explore the range of possible comparisons that can be drawn, for example, in the ways societies responded to industrialization, the impact of changing relations between ethnic groups, uneven economic development, including social stratification over the ownership of land, responses to environmental change, and changes in the relative economic and political weight of populations and states in the international system.

Taking the impact of industrialization on agrarian societies in the nineteenth century as an example, the American and European experience offers a range of fascinating contrasts. In the American Civil War, as we have seen, conflict between the sections led to the breakdown in the political community. The political parties became polarized on North–South lines in the 1850s and a sharp incompatibility between Southern and Northern interests developed when both sides saw their conflict over the control of the government as a mortal threat to their survival. In England, in contrast, slave-holding was abolished by Parliament, thanks to the growth of a liberal, educated and mainly Protestant middle class, which was aware of the horrors of slavery, and the much narrower social base of the slave-traders (who had also been undermined by American competition). Despite the sharp controversy in the early nineteenth century between landed interests and the rising urban and manufacturing interests over the Corn Laws, no great polarization occurred. Perhaps the English ruling class's genius for compromise is attributable to its financial success and its imperial advantages. Certainly, for many, nineteenth-century England was scarcely a peaceful one; nevertheless, the difference between the American case and the English case is that in the first, the regional differences broke the political community and led to a devastating civil war; while in the latter, the political community was able to absorb or exclude the competing interests.[2] This case contrasts too with the experience of Germany. Although relatively peaceful in the nineteenth century, the strains between the Junker classes and the Prussian military establishment they supported on the one hand, and the liberal middle-classes in the cities on the other, laid the basis for Germany's tortured development in the late nineteenth and early twentieth centuries.

Turning to changes in the relative status of ethnic groups, a crucial factor has been the capacity of political systems to accommodate different groups. Where party systems have provided strong electoral incentives for political co-operation between different ethnic groups, as for example in Estonia, Ukraine and Macedonia, it has been possible to contain ethnic tensions without violence. In Estonia, for example, although the Russian-speaking communities and the Estonian communities remain divided and have rather different identities, a combination of conflict resolution by the OSCE High Commissioner on National Minorities and a proportional voting system, which has encouraged elite-level political co-operation, has enabled at least a 'thin' form of political community.

Varshney's (2002) analysis of inter-ethnic riots in Indian cities lends support to this conclusion. He found a clear distinction between high levels of inter-ethnic association and co-operation in the cities with low levels of ethnic conflict, and high levels of intra-ethnic association but poor inter-ethnic communications in the cities with a high incidence of conflict. There are, of course, distinctive conditions in the various cities, but the finding again suggests the importance of some form of communal association in the prevention of conflicts.

In the case of environmental changes affecting relations between social groups, the presence of communities helps to overcome the dilemmas of collective action. Ostrom (1990) gives a number of examples of co-operation where communities have managed to regulate common pool resources such as fisheries, communal forests, irrigation system and grazing and hunting territories using self-organizing systems of governance that have worked over long periods. For example, a hundred fishermen in Alanya, Turkey, who had come into sometimes violent conflict through unrestrained use of a fishery, managed to set up a system to allocate fishing sites based on taking turns around the fishing sites, the first turn being chosen by a lottery. The system was set up by a co-operative representing half the fishers and came to be accepted by the others. The fishers monitored and enforced the system themselves and breaches were dealt with by amicable arguments. In this case the co-operative provided the team spirit on which a common approach to co-ordinating the fishermen could be based.

Chapter 6 discussed the process of stratification and uneven development that tends to result in the concentration of land ownership and the evolution of durable inequalities in land holdings. Land reforms are difficult to carry through peacefully, because of the sharp conflicts of interest between the landlords and the tenants. Nevertheless, it is possibly to identify examples of peaceful land reforms, and the Indian cases are particularly striking. A very significant feature of the land reforms carried out by the communist governments in Kerala and West Bengal was the efforts of their advocates to carry the community with them, through social mobilization and education, and compensation and provision of alternative opportunities for the landed groups. The opening up of an old society through democratization, which gave formerly marginalized groups some collective political power, created a new space in which change was possible. Here, of course, it was not only the presence of a community, but the transformation of that community during a period of change, that enabled the peaceful transition.

Coming to international systems, there is again evidence that the construction of community is a factor in the avoidance of warfare at times of changing power relations between states. Crutwell (1937) examines the power transition from Great Britain to the United States. Chapter 5 discussed the disputes that emerged in this case, which were patched up when the parties, especially Britain, realized there was more to gain from co-operation. At about the same time, proponents of a closer relationship developed the concept of the 'Atlantic Community', which became a political as well as a commercial partnership, based on an affinity of culture and an acceptance of common values. Similarly, the more recent and dramatic case of the peaceful demise of the Soviet Union can only be explained by the remarkable negotiation of new relationships and understandings achieved by Gorbachev. Here the metaphor of the 'Common European Home' served as an important legitimizing device for the shift away from a confrontational relationship, and the idea of the 'Euro-Atlantic Community', which took a concrete form in the newly institutionalized OSCE, again provided a basis of rules and values to accommodate the change. Kupchan and his colleagues (2001) discuss the role of new international orders in the accommodation of change, arguing that the negotiation of a new order encourages social learning in which states come to see one another as benign. The European Community is perhaps the prime example.

The case of climate change is particularly testing since it is urgent, global and deeply touches the living conditions and aspirations of people across the world. Chapter 7 explored the possibilities for conflict and the ways in which they might be transformed. But can there be a sufficient sense of community to underpin the co-operation that is required here? Is some minimum form of governance, development and political participation feasible at a global level?

It is, of course, too early to tell, but the possibility should not be ruled out. At times of crisis, people find new resources. As we have shown, the choice of action in conflicts creates the possibility of transforming contexts. The management of this conflict may require the extension of at least a thin form of political community, but in other settings this has been accomplished before.

Prevention of wars

Evidently no international orders to date have been perfectly effective in preventing wars. Nevertheless, at a more limited scale of space and time, institutions have successfully prevented conflicts. War-torn regions have become areas of peace. This is most striking at the level of the state, when political unification brings an end to wars between formerly sovereign units. The unifications of China, Japan, and England are examples of the introduction of common governance more or less durably putting an end to a state of war. Recently something similar appears to have happened to large groups of states as they have become more integrated by economic interdependence and political ties. They have formed security communities that have lost the fear of fighting one another. The dense institutional and economic relationships between them has come to approximate those that previously integrated communities within states. They have accepted common rules, share agreed norms, work together in international institutions and accept political bargaining and negotiation as a means of dealing with their disputes. In these respects parts of the world have adopted E.H.Carr's and Karl Deutsch's recipes for peaceful change.

These remain, however, partial orders. Major states are far from relinquishing war. The Euro-Atlantic community is still a highly militarized order that is frequently involved in external wars. To what extent is a more inclusive order, which might extend the benefits of co-operation more widely, a feasible possibility?

'The establishment of a global peaceful order', writes Michael Howard (2000), 'depends on the creation of a world community sharing the characteristics that make possible domestic order.' All kinds of preconditions, he argues, are necessary for this to become possible. Some argue that they include some form of state or state-like organization. Others argue that a minimum of governance without government would suffice. Co-operation is possible under anarchy, providing there is reciprocity. Between 'thick' and 'thin' conceptions of political community lie a vast range of possibilities. It would seem clear, however, that some minimum conditions are required. They take us back to the ideas of political theorists who, since Plato, have considered the essential conditions for political communities to form. In general, a community needs some sense of common identity, some minimal shared values and institutions, and public goods of some kind to underpin its co-operation.

The limitations of existing security communities become clear when judged against these standards. They provide benefits for their members but fail to provide sufficient benefits from those outside. Indeed, they sometimes operate at the expense of those outside. In this sense they are extensions of the state, which provides a domestic peace in the context of 'a state of warre'. Can there be some basis for a more universally accepted political community?

Patomäki (2002) discusses whether a global security community might be possible, and finds its condition in the 'self-transformative capacity of contexts'. This means 'the facility to challenge the context in the midst of everyday practices and the disengagement of the actors' from pre-existing roles and hierarchies. 'Since only agents in social relations can carry out context transformations and since this is a social activity, the conditions for individual self-transcendence and collective context-transformation are, in large part, social conditions' (2002: 201). We can interpret this idea to suggest that agents in societies can transform themselves and others, take on new identities and create new spaces that allow for the peaceful change of existing relationships, in the way in which this became possible on a smaller scale in Kerala. Peaceful change is possible then in the context of an emancipatory world politics.

We have come close to saying that peaceful change is the condition of peaceful change. But this accords with a 'process' view of peace. It is a matter, not of identifying conditions that will generate a state of peace with certainty, but of planting seeds of peace that grow into peace. In this sense, peaceful change in the individual, the community, and the world are interconnected. In A.J. Muste's aphorism, 'There is no way to peace; peace is the way.'

In a little noticed initiative the UN in 1998 adopted a proposal from President Khatami of Iran for a Culture of Dialogue. The programme set out a number of requirements for a Culture of Dialogue. These included knowledge about others, tolerance and respect, the search for unity in diversity, the recognition of dynamism of culture and civilizations, and a readiness to transform.

To create a capacity for a peaceful future, we need not only the institutions to avoid violent conflict, but also a capacity to foster mutual well-being and to 'think as a team'. In short, we need a culture of dialogue and peace.

Notes

1 Introduction

1 David Watson (ed.) *The Albanians of Rrogam*, consulting anthropologist Berit Backer, video, Granada: Disappearing World, 1992; see also Ali Eminov, Film Review, *American Anthropologist*, New Series, vol. 95, No. 2, June 1993, 515–17.

2 Marjorie Miller, 'Family Feuds Are No Game in Albania', *Los Angeles Times*, 12 June 1999.

3 A significant literature has developed on the meanings of peace (Forcey, 1989). Cox (1986: 127), in a philosophical discussion of the way the concept is used in Western culture, argues that peace must be understood as a *practice* of cultivating agreements. 'We can keep a more accurate perspective on what peace involves if we do not think of it as a thing that we make or a state that we reach but conceive of it as a process we undertake. It is an activity in which we engage ... It is a process of agreeing – the cultivation of a shared commitment to common expressions, projects and practices'. The view of peace as a process (Bailey, 1993) is thus linked to the cultivation of common agreements. Adam Curle (1971) writes: 'Peaceful relationships are those in which individuals or groups are enabled together to achieve goals which they could not have reached separately.' In contrast, 'unpeaceful relationships are those in which the units concerned damage each other so that, in fact, they achieve less than they could have done independently, and in one way or another harm each other's capacity for growth, maturation or fulfilment.'

Robert Schumann, the founding father of the European Community, expressed a similar view to Cox's: 'Peace is not solely the absence of war, but the achievement of common objectives and peaceful tasks undertaken together' (quoted by Alfred Tovias in Kacowicz, 2000, 150). This is expressed in more personal terms by the Indian teacher Sri Chinmoy: 'Peace is not the absence of war. It is the presence of love, harmony, satisfaction and oneness in the human family.' (Notice at Sri Chinmoy Peace Mile, Cutteslowe Park, Oxford.)

4 The Buddhist conception of life as 'Indra's net', in which each jewel reflects and adds lustre to the others, expresses the idea well.

5 For discussions of conflict emergence by conflict theorists and in international relations, see, for example, Kriesberg 1998, chapter 3; Bartos and Wehr 2002; Galtung 1996; Northedge and Donelan 1971, pp. 51–91.

6 For example the Arab–Israeli conflict began as a nationalist programme on the part of Zionists and resistance to it on the part of the Arabs who lived in Palestine. It then developed into a communal conflict, then after the establishment of Israel it became an international conflict linked to an internal conflict, and subsequently it spawned important internal conflicts among the Israelis and between different groups of Palestinians and other Arabs. Arab and Israeli nationalisms have defined themselves in relation to each other; in other words, actors and structure have defined each other. The conflict has

undergone drastic transformations and will no doubt undergo more before the conflict formation is dissolved.

7 A similar approach is taken in the rather sophisticated social-psychological understanding of conflict in the Buddhist world-view. Conflict arises out of *seeds*, seeds of our store-consciousness, which hold the ever-present potential for anger and resentment and false-perceptions and grasping. These seeds are watered and grow when we are hurt or suffer. They are then actualized as suspicion, hostile attitudes and behaviour, and sometimes as violence. The same seeds may continue to act over generations, so that the violence in a hurt suffered long ago becomes reborn in new people and re-enacted. So the conflictants tie a complex knot of emotions, perceptions and cognitions into which they and others become entrapped as they draw the knot ever tighter.

8 A.J.P. Taylor, 'How War Begins – (4) The First World War', BBC1, 1 August 1977, quoted in Suganami (1996: 159–60).

9 Alternative scenarios could have included a local war between Austria-Hungary and Serbia, had Russia decided not to oppose Vienna's attack on Serbia, an eastern front war between the Central Powers and Russia, had Moltke been less rigid in insisting on the Schlieffen Plan, or a continental war excluding Britain, had Berlin been more careful in avoiding actions that would bring Britain into the war.

10 For a discussion of causal powers and liabilities, which emphasizes that causality inheres in the causal powers of an object rather than the regularity of association of the cause and the effect, see Sayer (1992: 103–17).

2   A Theory of Emergent Conflict

1 Strictly, constant-sum and nonconstant-sum, but I adopt the common parlance.

2 Galtung's reference does not make the historical period entirely clear. Milan was divided between three brothers in 1354: Matteo II, who died in 1355; Galeazzo II (1354–78), and Bernabò (1354–85) all of whom lavished expenditure on the arts but were notorious for their cruelty and exorbitant taxation. The end of the twelfth century saw a long period of peace with growth of agriculture and trade. In the thirteenth century there was internal strife between the city, which wanted to protect the rights it had gained, and the nobility who supported the Emperor Frederick II, who attempted to revoke these rights. The conflict centred in part on control of the city council. The nobles hated its chief officer, the *capitano del popolo*. A civil war was prevented in 1258, through the Peace of St Ambrose, which declared the equality of nobles and people. Soldiers chosen by the *capitano del popolo* exercised effective lordship until 1277, when Archbishop Ottone Visconti seized power with the help of the nobles. A further series of power struggles between noble families continued up to and after the division of Milan between the three brothers. Another conflict between brothers took place in the early sixteenth century when Milan became a centre of competition between France and Spain. Charles V took the Duchy for himself in 1535. Rapoport (1960) quotes him: 'I wish what my brother wishes, namely the City of Milan'. The reference in Rapoport suggests that this may be the contest to which Galtung

referred. I have taken the idea of emergent conflict rather literally here by going back a further 200 years.

3   Boucher 1998: 173.
4   Boucher 1998: 174.
5   Boucher 1998: 61.
6   Thucydides, *History of the Peloponnesian War*, trans. Rex Warner, Harmondsworth: Penguin, 1954, p. 49.
7   Thucydides, p. 48.
8   Machiavelli, *The Discourses*, ed. Bernard Crick, Harmondsworth: Penguin, 1970, II, 19, 335–6 (quoted by Boucher 1998: 101).
9   Hobbes, Thomas, *Leviathan*, Harmondsworth: Penguin, 1981: 266 (quoted by Boucher 1998: 145).
10 Karl Marx, *Contribution to the Critique of Political Economy*, 20–1 (quoted by Boucher 1998: 364).
11 For a critical discussion of the application of evolutionary ideas to social change, see Sanderson 1990.
12 If we know the shapes of the curves, we can estimate the point at which differentiation occurs. For example, if the curves each took the form $V = 1 - (S_1 - e_1)^2$, a geometrical argument can indicate that differentiation takes place when the distance between the subgroups' preferred positions is $1/2 * \sqrt{(S_1 - e_1)}$.

I have represented differentiation here with respect to one variable, for simplicity of presentation. In practice social organizations operate in rich environments and adapt to multiple variables. The viability or preference curves should therefore be seen as curves in several dimensions. A party's overall welfare or viability will be some function of its welfare with respect to a number of variables. For example, if on a particular dimension welfare is measured by a bell-shaped curve such as $V = 1 - (S_1 - e_1)^2$, on multiple dimensions welfare might be $\Sigma a_i(1 - (S_i - e_i)^2)$ or $\Pi a_i(1 - (S_i - e_i)^2)$. The party may have negative payoffs with regard to some variables, yet be viable overall because these variables have a low weight in its overall viability.

13 A cognitive map represents logical or influence relationships in a systems diagram. For example, an actor would formulate links between perceived interests by linking one goal positively with another. These relationships can represent logical relations (such as: given interest X, the actor will adopt goal Y). If 'you have cotton production', then 'you will seek westward expansion'. A complex set of logical relations, or a network of links between elements, can then represent relations between different actors. At the simplest, we can represent an emerging conflict using the 'card-table' representation developed by Howard (1999) from the simplified payoff tables used in the analysis of options. Actors are seen to have a set of cards. In Howard's representation, each card is a strategy, but here I will represent a card as a position that an actor can take with respect to a variable. For example, 'develop cotton production' might be a card an actor 'plays', while other possible cards such as 'develop mixed agriculture' or 'develop industry' remain face down. Some cards are 'tied' together by functional relationships: if one has already been played, then a tied card must be played. (An existing position determines a goal.) In this representation the columns show combinations of cards played

by the actors, so that each column represents a possible scenario, at one point in time. Having set up the scene in this way, actors can then alter their positions by discarding cards and picking up new ones. They can move to new variables by taking up a new card. And indeed, an entire new actor can enter the scene. This representation has the virtue that it readily suggests the ease of adopting new positions, and the dynamic 'play' of social change as cards are taken up and discarded. It can highlight both the coming into being of a conflict when incompatible cards are played by different actors, and the scope for exploring alternative scenarios by examining the play of different cards.

14   This variable may already exist, or the parties may bring into existence themselves through their behaviour.

15   Collins 1981: 152–3.

16   There may, of course, be a general benefit from specialization on products of comparative advantage. But where one region has most of the strengths and another few of them, uneven development intensifies inequalities.

3   Co-operation and Conflict Transformation

1   For a more recent analysis see the discussion of the Tragedy of the Fishers in Bowles (2003).

5   Preventors of War

1   There is, as yet, little consensus on the explanation for these trends. Certainly the Cold War appears to have been responsible for fuelling many conflicts, and with its end armed groups have had to finance themselves from their own resources or the spoils of war, rather than from a convenient superpower. Hegre (2004a) points out that the reduction in the number of civil wars in the 1990s was the result of increased termination of conflicts, rather than any reduction in the number of new conflicts. This makes it difficult to associate the drop in the number of conflicts with any effects attributed, for example, to conflict prevention policies or the increasing numbers of democracies. Hegre 2004a: 243–52.

2   This describes the period after the collapse of the manor system in the Spring and Autumn Period (−770–476). From this stage intensive farming developed based on labour-intensive agriculture.

3   Hideysohi's achievement was shared with his predecessor Oda Nobunaga (1534–82) and his successor Tokugawa Ieyasu (1542–1616). See Storry (1960: 45–69).

4   The US claimed the right under the Monroe doctrine to intervene in a territorial dispute between Venezuela and British settlers in British Guiana. At one point President Cleveland threatened that the United States would resist the British 'by every means in its power'. The British Prime Minister responded that the crisis risked 'something of the unnatural horror of a civil war'. (Davidson and Sucharov 2001, in Kupchan et al. 2001: 101–37; Silver 2006).

5   Although the democratic peace proposition remains contested, the weight of evidence appears to support it. The more restrictive the definition of democracy, the stronger the relationship appears to be. For a review of evidence for the proposition, see Oneal and Russett 1999: 423–42. For a critical view, see Barbieri

and Schneider 1999: 387–404. See also Russett 1993; Chan 1997: 59–91; Gleditsch and Hegre 1997: 283–310; Russett and Oneal 2001.

6 The leading liberal states, and especially the former colonial powers, have been much the most active prosecutors of armed conflicts since the end of the Second World War. The leading participant has been the UK, which fought in 21 wars between 1946 and 2003, followed by the United States, which fought 16 wars and France which fought 10. The Soviet Union was next with nine, Australian and the Netherlands next with seven each, then Israel, Egypt, China and Thailand with six each.

7 Critics argue that the proxy variables that Collier and Hoeffler chose do not necessarily capture the real factors in conflict as claimed. For example, the central claim that there is a strong association between the share of primary commodity exports as a proportion of GDP and the incidence of conflicts may not necessarily capture the 'greed' of rebels, but the institutional weaknesses and political instability of oil-exporting states. Fearon and Laitin (2003) criticize the argument that the share of primary commodity exports in GDP explains the ability of rebels to finance insurgencies. Nathan argues that political repression is mis-specified as a grievance variable, since it also affects opportunity to rebel. These and other criticisms are discussed by Nathan 2005. The iconoclastic contrast between 'greed' and 'grievance' exaggerates the dichotomy between these two motives. Real conflicts are driven by a combination of factors, in which both political and economic motives and opportunities are important.

8 This was based on an analysis of civil wars with at least 1000 battle-deaths in the period 1816–1992.

9 Jongmann 2002.

10 Easterly (2000) reaches similar conclusions using different sources of data. He argues that quality of institutions (based on the International Country Risk Guide) reduces war casualties on national territory and lessens the probability of genocide.

11 The report goes on: 'effective structural prevention measures would strengthen the capacities of States to avoid the type of protracted armed conflict that weakened Afghanistan and enabled the rise within its territory of transnational terrorist networks'.

12 The CPR team suggests that 'the key characteristics of a society resilient to violent conflict include:

1. Political and social institutions which are largely inclusive, equitable, and accountable.
2. Economic, social, and ethnic diversity rather than polarization and dominance.
3. Growth and development that provide equitable benefits across the society.
4. Culture of dialogue rather than violence.'

13 However, on cost–benefit grounds, they rule out increasing general aid to the lowest income countries as a security-improving instrument, since they calculate that a 2 per cent increase in aid to these countries would cost $24bn a year, about ten times more than the economic benefits they calculate would

arise from the effects of the additional aid in preventing wars via the effect of per capita income.

7   Emergent Conflict over Climate Change

1   IPCC Third Assessment Report, 2001.
2   For a worked-out example of this kind of evolutionary game theory approach to bargaining, see Zott 2002: 727–53.
3   The change of goals achieved here is from 'business-as-usual' to 'restraint', which matches the shift from uncooperative to co-operative decision-making discussed by Parson and Zackhauser, who see environmental decision-making as going from 'unconcerned' to 'uncooperative' to 'co-operative'. Parson and Zackhauser 1995: 212–34.
4   For a good analysis of the negotiations to date and their political background, see Paterson 1996.
5   On these grounds, the Copenhagen Consensus report argued that other development needs should take a higher priority than action to mitigate climate change. Lomborg 2004.
6   The British government's Stern Review is considering a zero discount rate, but others may take different views.
7   Damage $= 100 * (-0.0045\,T + 0.0035\,T^2)$. The formula is given in Nordhaus's RICE model.
8   There is some evidence that the POLES model on which this is based over-estimates abatement costs, especially at high levels of abatement.
9   The Multi-Stage Scenario neatly combines several principles that have been pressed for the design of a climate regime, including the principle that responsibility for carbon emissions and capability to respond should influence obligations, that countries with low per capita incomes should be exempt from commitments, and that the principle of equal per capita emissions should apply. For an account of how a combination of different preferences can decrease conflict of interest in multilateral negotiations, see Sebenius 1984.
10 For a discussion of alternative designs for a climate regime see, for example, Victor 2001.

8   Conclusions: Peaceful Change and Political Community

1   'In neither the everyday nor the narrower economic sense of the term does rationality imply self-interest', writes Herbert Gintis (2000). Not only is there strong evidence of altruism and reciprocating behaviour, but also laboratory subjects are loss averse and more status quo oriented than the utility-maximizing model would suggest.
2   Lewis Coser cites the accommodation of the Chartists as an example of conflict management:

> The Chartists first compelled attention to the hardness of the workmen's lot, and forced thoughtful minds to appreciate the deep gulf between the two nations which lived side by side without knowledge or care for each other. Though remedy came slowly and imperfectly, and was seldom

directly from Chartist hands, there was always the Chartist impulse behind the first timid steps towards social and economic betterment. The cry of the Chartists did much to force public opinion to adopt the policy of factory legislation in the teeth of the opposition of the manufacturing interests. It compelled the administrative mitigation of the harshness of the New Poor Law. It swelled both the demand and the necessity for popular education. It prevented the unqualified victory of the economic gospel of the Utilitarians.... The whole trend of modern social legislation must well have gladdened the hearts of the ancient survivors of Chartism. (Coser 1967, quoting Mark Howell).

Bibliography

Adler, Emmanuel, 1998. 'Condition(s) of Peace', *Review of International Studies* 24 (December): 165–91.

Adler, Emmanuel and Michael Barnett, eds, 1998. *Security Communities*. Cambridge: Cambridge University Press.

Arendt, Hannah, 1970. *On Violence*. London: Allen Lane /The Penguin Press.

Athanasiou, Tom and Paul Baer, 2002. *Dead Heat: Global Justice and Global Warming*. New York: Seven Stories Press.

Axelrod, Robert, ed. 1976. *Structure of Decisions: the Cognitive Maps of Political Elites*. Princeton, NJ: Princeton University Press.

Axelrod, Robert, 1970. *Conflict of Interest: A Theory of Divergent Goals with Applications to Politics*. Chicago: Markham.

Axelrod, Robert, 1972. *Framework for a General Theory of Cognition and Choice*. Berkeley: University of California Press.

Axelrod, Robert, 1984. *The Evolution of Cooperation*. New York: Basic Books.

Azar, Edward, 1990. *The Management of Protracted Social Conflict: Theory and Cases*. Aldershot: Dartmouth.

Baechler, Günter, 1999. 'Environmental Degradation and Violent Conflict: Hypothethes, Research Agendas and Theory-Building', in Mohamed Suliman, ed., *Ecology, Politics and Violent Conflict*. London: Zed: 76–112.

Bailey, Sydney, 1993. *Peace is a Process*. London: Quaker Home Service.

Barbieri, Katherine and Gerard Schneider, 1999. 'Globalization and Peace', *Journal of Peace Research* 36(4): 387–404.

Bardsley, Nicholas, 2001. 'Collective Reasoning: A Critique of Martin Hollis's Position', *Critical Review of International, Social and Political Philosophy* 4(4): 171–92.

Bartos, Otomar J. and Paul Wehr, 2002. *Using Conflict Theory*. Cambridge: Cambridge University Press.

Berdal, Mats and David M. Malone, eds. 2000. *Greed and Grievance: Economic Agendas in Civil Wars*. Boulder: Lynne Rienner.

Bertalannfy, L. von, 1968. *General Systems Theory*. New York: Braziller.

Besançon, Marie L., 2005. 'Relative Resources: Inequalities in Ethnic Wars, Revolutions and Genocides', *Journal of Peace Research* 42(4): 393–415.

Binmore, Ken, 1992. *Fun and Games: A Text on Game Theory*. Lexington, MA: D.C. Heath and Co.

Binningsbø, Helga Malmin, 2005. Consociational Democracy and Postconflict Peace: Will Power–Sharing Institutions Increase the Probability of Lasting Peace After Civil War? Paper presented at the Thirteenth National Conference in Political Science, Hurdasjøen, 5–7 January.

Binswanger, Hans P., Klaus Deininger and Gershon Feder, 1995. 'Power, Distortions, Revolt and Reform in Agricultural Land Relations', in Jere Behrman and T.N. Srinivasan, eds, *Handbook of Development Indicators*. Elsevier: North–Holland. 3B: 2659–772.

Bloch, Marc, 1962. *Feudal Society*. London: Routledge & Kegan Paul.

Boix, Carles, 2004. Political Violence around the World. Paper prepared for the Yale Conference on Order, Conflict and Violence, 30 April–1 May, 2004.

Boucher, David, 1998. *Political Theories of International Relations: From Thucydides to the Present.* Oxford: Oxford University Press.

Boulding, Kenneth, 1962. *Conflict and Defense.* New York: Harper and Row.

Boulding, Kenneth, 1970. *A Primer on Social Dynamics: History as Dialectics and Development.* New York: Free Press.

Boulding, Kenneth, 1978. *Stable Peace.* Austin: University of Texas Press.

Bowles, Samuel, 2004. *Microeconomics: Behavior, Institutions and Evolution.* Princeton: Princeton University Press.

Brams, Steven J., 1990. *Negotiation Games: Applying Game Theory to Bargaining and Arbitration.* New York and London: Routledge.

Brauch, Günther, 2002. 'Climate Change, Environmental Stress and Conflict', in Federal Ministry for the Environment, ed., *Climate Change and Conflict.* Berlin: Federal Ministry for the Environment: 9–112.

Braudel, Fernand, 1979. *The Perspective of the World (Le temps du monde)*: Harper and Row.

Brogan, Hugh, 1986. *Penguin History of the United States of America.* London: Penguin.

Buhaug, Halvard, 2005. *Exit, Voice and Violence: Determinants of Territorial and Governmental Conflict, 1946–99.* Norwegian University of Science and Technology. Paper prepared for the Annual National Political Science Conference, Hurdalsjøen, 5–7 January. http:\\www.svt.ntnu.no/iss/halvard.buhaug/papers.htm .

Bull, Hedley and Adam Watson, eds. 1984. *The Expansion of International Society.* Oxford: Oxford University Press.

Burton, John, 1969. *Conflict and Communication.* London: Macmillan.

Burton, John, 1987. *Resolving Deep-rooted Conflict: A Handbook.* Lanham, MD: University Press of America.

Buzan, Barry and Richard Little, 2000. *International Systems in World History.* Oxford: Oxford University Press.

Buzan, Barry, Charles Jones and Richard Little, 1993. *The Logic of Anarchy: Neorealism to Structural Realism.* New York: Columbia University Press.

Cain, Mead, 1983. 'Landlessness in India and Bangladesh: A Critical Review of National Data Sources', *Economic Development and Cultural Change* 32: 149–66.

Campbell, D. and G.M. Dillon, 1993. *The Political Subject of Violence.* Manchester: Manchester University Press.

Carr, Edward Hallam, 1939. *The Twenty Years Crisis.* London: Macmillan.

Cedermann, Lars-Erik, 1997. *Emergent Actors in World Politics: How States and Nations Develop and Dissolve.* Princeton, NJ: Princeton University Press.

Chan, Stephen, 1997. 'In Search of Democratic Peace: Problems and Promise', *Mershon International Studies Review* 41 (Supplement 1): 59–91.

Chandran, S. and M. Joseph, 2002. 'Caste Violence and Class in Bihar: The Ranvir Sena', in M. Mekenkamp, P. van Tongeren and H. van de Heen, eds, *Searching for Peace in Central and South Asia: An Overview of Conflict Prevention and Peacebuilding Activities.* Boulder: Lynne Rienner.

Chi, Ch'ao-Ting, 1970. *Key Economic Areas in Chinese History, As Revealed in the Development of Public Works for Water Control.* New York: Augustus M. Kelley.

Christodoulou, Demetrios, 1990. *Unpromised Land: Agrarian Reform and Conflict Worldwide.* London: Zed.

184 *Bibliography*

Cohen, Raymond, 1996. 'On Diplomacy in the Ancient Near East: the Amarna Letters', *Diplomacy and Statecraft* 7: 246.

Collier, Paul and Anke Hoeffler, 2004a. 'Conflicts', in Bjørn Lomborg, ed., *Global Crises, Global Solutions*. Cambridge: Cambridge University Press.

Collier, Paul and Anke Hoeffler, 2004b. 'Greed and Grievance in Civil War', *Oxford Economic Papers* 56(4): 563–95.

Collier, Paul and Anne Hoeffler, 1998. 'On Economic Causes of Civil War', *Oxford Economic Papers* 50 (October): 563–73.

Collier, Paul, V.L. Elliott, Håvard Hegre, Anke Hoeffler, Marta Reynal–Querol and Nicholas Sambanis, 2003. *Breaking the Conflict Trap*. Oxford: World Bank and Oxford University Press.

Collins, Bruce, 1981. *The Origins of America's Civil War*. London: Edward Arnold.

Coser, Lewis, 1956. *The Functions of Social Conflict*. London: Routledge.

Coser, Lewis, 1967. *Continuities in the Study of Social Conflict*. New York: Free Press.

Cousens, Elizabeth M., 2001. 'Introduction', in Elizabeth M. Cousens and Chetan Kumar, eds, *Peacebuilding as Politics*. Boulder and London: Lynne Rienner: 1–20.

Covington, Coline, Paul Williams, Jane Arundale and Jean Knox, eds. 2002. *Terrorism and War: Unconscious Dynamics of Political Violence*. London: Karnac.

Cox, Gray, 1986. *The Ways of Peace: A Philosophy of Peace As Action*. New York: Paulist Press.

Cramer, Christopher, 2005. Inequality and Conflict: A Review of An Age-Old Concern. *UNRISD Papers on Identities, Conflict and Cohesion*.

Criqui, P., A. Kitous, M. Berk, M. den Elzen, B. Eickhout, P. Lucas, D. van Vuuren, N. Kouvaritakis and D. Vanregemorter, 2003. Greenhouse Gas Reduction Pathways in the UNFCC Process up to 2025. Brussels: European Commission, DG Environment.

Crutwell, Charles Robert Mowbray Fraser, 1937. *History of Peaceful Change in the Modern World*. London, New York: Oxford University Press.

Curle, Adam, 1971. *Making Peace*. London: Tavistock.

Dahrendorf, R., 1957. 'Towards a Theory of Social Conflict', *Journal of Conflict Resolution* 2(2): 170–83.

Daudelin, Jean, 2003. *Land and Violence in Post-Conflict Situations*. Ottawa: The North–South Institute.

Davidson, Jason and Mira Sucharov, 2001. 'Peaceful Power Transitions: The Historical Cases', in Charles A. Kupchan, Emmanuel Adler, Jean-Marc Coicaud and Yuen Foong Khong, eds, *Power in Transition: The Peaceful Change of International Order*. Tokyo, New York, Paris: United Nations University Press: 101–37.

de Soysa, Indra, Nils Petter Gleditsch and Margareta Sollenberg with Michael Gibson, and Arthur Westing, 1999. To Cultivate Peace: Agriculture in a World of Conflict. Oslo: Peace Research Institute Oslo.

de Ste Croix, G.E.M, 1972. *The Origins of the Peloponnesian War*. London: Duckworth.

De Waal, Frans, 1989. *Peacemaking Among Primates*. Cambridge MA: Harvard University Press.

Deininger, Klaus, 1999. 'Making Negotiated Land Reform Work: Initial Experience from Colombia, Brazil and South Africa', *World Development* 27(4): 651–72.

Deininger, Klaus, 2003. *Land Policies for Growth and Poverty Reduction*. Oxford: Oxford University Press and the World Bank.

Dillon, Mick and Julian Reid, 2000. 'Global Liberal Governance: Biopolitcs, Security and War', *Millennium* 30(1): 41–66.

Doyle, Michael W. and Nicholas Sambanis, 2000. 'International Peacebuilding: A Theoretical and Quantitative Analysis', *American Political Science Review* 94(4): 779–801.

Dugan, Mairie, 1996. 'A Nested Model of Conflict', *Women in Leadership* 1(1): 9–10.

Dukes, E. Franklin, 1999. 'Structural Forces in Conflict and Conflict Resolution', in Ho-Won Jeong, ed., *Conflict Resolution Dynamics: Process and Structure*. Aldershot: Ashgate: 155–71.

Easterly, William. 2000. 'Can Institutions Resolve Ethnic Conflict', unpublished, World Bank, February.

Eden, Colin, 1988. 'Cognitive Mapping', *European Journal of Operational Research* 36: 1–13.

Eden, Colin and Fran Ackermann, 1998. *Making Strategy: The Journey of Strategic Management*. London: Sage Publications.

Elbadawi, I. and N. Sambanis, 2002. 'How Much War Will We See', *Journal of Conflict Resolution* 46(3): 307–34.

El-Ghonemy, M. Riad, 1990. *The Political Economy of Rural Poverty: The Case for Land Reform*. London: Routledge.

Eswaran, Mukesh and Ashok Kotwal, 1986. 'Access to Capital and Agrarian Production Organisation', *Economic Journal* 96(382): 482–98.

Etzioni, Amitai, 1964. 'On Self-Encapsulating Conflicts', *Journal of Conflict Resolution* 8(3): 242–55.

Fabbro, David, 1978. 'Peaceful Societies: An Introduction', *Journal of Peace Research* 15(1): 67–83.

Fearon, James D., 2004. 'Why Do Some Civil Wars Last So Much Longer Than Others?', *Journal of Peace Research* 41(3): 275–301.

Fearon, James D. and David Laitin, 1996. 'Explaining Interethnic Cooperation', *American Political Science Review* (4): 715–35.

Fearon, James D. and David Laitin, 2003. 'Ethnicity, Insurgency, and Civil War', *American Political Science Review* 97(1): 75–90.

Ferguson, R. Brian, 1990. 'Explaining War', in Jonathan Haas, ed., *The Anthropology of War*. Cambridge: Cambridge University Press: 26–55.

Finnemore, Martha, 1996. *National Interests in International Society*. Ithaca: Cornell University Press.

Fisher, R. and W. Ury, 1981. *Getting to Yes*. Boston: Houghton Mifflin.

Flannery, Kent V. and J. Marcus, 2003. 'The Origin of War: New Carbon-14 Dates from Ancient Mexico', *Proceedings of the National Academy of Sciences* 100(20): 11801–5.

Food and Agriculture Organization of the United Nations (FAO), 2004. *FAOSTAT on-line Statistical Service*. Rome: FAO. Electronic Database available at: http://apps.fao.org.

Forcey, Linda, ed. 1989. *Peace: Meanings, Politics, Strategies*. New York: Praeger.

Galtung, Johan, 1969. 'Conflict as a Way of Life', in H. Freeman, ed., *Progress in Mental Health*. London: Churchill.

Galtung, Johan, 1984. *There Are Alternatives! Four Roads to Peace and Security*. Nottingham: Spokesman.

Galtung, Johan, 1989. *Solving Conflicts: A Peace Research Perspective*. Honolulu: University of Hawaii Press.

Galtung, Johan, 1996. *Peace by Peaceful Means*. London: Sage.

Gates, Scott, Håvard Hegre, Mark P. Jones and Håvard Strang, 2001. On the Shoulders of Giants: a Multidimensional Institutional Representation of Political

Systems (MIRPS). Paper presented at the Uppsala Conference on Data Collection, 2001.

Gilbert, Margaret, 1992. *On Social Facts*. Princeton, NJ: Princeton University Press.

Gintis, Herbert, 2000. *Game Theory Evolving*. Princeton, NJ: Princeton University Press.

Gleditsch, Nils Petter, 2001. 'Armed Conflict and the Environment', in Paul Diehl and Nils Petter Gleditsch, eds, *Environmental Conflict*. Oxford: Westview: 251–72.

Gleditsch, Nils Petter and Håvard Hegre, 1997. 'Democracy and Peace, Three Levels of Analysis', *Journal of Conflict Resolution* 41(2): 283–310.

Gleditsch, Nils Petter, Peter Wallensteen, Mikael Erikkson, Margaret Sollenberg and Håvård Strand, 2002. 'Armed Conflicts 1946–2001: A New Dataset', *Journal of Peace Research* 39(5): 615–37.

Griffin, Keith, Azizur Rahman Khan and Amy Ickowitz, 2000. Poverty and the Distribution of Land. Riverside: Department of Economics, University of California, Riverside.

Grubb, Michael, 2003. 'The Economics of the Kyoto Protocol', *World Economics* 4(3):143–89.

Gupta, Joyeeta, 2001. *Our Simmering Planet: What To Do About Global Warming*. London: Zed.

Gurr, Ted Robert, 2000. *Peoples versus States: Minorities at Risk in the New Century*. Washington D.C: United States Institute of Peace.

Gurr, Ted Robert, Monty G. Marshall and Khosla Deepa, 2002. Peace and Conflict 2001: A Global Survey of Armed Conflicts, Self-Determination Movements and Democracy. College Part: CIDCM, University of Maryland.

Hare, Bill and Malte Meinshausen, 2004. How Much Warming Are We Committed To and How Much Can We Avoid? Potsdam: Potsdam Institute for Climate Impact Research.

Harris, Peter and Ben Reilly, eds. 1998. *Democracy and Deep-Rooted Conflict*. Stockholm: Institute for Democracy and Electoral Assistance.

Hegre, Håvard, 2003. 'Development and the Liberal Peace: What Does it Take to be a Trading State?', in Gerald Schneider, Katherine Barbieri and Nils Petter Gleditsch, eds, *Globalization and Armed Conflict*. Lanham: Rowman and Littlefield: 205–31.

Hegre, Håvard, 2004a. 'The Duration and Termination of Civil War', *Journal of Peace Research* 41(3): 243–52.

Hegre, Håvard, 2004b. Disentangling Democracy and Development as Determinants of Armed Conflict. PRIO, Centre for the Study of Civil War.

Hegre, Håvard and Nicholas Sambanis, 2005. 'Sensitivity Analysis of the Empirical Literature on Civil War Onset', *Journal of Conflict Resolution* 50(4): 508–35.

Hegre, Håvard and Nicholas Sambanis, 2006. 'Sensitivity Analysis of Empirical Results on Civil War Onset', *Journal of Conflict Resolution* 50(4): 508–35.

Hegre, Håvard, Tanja Ellingsen, Nils Petter Gledditsch and Scott Gates, 2001. 'Towards a Democratic Civil Peace? Democracy, Political Change and Civil War, 1816–1992', *American Political Science Review* 95(1): 33–48.

Heller, Patrick, 2000a. 'Social Capital and the Developmental State', in Govindan Parayil, ed., *Kerala: The Development Experience*. London: Zed: 66–87.

Heller, Patrick, 2000b. 'Degrees of Democracy: Some Comparative Lessons from India', *World Politics* 52(4): 484–519.

Henderson, Errol A. and J. David Singer. 2000. 'Civil War in the Post-colonial World, 1946-92', *Journal of Peace Research*, vol. 37.

Herring, Ronald J., 1983. *Land to the Tiller: The Political Economy of Agrarian Reform in South Asia*. New Haven and London: Yale University Press.

Hicks, John, 1969. *A Theory of Economic History*. Oxford: Oxford University Press.

Hinsley, F.H., 1963. *Power and the Pursuit of Peace*. Cambridge: Cambridge University Press.

Hinsley, F.H., 1987. 'Peace and War in Modern Times', in Raimo Vayrynen, ed., *The Quest for Peace: Transcending Collective Violence and War Among Societies, Cultures and States*. London: Sage.

Hirschleifer, Jack, 2001. *The Dark Side of the Force: Economic Foundations of Conflict Theory*. Cambridge: Cambridge University Press.

Hirschman, Albert O., 1970. *Exit, Voice and Loyalty. Responses to Decline in Firms, Organizations and States*. Cambridge, MA: Harvard University Press.

Holland, John H., 1992. *Adaptation in Natural and Artificial Systems*. Cambridge, MA: MIT Press.

Holland, John H., 1995. *Hidden Order: How Adaptation Builds Complexity*. Cambridge, Mass: Perseus.

Hollis, Martin, 1977. *Models of Man*. Cambridge: Cambridge University Press.

Hollis, Martin, 1996. *Reason in Action: Essays in the Philosophy of Social Science*. Cambridge: Cambridge University Press.

Holsti, K.J., 1991. *Peace and War: Armed Conflicts and International Order, 1648–1989*. Cambridge: Cambridge University Press.

Holsti, K.J., 1996. *The State, War, and the State of War*. Cambridge: Cambridge University Press.

Homer-Dixon, Thomas, 1991. 'On the Threshold: Environmental Changes as Causes of Acute Conflict', *International Security* 16(2): 76–116.

Homer-Dixon, Thomas, 1994. 'Across the Threshold: Empirical Evidence on Environmental Scarcities as Causes of Violent Conflict', *International Security* 19(1): 5–40.

Homer-Dixon, Thomas, 2001. *Environment, Scarcity and Violence*. Princeton, NJ: Princeton University Press.

Horowitz, D., 1985. *Ethnic Groups in Conflict*. Berkeley and London: University of California Press.

Howard, Michael, 1976. *War in European History*. Oxford: Oxford University Press.

Howard, Michael, 1978. *War and the Liberal Conscience*. Oxford: Oxford University Press.

Howard, Michael, 1983. *The Causes of Wars*. London: Unwin.

Howard, Michael, 2000. *The Invention of Peace: Reflections on War and International Order*. London: Profile.

Howard, Nigel, 1999. Confrontation Analysis: How to Win Operations other than War. Washington: Department of Defense C4ISR Co-operative Research Programme.

Janis, I.L., 1972. *Victims of Groupthink*. New York: Houghton Mifflin.

Jongmann, Albert, 2000. The World Conflict and Human Rights Map; 2000. Leiden: Leiden University: PIOOM Foundation.

Kacowicz, Arie M., 1994. *Peaceful Territorial Change*. Columbia, SC: University of South Carolina Press,.

Kacowicz, Arie M., 1995. 'Explaining Zones of Peace: Democracies As Satisfied Powers?', *Journal of Conflict Resolution* 32(3): 265–76.

Kacowicz, Arie M., 1998. *Zones of Peace in the Third World: South America and West Africa in Comparative Perspective*. New York: State University of New York Press.

Kacowicz, Arie M., 2000. 'Stable Peace in South America: The ABC Triangle 1979–1999', in Arie M. Kacowicz, Yaacov Bar-Siman-tov, Ole Elgström, Magnus Jerneck, ed., *Stable Peace Among Nations*. Lanham, MD: Rowman & Littlefield: 200–19.

Kacowicz, Arie M., ed. 2000. *Stable Peace Among Nations*. Lanham, MD; Oxford: Rowman & Littlefield.

Kadaré, Ismail, 1990. *Broken Spring*. Lanham, MD: New Amsterdam Books.

Kaldor, Mary, 2003. 'The Idea of Global Civil Society', *International Affairs* 79(3): 583–93.

Kaufman, Daniel, Aart Kraay and Pablo Zoido-Lobaton, 1999. Aggregating Governance Indicators. Washington: World Bank.

Kaufman, Daniel, Aart Kraay and Pablo Zoido-Lobaton. 2000. 'Governance Matters: from Measurement to Action', *Finance and Development* (June).

Keegan, John, 1994. *A History of Warfare*. New York: Random House.

Kelly, Raymond C., 2003. *Warless Societies and the Origin of War*. Ann Arbor: University of Michigan Press.

Keohane, 1984. *After Hegemony: Cooperation and Discord in the World Political Economy*. Princeton, NJ: Princeton University Press.

Keohane, Robert and Joseph S. Nye, 1989. *Power and Interdependence*. Harvard: Harper Collins.

Keohane, Robert O., 1989. 'Neoliberal Institutionalism: A Perspective on World Politics', in Robert O. Keohane, ed., *International Institutions and State Power: Essays in International Relations Theory*. Boulder, CO: Westview Press.

Keohane, Robert O., ed. 2002. *Power and Governance in a Partially Globalized World*. London and New York: Routledge.

King, Russell, 1977. *Land Reform: A World Survey*. London: G. Bell and Sons.

Klare, Michael, 2005. *Blood and Oil*. London: Penguin.

Kratochwil, F.V., 1998. 'Politics, Norms and Peaceful Change', *Review of International Studies* 24: 193–218.

Kriesberg, Louis, 1998. *Constructive Conflicts: From Escalation to Resolution*. Lanham, MD: Rowman & Littlefield.

Krishnakumar, R., 2004. Reversing Land Reforms. *Frontline* 21(4), February: 14–27.

Krus, D.J., E.A. Nelsen and J.M. Webb, 1998. 'Recurrence of War in Classical East and West civilizations', *Psychological Reports* 84: 139–43.

Kupchan, Charles A., Emmanuel Adler, Jean-Marc Coicaud and Yuen Foong Khong, 2001. *Power in Transition: The Peaceful Change of International Order*. Tokyo, New York, Paris: United Nations University Press.

Lederach, J. 1995a: *Preparing for Peace: Conflict Transformation Across Cultures*. New York: Syracuse University Press.

Lederach, J. 1995b: 'Conflict Transformation in Protracted Internal Conflicts: The Case for a Comprehensive Framework', in Rupesinghe, ed., 201–22.

Lederach, J. 1997 *Building Peace: Sustainable Reconciliation in Divided Societies*. Washington, D.C: United States Institute of Peace.

Lee, J.S. 1931. 'The Periodic Recurrence of Internecine Wars in China', *China Journal*, March-April.

Lemke, D. 2002. *Regions of War and Peace*. Cambridge: Cambridge University Press.

Levins, Richard, 1968. *Evolution in Changing Environments*. Princeton, NJ: Princeton University Press.

Libiszewski, Stephan, 1999. 'International Conflicts Over Freshwater Resources', in Mohamed Suliman, ed., *Ecology, Politics and Violent Conflict*. London and New York: Zed: 115–38.

Lichbach, Mark Irving, 1989. 'An Evaluation of "Does Economic Inequality Breed Political Conflict" Studies', *World Politics* 41(4): 431–70.

Linklater, Andrew, 1998. *The Transformation of Political Community*. Cambridge: Polity.

Lipjhart, Arend, 1977. *Democracy in Plural Societies*. New Haven, CT: Yale University Press.

Lipton, Michael and Martin Ravallion, 1995. 'Poverty and Policy', in J. Behrman and T.N. Srinivasan, eds, *Handbook of Development Indicators*. Elsevier: North-Holland. 3B: Chapter 41.

Lomborg, Bjørn, ed. 2004. *Global Crises, Global Solutions*. Cambridge: Cambridge University Press.

Lonergan, Steve C., 2001. 'Water and Conflict: Rhetoric and Reality', in Paul Diehl and Nils Petter Gleditsch, eds, *Environmental Conflict*. Oxford: Westview.

Luard, 1986. *War in International Society*. London: I.B.Tauris Ltd.

Luce, Robert Duncan and Howard Raiffa, 1957. *Games and Decisions*. New York: Wiley.

Lujala, Päivi, Nils Petter Gleditsch and Elisabeth Gilmore, 2005. 'A Diamond Curse? Civil War and a Lootable Resource', *Journal of Conflict Resolution*.

Mack, Andrew, 2006. The Human Security Report: Human Security Institute.

MacMillan, John, 2004. 'Review of International Studies', *Liberalism and the Democratic Peace* 30(2): 179–200.

Magnusson, Magnus, 1966. *Njal's Saga*. London: Penguin.

Marshall, Monty G., Robert T. Gurr and Barbara Harff, 2002. 'Internal Wars and Failures of Governance, 1955–2002', http://www.cidcm.umd.edu/inscr/stfail.

McAdam, Doug, 1999. *Political Process and the Development of Black Insurgency, 1930–1970*. Chicago: University of Chicago Press.

McConnell, John, 1995. *Mindful Mediation: A Handbook for Buddhist Peacemakers*. Bangkok: Buddhist Research Institute, Mahachula Buddhist University.

Miall, Hugh, 1992. *The Peacemakers: Peaceful Settlement of Disputes Since 1945*. London: Macmillan.

Midlarsky, Manus I., 1988. 'Rulers and the Ruled: Patterned Inequality and the Onset of Mass Political Violence', *American Political Science Review* 82(2): 491–509.

Mitchell, C.R., 1981. *The Structure of International Conflict*. London: Macmillan.

Mitchell, Sara McLaughlin, Scott Gates and Håvard Hegre, 1999. 'Evolution in Democracy–War Dynamics', *Journal of Conflict Resolution* 43(6): 771–92.

Moore, Barrington, 1967. *Social Origins of Dictatorship and Democracy*. London: Penguin.

Moore, William H., Ronald Lindstrom and Valerie O'Regan, 1996. 'Land Reform, Political Violence and the Economic Inequality–Political Conflict Nexus', *International Interactions* 21(4): 335–63.

Mueller, John, 1989. *Retreat from Doomsday: The Obsolescence of Major War*. New York: Basic Books.

Muller, Edward N. and Mitchell A. Seligson, 1987. 'Inequality and Insurgency', *American Political Science Review* 81: 425–51.

Muller, Edward N., Mitchell A. Seligson, and Fu Hung-der, 1989. 'Land Inequality and Political Violence', *American Political Science Review* 83(2): 577–96.

Murshed, S. Mansoob and Scott Gates, 2005. 'Spatial Horizontal Inequality and the Maoist Insurgency in Nepal', *Review of Development Economics* 9(1): 121–34.

Nash, John, 1951. 'Non-co-operative games', *Annals of Mathematics* 54: 286–95.

Nathan, Laurie, 2005. 'The Frightful Inadequacy of Most of the Statistics: A Critique of Collier and Hoeffler on Causes of War', *Crisis States Discussion Papers*, No. 11. http:\\ www.crisisstates.com/download/dp/dp11.pdf.

Nicholson, Michael, 1989. *Formal Theories in International Relations*. Cambridge: Cambridge University Press.

Nicholson, Michael, 1992. *Rationality and the Analysis of International Conflict*. Cambridge: Cambridge University Press.

Nordhaus, W.D. and J. Boyer, 2000. *Warming the World: Economic Models of Global Warming*. Cambridge, MA: MIT Press.

Northedge, F.S. and M.D. Donelan, 1971. *International Disputes: The Political Aspects*. London: Europa Publications, for the David Davies Memorial Institute of International Studies.

Nossiter, T.J., ed. 1982. *Communism in Kerala: A Study in Political Adaptation*. London: Hurst (for the Royal Institute of International Affairs).

O'Laughlin, John, 2004. 'The Political Geography of Conflict: Civil Wars in the Hegemonic Shadow', in C. Flint, ed, *The Geography of War and Peace*. New York: Oxford University Press.

Oneal, John R. and Bruce Russett, 1999. 'Assessing the Liberal Peace', *Journal of Peace Research* 36(4): 423–42.

Oomen, M.A., 1971. Land Reforms and Socio-Economic Change in Kerala. *C.I.S.R.S. Social Research No. 8*. Bangalore: Christian Institute for the Study of Religion and Society.

Østby, Gudrun 2005a. Horizontal Inequalities and Civil Conflict. Paper prepared for the 1st PIDDCP (Political Institutions, Development and a Domestic Civil Peace) conference, Oxford, PRIO, Centre for the Study of Civil War.

Østby, Gudrun 2005b. *Inequality, Institutions, and Instability: Horizontal Inequalities, Political Institutions, and Civil Conflict in Developing Countries 1986–2003*. Political Institutions, Development and a Domestic Civil Peace, Oxford.

Ostrom, Elinor, 1990. *Governing the Commons: The Evolution of Institutions for Collective Action*. Cambridge: Cambridge University Press.

Otterbein, Keith F., 1973. *The Evolution of War: A Cross-Cultural Study*. New Haven: HRAF Press.

Parson, Edward A. and Richard J. Zackhauser, 1995. 'Co-operation in the Unbalanced Commons', in Kenneth Joseph Arrow, ed., *Barriers to Conflict Resolution*. New York: W.W. Norton & Co.: 212–34.

Paterson, Matthew, 1996. *Global Warming and Global Politics*. London: Routledge.

Patomäki, Heikki, ed. 1995. *Peaceful Changes in World Politics*. Tampere: Tampere Peace Research Institute.

Patomäki, Heikki, 2001. 'The Challenge of Critical Theories: Peace Research at the Start of a New Century.' *Journal of Peace Research* 38(6): 723–37.

Patomäki, Heikki, 2002. *After International Relations: Critical Realism and the (Re)construction of World Politics*. London and New York: Routledge.

Peluso, Nancy Lee and Michael Watts, eds. 2001. *Violent Environments*. Ithaca, NY: Cornell University Press.

Pogge, Thomas, 2002. *World Poverty and Human Rights*. Cambridge: Polity.

Pondy, Louis R., 1969. 'Towards a Theory of Internal Resource Allocation', in Mayer Zald, ed., *Power in Organizations*. Nashville, Tenn.: Vanderbilt University Press.

Pondy, Louis R., 1970. 'Interdependence, Conflict and Co-ordination in Organizations', *Graduate School of Business Administration* Paper no. 32.

Prosterman, Roy L. and Jeffrey M. Riedinger, 1987. *Land Reform and Democratic Development*. Baltimore: Johns Hopkins University Press.

Prosterman, Roy L. and Tim Hanstad, 2000. *Land Reform: A Revised Agenda for the 21st Century*. Seattle: Rural Development Institute.

Pruitt, D.G. and J.Z. Rubin, 1986. *Social Conflict: Escalation, Stalemate and Settlement*. New York: Random House.

Raknerud, Arvid and Håvard Hegre, 1997. 'The Hazard of War: Reassessing the Evidence for the Democratic Peace', *Journal of Peace Research* 34(4): 385–404.

Raleigh, Clionadh and Henrik Urdal, 2005. Climate Change, Environmental Degradation and Armed Conflict: PRIO.

Ramsbotham, Oliver, Tom Woodhouse and Hugh Miall, 2005. *Contemporary Conflict Resolution*. Cambridge: Polity.

Rapoport, Anatol, 1960. *Fights, Games and Debates*. Ann Arbor: University of Michigan Press.

Rapoport, Anatol, 1974. *Conflict in Man-made Environment*. Harmondsworth: Penguin.

Rapoport, Anatol, 1989. *The Origins of Violence*. New York: Paragon.

Rasmussen, Mikkel Vedby, 2003. *West, Civil Society and the Construction of Peace*. Basingstoke: Palgrave Macmillan.

Reynal-Querol, Marta, 2001. 'Ethnicity, Political Systems and Civil War', *Journal of Conflict Resolution* 46(1): 29–54.

Richardson, Lewis Fry, 1960. *Statistics of Deadly Quarrels*. Pittsburgh: Boxwood Press.

Robarchek, Clayton, 1990. 'Motivations and Material Causes: On the Explanation of conflict and war', in Jonathan Haas, ed., *The Anthropology of War*. Cambridge: Cambridge University Press: 56–76.

Rosecrance, Richard, 1986. *The Rise of the Trading State: Commerce and Conquest in the Modern World*. New York: Basic Books.

Ross, Marc Howard, 1993. *The Management of Conflict: Interpretations and Interests in Comparative Perspective*. New Haven: Yale University Press.

Rubinstein, Ariel, 1982. 'Perfect Equilibrium in a Bargaining Model', *Econometrica* 50(1): 97–109.

Rubinstein, Richard E., 1999. 'Conflict Resolution and the Structural Sources of Conflict', in Ho-Won Jeong, ed., *Conflict Resolution Dynamics: Process and Structure*. Aldershot: Ashgate: 173–95.

Rupesinghe, Kumar, (ed.) 1995. *Conflict Transformation*. London: Macmillan.

Russett, Bruce M., 1964. 'Inequality and Instability: The Relation of Land Tenure to Politics', *World Politics* 16(3): 442–54.

Russett, Bruce, 1993. *Grasping the Democratic Peace: Principles for a Post-Cold War World*. Princeton, NJ: Princeton University Press.

Russett, Bruce and John R. Oneal, 2001. *Triangulating Peace: Democracy, Interdependence, and International Organizations*. New York: W.W. Norton & Company. Sahlins, M.D., 1974. *Stone Age Economics*. London: Tavistock.

Sambanis, Nicholas, 2002. 'A Review of Recent Advances and Future Directions in the Quantitative Literature on Civil War', *Defence and Peace Economics* 13(3): 215–43.

Sayer, R. Andrew, 1992. *Method in Social Science: A Realist Approach*. London: Routledge.

Schelling, Thomas C., 1960. *The Strategy of Conflict*. Cambridge, MA: Harvard University Press.

Schellnhuber, Hans Joachim, ed. 2006. *Avoiding Dangerous Climate Change*. Cambridge: Cambridge University Press.

Schmid, Alex, 1997. 'Early Warning of Violent Conflicts', in Alex P. Schmid, ed., *Violent Crime and Conflicts*. Milan: ISPAC (International Scientific and Professional Advisory Council of the United Nations Crime Prevention and Criminal Justice Programme).

Schneider, Gerald, Katherine Barbieri and Nils Petter Gleditsch, eds. 2003. *Globalization and Armed Conflict*. Lanham, MD: Rowman & Littlefield.

Searle, John, 1990. 'Collective Intentions and Actions', in Philip R. Cohen, Jerry Morgan and Martha Pollack, eds, *Intentions in Communication*. Cambridge, MA: MIT Press: 401–16.

Sebenius, James K., 1984. *Negotiating the Law of the Sea*. Cambridge, MA: Harvard University Press.

Sen, Amartya, 1984. *Resources, Values and Development*. Oxford: Blackwell.

Sen, Amartya, 1999. *Development as Freedom*. Oxford and Delhi: Oxford University Press.

Sen, Amartya, 2002. *Rationality and Freedom*. Cambridge, MA and London: Belknap Press of Harvard University Press.

Silver, Lara, 2006. The Use of Metaphor in Constructing the 'Atlantic Community'. Unpublished paper, University of Kent, Department of Politics and International Relations.

Simmel, George, 1964. *Conflict and the Web of Group-Affiliations*. New York: Free Press.

Sisk, Timothy D., 1997. *Power Sharing and International Mediation in Ethnic Conflicts*. Washington D.C.: United States Institute of Peace.

Skocpol, Theda, 1979. *States and Social Revolutions: A Comparative Analysis of France, Russia & China*. Cambridge: Cambridge University Press.

Sommerfhof, G., 1969. 'The Abstract Characteristics of Living Things', in F.E. Emery, ed., *Systems Thinking*. Harmondsworth: Penguin: 147–202.

Sorokin, Pitrim. 1962. *Social and Cultural Dynamics*, vol. 3, New York: Bedminister Press.

Spencer, Charles S., 2003. 'War and Early State Formation in Oaxaca, Mexico', *Proceedings of the National Academy of Sciences* 100(20): 11185–7.

Spruyt, Hendrik, 1994. *The Sovereign State and Its Competitors: An Analysis of System Change*. Princeton, NJ: Princeton University Press.

Stampp, Kenneth M., ed. 1965. *The Causes of the Civil War*. Englewood Cliffs, NJ: Prentice-Hall.

Stewart, Frances, 2001. Horizontal Inequalities: A Neglected Dimension of Development. Oxford: Centre for Research on Inequality, Human Security and Ethnicity.

Stewart, Frances and Meghan O'Sullivan, 1998. Democracy, Development and Conflict – Three Cases. Oxford: Queen Elizabeth House. Working Paper QEHWPS15.

Storry, Richard. 1960. *A History of Modern Japan*. Harmondsworth, Penguin.

Suganami, Hidemi, 1996. *On the Causes of War*. Oxford: Clarendon Press.

Sugden, Robert, 1986. *The Economics of Rights, Co-operation and Welfare*. Oxford: Blackwell.

Sugden, Robert, 1993. 'Thinking as a Team: Towards an Explanation of Non-selfish Behaviour', *Social Philosophy and Policy* 10: 69–89.

Sussmann, H.J., 1978. 'Catastrophe Theory as Applied to the Social and Biological Sciences: A Critique', *Synthese* 31.

Taylor, Michael, 1987. *The Possibility of Cooperation.* Cambridge: Cambridge University Press.
Thiesenhusen, W., ed. 1989. *Searching for Agrarian Reform in Latin America.* London: Unwin Hyman.
Tilly, Charles, 1990. *Coercion, Capital and European States, AD990–1992.* Oxford: Blackwell.
Tilly, Charles, 1998. 'International Communities, Secure or Otherwise', in Emmanuel Adler and Michael Barnett, eds, *Security Communities.* Cambridge: Cambridge University Press: 397–412.
Tilly, Charles, 2003. *The Politics of Collective Violence.* Cambridge: Cambridge University Press.
Tilly, Charles, ed. 1978. *From Mobilization to Revolution.* Reading, MA: Addison-Wesley Pub. Co.
Tuma, Elias H., 1965. *Twenty-Six Centuries of Agrarian Reform: A Comparative Analysis.* Berkeley: University of California Press.
UN Secretary-General's *Report on the Prevention of Armed Conflict,* 2001. Paragraph 29. United Nations.
Vanhanen, Tatu, 1997. *Prospects of Democracy.* London: Routledge.
Varshney, Ashutosh, 2002. *Ethnic Conflict and Civic Life.* New Haven and London: Yale University Press.
Väyrynen, Raimo, 1991. 'To Settle or To Transform? Perspectives on the Resolution of National and International Conflicts', in Raimo Väyrynen, ed., *New Directions in Conflict Theory: Conflict Resolution and Conflict Transformation.* London: Sage: 1–25.
Victor, David G., 2001. *The Collapse of the Kyoto Protocol and the Struggle to Slow Global Warming.* Princeton and Oxford: Princeton University Press.
Volkan, V.D., J.V. Montville and D.A. Julius, eds, 1991. *The Psychodynamics of International Relations.* Lexington, MA: Lexington Books.
Wallensteen, P., 1984. 'Universalism vs. Particularism: On the Limits of Major Power Order', *Journal of Peace Research* 21(3): 243–57.
Wallensteen, P., 1984. 'Universalism vs. Particularism: On the Limits of Major Power Order', *Journal of Peace Research* 21(3): 243–57.
Waltz, Kenneth, 1959. *Man, the State and War.* Columbia: Columbia University Press.
Watson, Adam, 1992. *The Evolution of International Society.* London and New York: Routledge.
Weber, Max, 1922. *The Theory of Social and Economic Organisation.* New York: Oxford University Press.
Wendt, Alexander, 1999. *Social Theory of International Politics.* Cambridge: Cambridge University Press.
Williams, Andrew, 1998. *Failed Imagination? New World Orders of the Twentieth Century.* Manchester and New York: Manchester University Press.
Winters, P., R. Murgai, E. Sadoulet, A. de Janvry and G. Frisvold, 1999. 'Climate Change and Agriculture: Effects on Developing Countries', in F.F. Frisvold and B. Kuhn, eds, *Global Environmental Change and Agriculture.* Cheltenham: Edward Elgar.
Wolfers, Arnold, 1962. *Discord and Collaboration: Essays on International Politics.* Baltimore: Johns Hopkins Press.
Woodcock, Alexander and Monte Davis, 1978. *Catastrophe Theory.* Harmondsworth: Penguin.

World Bank. Conflict Prevention and Reconstruction Team (CPR) Social Development Department, World Bank Conflict Analysis Framework (CAF) Draft, April 11. http://siteresources.worldbank.org/INTCPR/214574111 2883508044/20657757/CAFApril2005.pdf

Wright, Q., 1942. *A Study of War*. Chicago: University of Chicago Press.

Zahler, R.S. and H.J. Sussman, 1977. 'Claims and Accomplishments of Applied Catastrophe Theory', *Nature* (27 October).

Zeuthen, Frederik, 1930. *Problems of Monopoly and Economic Warfare*. London: Routledge & Sons.

Zott, Christoph, 2002. 'When Adaptation Fails: An Agent-Based Explanation of Inefficient Bargaining Under Private Information', *Journal of Conflict Resolution* 46(6): 727–53.

Index